World of Warcraft and Philosophy

Popular Culture and Philosophy®

Series Editor: George A. Reisch

VOLUME 1
Seinfeld and Philosophy: A Book about Everything and Nothing (2000)

VOLUME 2
The Simpsons and Philosophy: The D'oh! of Homer (2001)

VOLUME 3
The Matrix and Philosophy: Welcome to the Desert of the Real (2002)

VOLUME 4
Buffy the Vampire Slayer and Philosophy: Fear and Trembling in Sunnydale (2003)

VOLUME 5
The Lord of the Rings and Philosophy: One Book to Rule Them All (2003)

VOLUME 6
Baseball and Philosophy: Thinking Outside the Batter's Box (2004)

VOLUME 9
Harry Potter and Philosophy: If Aristotle Ran Hogwarts (2004)

VOLUME 12
Star Wars and Philosophy: More Powerful than You Can Possibly Imagine (2005)

VOLUME 13
Superheroes and Philosophy: Truth, Justice, and the Socratic Way (2005)

VOLUME 15
The Chronicles of Narnia and Philosophy: The Lion, the Witch, and the Worldview (2005)

VOLUME 17
Bob Dylan and Philosophy: It's Alright Ma (I'm Only Thinking) (2006)

VOLUME 18
Harley-Davidson and Philosophy: Full-Throttle Aristotle (2006)

VOLUME 19
Monty Python and Philosophy: Nudge Nudge, Think Think! (2006)

VOLUME 20
Poker and Philosophy: Pocket Rockets and Philosopher Kings (2006) Edited by Eric Bronson

VOLUME 21
U2 and Philosophy: How to Decipher an Atomic Band (2006)

VOLUME 22
The Undead and Philosophy: Chicken Soup for the Soulless (2006)

VOLUME 23
James Bond and Philosophy: Questions Are Forever (2006)

VOLUME 24
Bullshit and Philosophy: Guaranteed to Get Perfect Results Every Time (2006)

VOLUME 25
The Beatles and Philosophy: Nothing You Can Think that Can't Be Thunk (2006)

VOLUME 26
South Park and Philosophy: Bigger, Longer, and More Penetrating (2007) Edited by Richard Hanley

VOLUME 27
Hitchcock and Philosophy: Dial M for Metaphysics (2007) Edited by David Baggett and William A. Drumin

VOLUME 28
The Grateful Dead and Philosophy: Getting High Minded about Love and Haight (2007) Edited by Steven Gimbel

VOLUME 29
Quentin Tarantino and Philosophy: How to Philosophize with a Pair of Pliers and a Blowtorch (2007) Edited by Richard Greene and K. Silem Mohammad

VOLUME 30
Pink Floyd and Philosophy: Careful with that Axiom, Eugene! (2007) Edited by George A. Reisch

VOLUME 31
Johnny Cash and Philosophy: The Burning Ring of Truth (2008) Edited by John Huss and David Werther

VOLUME 32
Bruce Springsteen and Philosophy: Darkness on the Edge of Truth (2008) Edited by Randall E. Auxier and Doug Anderson

VOLUME 33
Battlestar Galactica and Philosophy: Mission Accomplished or Mission Frakked Up? (2008) Edited by Josef Steiff and Tristan D. Tamplin

VOLUME 34
iPod and Philosophy: iCon of an ePoch (2008) Edited by D.E. Wittkower

VOLUME 35
Star Trek and Philosophy: The Wrath of Kant (2008) Edited by Jason T. Eberl and Kevin S. Decker

VOLUME 36
The Legend of Zelda and Philosophy: I Link Therefore I Am (2008) Edited by Luke Cuddy

VOLUME 37
The Wizard of Oz and Philosophy: Wicked Wisdom of the West (2008) Edited by Randall E. Auxier and Phillip S. Seng

VOLUME 38
Radiohead and Philosophy: Fitter Happier More Deductive (2009) Edited by Brandon W. Forbes and George A. Reisch

VOLUME 39
Jimmy Buffett and Philosophy: The Porpoise Driven Life (2009) Edited by Erin McKenna and Scott L. Pratt

VOLUME 40
Transformers and Philosophy (2009) Edited by John Shook and Liz Stillwaggon Swan

VOLUME 41
Stephen Colbert and Philosophy: I Am Philosophy (And So Can You!) (2009) Edited by Aaron Allen Schiller

VOLUME 42
Supervillains and Philosophy: Sometimes, Evil Is Its Own Reward (2009) Edited by Ben Dyer

VOLUME 43
The Golden Compass and Philosophy: God Bites the Dust (2009) Edited by Richard Greene and Rachel Robison

VOLUME 44
Led Zeppelin and Philosophy: All Will Be Revealed (2009) Edited by Scott Calef

VOLUME 45
World of Warcraft and Philosophy: Wrath of the Philosopher King (2009) Edited by Luke Cuddy and John Nordlinger

IN PREPARATION:

Mr. Monk and Philosophy (2010) Edited by D.E. Wittkower
Anime and Philosophy (2010) Edited by Josef Steiff and Tristan Tamplin
Soccer and Philosophy (2010) Edited by Ted Richards
Facebook and Philosophy (2010) Edited by D.E. Wittkower
Manga and Philosophy (2010) Edited by Josef Steiff and Adam Barkman
The Red Sox and Philosophy (2010) Edited by Michael Macomber
Martial Arts and Philosophy (2010) Edited by Graham Priest and Damon Young
The Onion and Philosophy (2010) Edited by Sharon M. Kaye

For full details of all Popular Culture and Philosophy® books, visit www.opencourtbooks.com.

Popular Culture and Philosophy®

World of Warcraft and Philosophy

Wrath of the Philosopher King

Edited by
LUKE CUDDY
and
JOHN NORDLINGER

OPEN COURT
Chicago and La Salle, Illinois

This is dedicated to Blizzard Entertainment for all their hard work in creating, designing, and implementing World of Warcraft *and the other games of the* Warcraft *franchise. It's also dedicated to the vast community of* World of Warcraft *players, guild leaders, and other denizens of Azeroth.*

Volume 45 in the series, Popular Culture and Philosophy™, edited by George A. Reisch

To order books from Open Court, call toll-free 1-800-815-2280, or visit our website at www.opencourtbooks.com.

Open Court Publishing Company is a division of Carus Publishing Company.

First printing 2009

Printed and bound in the United States of America.

Library of Congress Cataloging-in-Publication Data

World of Warcraft and philosophy : wrath of the philosopher king / edited by Luke Cuddy and John Nordlinger..
p. cm.—(Popular culture and philosophy ; v. 45)
Includes bibliographical references and index.
ISBN 978-0-8126-9673-8 (trade paper : alk. paper)
1. World of Warcraft. 2. Computer games—Philosophy.
I. Cuddy, Luke, 1980- II. Nordlinger, John, 1963-
GV1469.25.W64W64 2009
794.801—dc22

2009033112

Contents

Acknowledgments

First, thanks to George and David at Open Court for supporting our judgment. We would also like to thank the contributing authors, who have managed to limit their online game playing in order to write compelling and entertaining articles. Luke is grateful to his friend Brad Gaston for having the integrity to discuss the game in detail. Crystel from the coffee shop, too, is deserving of gratitude for sitting with Luke and discussing *World of Warcraft* for several hours. He would also like to thank Michael Jenkins and Justin Murray of SDSU for their honest and useful reviews of a rough draft of the full manuscript. One last heartfelt thanks to Luke's good friend, Jason Vandusen, of *Vandusen Design* <vandusendesign.com>. Jason's excellent design work and advice were essential to the final product. John is thankful to his guild on *World of Warcraft* (TerrorNova—Eitrigg) and on Everquest2 (Truthseekers—Antonia Bayle) for helping him learn the subtleties of existing in virtual worlds and the nuances of PvP.

Read a Philosophy Book

Within these pages, discover the necessary tools to become an Apprentice, Journeyman, Expert, Artisan, Master, and Grand Master Philosopher.

Obtain Book: 1/1 (Complete)
Apprentice Philosopher: 0/1
Journeyman Philosopher: 0/1
Expert Philosopher: 0/1
Artisan Philosopher: 0/1
Master Philosopher: 0/1
Grand Master Philosopher: 0/1
Brag to Guild about Philosophical Mastery: 0/1 (Optional)

Description

For years, you've wanted to take your game to the next level. Now is your chance, Reader! In the pages that follow are the appropriate theories and ideas to help you step it up intellectually, to help you give your game some meaningful philosophical insight. As a Massively Multiplayer Online Role Playing Game (MMORPG) owing its success to previous installments of the genre and the original real-time strategy games, *World of Warcraft (WoW)* is just itching for philosophical analysis. The cultural reach of *WoW* is incredible, and we couldn't hope to do justice to it in a short introduction. We do consider *WoW* to be a profound cultural phenomenon and, quite frankly, a great game. Though our focus with this book is *WoW* and its expansions, the authors also touch on the *Warcraft* franchise, lore, and other media.

If you're new to philosophy, you also might be wondering what philosophy is in the first place and why we would presume to mix it with your *World of Warcraft*! Well, what *does* it mean when a person gives you his "philosophy" of, say, leveling up a character? It doesn't mean that he will give you specific examples, but rather an overarching guide of the principles that inform his leveling up process. For any gamer, such principles are important because, without them, he would be lost.

The secret is that we all have such guiding principles, Reader, whether we're aware of them or not. They direct us when we play and they direct us when we order the latest strategy guide from *Amazon*. The beginning stage of becoming a philosopher is learning to recognize and understand the justifications for these guiding principles in ourselves, as we play and as we live.

To put it another way, philosophy is a tradition that poses and occasionally answers questions. In some cases questions are not specifically answered. In other cases investigating a certain question leads to more questions! Of course, to think that there is an easy answer to every question out there is to be a bit naive, or to attribute a simplicity to the world that is unwarranted. The ancient philosopher Socrates made the famous statement that *he knew he did not know*, and this claim in itself opened him up to being the wisest person in Athens. There are some things we know and there are other things we don't, as individuals and as a species. Socrates taught that it's best to be honest about what we don't know rather than pretend to have reached some level of understanding which we clearly haven't reached. Part of the philosopher's task is to humbly ponder the seemingly unknowable things, occasionally reaching acceptable answers and advancing general human knowledge.

And this is just what the authors do in this book in relation to *WoW*. Videogames are still a very new cultural phenomenon in the eyes of human history—MMORPGs even more so. It is our belief that *WoW* can teach us not just about huge virtual worlds and videogames, but also about people and society. In some cases, *WoW* serves as a model for examining the potential of economic, ethical, or political theories. While the world is virtual, the people controlling the toons in that world are real. The folks at Blizzard are real.

This quest does not necessarily need to be completed in order. Depending on your current level of understanding, you may decide to skip ahead to chapters that seem most interesting to you. This is perfectly natural for philosophy, Reader! Different sorts of people are drawn to philosophy for different reasons.

If you're a beginner, however, we recommend you start at the apprentice level, where there is a more eclectic selection of material. However, at the beginning of each section we provide an overview of the major themes covered, in addition to some of the big questions the authors tackle in that section.

Whether or not you fully complete your quest, we hope that you emerge from the experience with a more open mind, a deeper appreciation for and understanding of your life as a gamer and person, and a greater respect for the issues that arise from in depth gameworlds like *WoW*.

Rewards

You will receive: **+21 Intellect!**
(We know what you're thinking, but isn't the inherent joy of gaining knowledge worth it?)

Apprentice Philosopher

Aggro Your Brain by reading…

You Can Kill Your Friends but You Can't Save Gnomeregan (EVANS): 0/1
Render Unto Caesar (HAW): 0/1
Finding Adam Smith in Azeroth (KOSMINSKY): 0/1
A Meaningless World . . . of *Warcraft* (CUDDY): 0/1
A Mage in Motion (FERRET): 0/1

Description

In this section, Reader, you will be introduced to a few different philosophical topics to whet your appetite—we present you with a philosopher's knapsack of sorts. Included is a story that originally appeared in the magazine of *Fantasy and Science Fiction (F&SF)*. We are grateful to Gordon Van Gelder at *F&SF* and to the author of the story himself for allowing us to reprint it here. The story provides a playful introduction to the idea that games like *WoW* blur the line between the gameworld and the real world.

Here you will also find questions about ethics, economics, life's meaning, and the nature of reality itself. Most of us players of *WoW* have, at some point or another, wondered about the ethical positions of other players (perhaps the first time you were the victim of a ninja?). Those of you whose avatars are permanent fixtures of an auction house might have occasionally entertained questions about the economy in Azeroth. Is *WoW*'s economy perfect in any intelligible sense? Or maybe you've wondered if life has any inherent meaning and, if it doesn't, whether *WoW* can be a response to meaninglessness. If your brain works on a more abstract level, you might have wondered if either you, or your toon, are free in any meaningful sense. What sorts of laws of physics exist in *WoW*? Does true motion occur?

Rewards

You will receive: **+5 Intellect!**

1
You Can Kill Your Friends but You Can't Save Gnomeregan

MONICA EVANS

Imagine attending the funeral of a very dear friend, in some cold cemetery on a winter morning, when a group of teenagers crashes the ceremony: running up and down the aisles, punching the mourners in the face, overturning your dead friend's coffin, and screaming obscenities the whole time. And laughing.

Horrible, isn't it?

Now imagine you're playing some war-like game—paintball, perhaps—and you have just discovered that, rather than preparing for your attack, the opposing team has decided to put down their weapons and hold a poetry reading in the middle of the warzone. And that not only are they going to be completely defenseless for the duration, they've announced the exact date, time, and place on their public website, with a note saying "Please don't bother us."

Tempting, isn't it?

From an ethical standpoint, the scenarios above are easy to categorize. The first is shocking, nearly unthinkable in its lack of respect or consideration for the funeral-goers. The second is ruthless but unquestionably fair in a war-game setting, particularly one in which the main goal is to take out the opposing team. Of course, these scenarios are described as if they occurred in life. In the digital world, things aren't so simple, particularly when you consider that both of the above scenarios can occur at the same time—as they did in March 2006, when a *World of Warcraft (WoW)* guild named "Serenity Now" crashed an in-game funeral held to honor a real person, killed the avatars of everyone in attendance, and posted a video of the massacre on their website as an advertisement for their "hardest-of-the-hard-core" Player versus Player (PvP) guild.

The issue isn't whether the members of "Serenity Now" had any right to do what they did, or whether the funeral raid is an example of player behavior at its worst or large-scale strategy at its best. The issue is one of perception: that ethical or morally-correct behavior in a Massively Multiplayer Online Role Playing Game (MMORPG) is directly related to each player's understanding of the game world, rules, and culture. To the funeral attendees, *World of Warcraft* is an extension of real life, and in-game events can be just as real, important, and meaningful as real life events. To the "Serenity Now" members, *World of Warcraft* is a game first and foremost, one that encourages competition and rewards players for the domination of other players through skill, tactics, or surprise. And both groups are correct in their perceptions. The problem occurred when these two groups and their opposing world views came into conflict, to the point that the original video of the incident has attracted over 3.7 million views on YouTube, and comments are still going strong at the time of this writing.[1]

So *World of Warcraft*, for the new initiate, can be an ethical minefield. How do you deal with situations in which every player has a completely different outlook on what constitutes "good" behavior? What are the rules for digital ethics? And how much, if any of it, applies to your real life?

Plato, Thrall, and Two Cloaked Rogues Walk Into a Bar . . .

When talking about ethics and MMORPGs, one of the most popular references is the story of the Ring of Gyges from Plato's *Republic*. The ring is a mythical artifact that allows the wearer to turn invisible at will. It is found by an ordinary shepherd, who upon discovering its powers immediately travels to the capital, seduces the queen, kills the king, takes over the kingdom, and generally acts like a very bad man. (Think Arthas after he picks up Frostmourne, but without the demon lords or undead army.) The point of the story, according to the teller,[2] is that no man is so perfectly virtuous that he could resist the temptation the ring offers: the ability to commit all kinds of evil acts and get away with them.

---

[1] "Serenity Now bombs a world of warcraft funeral," YouTube.com (March 19th, 2006) <www.youtube.com/watch?v=IHJVolaC8pw>.

[2] Glaucon in Plato, *Republic*, Book 2, lines 359c8–360d6.

In other words, we act like good people not out of our own inherent goodness, but because we fear retribution from the rest of society.

For someone who has heard of *World of Warcraft* but never played it, this may seem like a perfect analogy. How like a virtual world! Absolute anonymity at all times, with no possibility of real-life consequence, allowing players to give in to their basest, least virtuous desires at every single moment. And yet, those of us who play the game can see this isn't the case. *WoW* is populated with about the same ratio of good friends, indifferent strangers, and complete and total jerks as any large group of people in any space, virtual or not. And while MMORPGs necessarily limit the sorts of actions that are possible in each gamespace—at the very least, for game design or technological restraints—these limits still allow players to commit a wide variety of evil, immoral, ruthless, or just plain irritating actions against each other. So why are there so many ordinary citizens among the griefers[3] in *World of Warcraft*?

Plato's story of the Ring of Gyges argues that morality is a social construction—and *World of Warcraft* players are a society. They depend on each other for raid groups, form guilds with in-game and real-life friends, trade goods and services in every major capital city, and slaughter each other in prescribed PvP-combat areas. And each of their characters builds a reputation, for good or ill, over time, based on their previous actions. There are few actions a player can take that will create real-life consequences (having your account banned by Blizzard, for example), but there are many, many ways in which players can bring down the wrath of an in-game society on themselves, as many a ninja-looter[4] has discovered upon being kicked from their guild. So again, we have the same range of ethical behavior. Some players act badly and suffer in-game, secure that their anonymity will protect them from real-life consequences. Others try to act in a morally right way because they value this society of players, from close guildmates to the multitude of strangers that happen to exist on the same server.

---

[3] A derogatory term, sometimes, for players that enjoy online games by anonymously annoying or frustrating other players.

[4] A player who, once a final boss is downed in a dungeon, steals the rare equipment that drops and vanishes, leaving the other four to twenty-four players in the lurch. This is quite possibly the greatest sin players can commit in-game, as it involves equal parts theft, betrayal, and time wasting.

The Ring of Gyges isn't a perfect analogy for a virtual world, considering that only one person is allowed freedom from retribution. Anonymity is more complicated than that in *World of Warcraft*, as the game's design essentially hands every player their own personal Ring of Gyges. Think how different the shepherd's story would have been if everyone involved could turn invisible at will, particularly the palace guards!

No One Expects the Borean Inquisition . . . or Do They?

Whether we believe morality is a social construction or not, we can at least agree that ethical decisions must occur between people, not computers.[5] That said, there are a number of computer-driven situations in *World of Warcraft* that inspire ethical questions, particularly in the latest expansion, *Wrath of the Lich King*. One of the developers' goals was to make the player's experience more ethically conflicted, in light of the fact that the expansion's focal character, former Paladin and current Lich King Arthas Menethil, is a decidedly conflicted character himself:

> We want to add some layers of psychology that put you in strange moral situations . . . that mimic some of Arthas' own experiences. . . . By the time you stand toe-to-toe with this bastard, do you still have your pretty principles and highfalutin morality, or is it a mirror reflection? Arthas is after that as much as global domination. It's a hook that makes it personal[6] that [previous expansions] didn't have.[7]

In game terms, these layers of psychology are usually presented as part of long quest chains, where players are asked to do perhaps immoral or questionable things to achieve in-game rewards. But

---

[5] At the time of this writing, artificial intelligence isn't quite to the level that we have ethical concerns about it; and while artificial life does exist, and does inspire ethical issues (see Steve Grand's *Creatures*), I can safely say that it does not exist in *World of Warcraft*.

[6] Never mind that *World of Warcraft's* nature often makes it difficult to personalize. Try as you might, it's hard to really feel the "killing" of Illidan for the fourteenth time with some dozen Ventrilo voices arguing over *Family Guy* reruns and whether the Crystal Spire of Karabor is meant for "shammies" or "pallies."

[7] Designer Chris Metzen in an interview with game review site *1up.com*, September 2007.

what the developers describe above is a very narrative way to deal with ethics: not to offer real choices with real consequences, but to force players into bad situations and present them with the results, hopefully inspiring deeper consideration of the ethical values in question. Of course, players are guaranteed loot and experience for finishing these quests, whether they agreed with—or even paid attention to—the ethical dilemmas presented. And any questionable actions a player may have committed during the quest are reset in preparation for the next player to come along, often while the first player is still deciding on a reward.

The problem with narrative ethical dilemmas is that few of them, if any, have real or lasting consequences for players, partially because of the limitations of game mechanics. The lost capital city of Gnomeregan, now an instanced dungeon, is meant to be fought through. Infected Gnome citizens can be killed but never saved; they weren't designed for it, and saving them would throw off the carefully balanced challenges in the dungeon. Players can sympathize with boss character (of the Deadmines) Edwin Van Cleef and his struggle against the corrupt nobles of Stormwind, but you can't join his side, and killing him is the only way to find out the end of his personal story. Likewise, players that choose to be Death Knights, evil servants of the Lich King, can't also choose to stay evil and remain with Arthas. The first series of quests details each knight's redemption and newfound moral center, as well as shifting their allegiance to either the Alliance or the Horde.

When presented with a narrative situation that is ethically questionable, the only choice players have is to refuse to interact with it. Such is the case with the infamous "torture quest" in the Borean Tundra, in which a member of the Kirin Tor, a powerful organization of mages, asks you to intervene with a prisoner you've just captured, saying that his faction's code of conduct frowns upon taking certain "extreme measures. . . . You, however, as an outsider, are not bound by such restrictions and could take any steps necessary in the retrieval of information. Do what you must. . . . I'll just busy myself organizing these shelves here. . . ." Mechanically, the quest is similar to countless others in which you "use" an item on a Non-Player Character some arbitrary number of times, but the content seems to bother a number of people—among them, Richard Bartle, one of the first Multi-User Dungeon developers and author of *Designing Virtual Worlds*, who said the following on his blog:

> I was expecting for there to be some way to tell the guy who gave you the quest that no, actually I don't want to torture a prisoner, but there didn't seem to be any way to do that. Worse, the quest is part of a chain . . . So, either you play along and zap the guy, or you don't get to go to the Nexus.

One could make the argument that giving up access to the Nexus, one of the first new dungeons players have access to, is ethically right in this situation. On the other hand, it's nearly impossible to get to this quest without killing any number of human enemies, which makes the dilemma somewhat less substantive. If you've already killed a dozen people, why is torturing one more the point at which ethics are concerned? And why has no one complained about the thousands of human enemies players have been killing in *World of Warcraft* since its release?

The real issue with the torture quest, of course, is that there's no torture to speak of. The prisoner in question respawns unhurt and unchanged for every player that obtains the quest, as does every one of his brethren that players may have killed previously. The "torture" in this case is a purely narrative construction, one that Bartle argues is dealt with too casually for the subject matter, and one that should make us think about our narrative proclivities in games. Ultimately, though, it's a tempest in a teapot, and not nearly as tough to deal with as the real ethical questions in games.

Make Love, Not Warcraft: Why We Keep Giving Away Free Stuff

In the end, a player's personal ethics in world will depend on two things: how much the player is emotionally or socially invested in that world, and whether the world is viewed as part of the player's real life or not. Only then can we start looking at whether traditional real world systems of ethics apply to MMORPGs, and the ways in which real world issues are transformed by the gamespace.

A good place to start looking for in-game guidance might be utilitarianism.[8] The essential principle of utility is to maximize plea-

[8] Advocated by a number of people, classically in John Stuart Mill's book *Utilitarianism* (1863).

sure and minimize pain. (Change those words to "enjoyment" and "frustration", and this is a pretty good philosophy for *World of Warcraft* designers.) As an ethical guide, a utilitarian might argue that the right decision is the one that brings the most happiness into a system; in essence, to do what serves the greater good, not just the pleasure of the individual player. This might explain what some players have found so surprising in *World of Warcraft*: that a number of people are, quite frankly, nice. "Good samaritan" players are easy to spot: they're the level 80s that always have a spare twenty silver for struggling newbies, that give away expensive enchantments for free while improving their trade skills, and that often run low-level characters through dungeons they couldn't handle on their own, usually for the fun of it.

But while only a select few spend the majority of their time helping others, it's quite common for players to help each other out, particularly when between quests, raids, or battlegrounds. It takes very little effort on the part of a high-level player to bring a great deal of happiness to a lower-level player. Additionally, Blizzard's design principles encourage every player to eventually reach the highest level, in essence making it easy for players to inject pleasure into the system. Likewise, a utilitarian perspective explains the universal loathing for ninja-looters, thieves not just of difficult-to-obtain items but of time and opportunity, who commit a supremely selfish act that brings a huge amount of unhappiness to a number of players, arguably much more than the momentary happiness it brings to the looter.

This utilitarian perspective can't extend to issues of in-game justice. One of John Stuart Mill's arguments under utilitarianism is that the severity of a criminal's punishment should be greater than the pleasure gained from the crime, and that the main purpose of this punishment is to deter further criminal acts. There are certainly rules of etiquette among players, but while ninja-looters may be reviled, they are never tried, convicted, and formally punished by other players. The world in total is owned and controlled by Blizzard Entertainment, and Blizzard rarely steps in to punish anyone, particularly over actions that are made possible—and arguably implicitly condoned—by the game's design.

This held true when a guild named "The Imperial Order" held the Detheroc server hostage during a sponsored world event, preventing every player on that server from accessing new game content[9]. The situation resolved itself without Blizzard's interference, but it brings up an interesting point about justice: that as much as individual players can make decisions based on personal ethics, a system of player-controlled justice is something neither the game world nor the game developers allow. Azeroth has room for multiple societies, but the digital world is first and foremost someone's carefully created and balanced property, and players only have a say in the things they can personally control.

Combat Mechanics: Why It's Okay to Kill Your Friends

Where utilitarianism focuses on the consequences of actions, deontological ethics focus on the rightness or wrongness of intent and motive. Looking for ethical guidelines, some players might turn to Immanuel Kant for perspective. Kant argues in the second formulation of the famous Categorical Imperative[10] that human beings should always be treated as ends, not just as means, and with the respect that all rational beings deserve. This certainly applies to players who have achieved their personal goals halfway into a dungeon instance, but stay with the party until the final boss has been downed. Even players that clearly consider *World of Warcraft* to be "just a game" rarely desert their group, understanding that each avatar has a human behind it who is worthy of both respect and the chance for "phat loots." (Hailing back to Mill, most players also realize that deserting a party does little for their reputation, and may make finding future groups more difficult).

Kant's arguments also make a good case for killing other players. The first formulation of the Categorical Imperative states, "Act only according to that maxim whereby you can at the same time

---

[9] This guild had similar motivations to the "Serenity Now" raiders: gaining attention. Their justification for refusing to open the Ahn'Qiraj content for their server was, in their words, "Nobody remembers the fair and quietly intelligent people we meet in their daily lives, but everyone remembers those who ruin their day. . . ." The guild held Detheroc hostage just long enough to get noticed, but not so long that players really suffered from what was apparently an elaborate prank. "Terrorist Guild holds WOW Hostage," Kotaku.com (February 20th, 2006) <http://kotaku.com/gaming/wow/terrorist-guild-holds-wow-server-hostage-155844.php>.

[10] Defined in *Groundwork for the Metaphysics of Morals* (1785).

will that it should become a universal law." In *World of Warcraft*, there is no penalty for death other than the loss of time (arguably the only "currency" in game that matters), and a small fee for equipment repairs. Losing a fight and reclaiming your corpse can be embarrassing, frustrating, and sometimes time-consuming, but it's always fair. For PvP to work as a game mechanic, character death must be equally possible for all player characters—hence, why killing your friends can be so much fun.

This perspective bolsters the argument of the funeral raiders: that their intent was game-centric, a fair ambush. It's worth noting that ethical concerns were raised more over the posted video than the ambush itself, which suggested that the raiders enjoyed the massacre specifically because they felt it was less than sporting. For the attendees, the issue was less that they were killed than that they were killed in that time and place, while trying to honor their friend, an argument that doesn't necessarily hold up under the strictures of universal law. They might also argue, however, that respect for the death of a friend and fellow player is something everyone has a right to, and that the raiders treated them as means to more honor points, not with the respect that all players deserve. Once again, ethical considerations come down to the individual beliefs of the players.

Achievement Unlocked: Ethical Considerations

For raiders and griefers, role-players and power-levelers, gold farmers, and good samaritans, *World of Warcraft* presents a different but ultimately unifying experience. There are as few solid answers to the common in-game ethical dilemmas as there are in the real world, and as many differing perspectives by which to guide your actions as a player. But while *WoW* is first and foremost a game, there should be no question that the gamespace, the players, and the multitude of player-built societies on multiple servers are deserving of serious ethical consideration by any person that enters that digital realm. There are millions of people behind the avatars, all self-motivated, all born of a particular belief system, culture, and personality, and all searching for some kind of meaningful experience through the game.

Luckily, when it gets too overwhelming, there are at least some basic rules of etiquette, if not of ethics, that can help the newbie player along, as stated by the designers of the game themselves:[11] Be polite. Take the high road. Give away items. Try teaming up. Help other players. Don't be greedy.

And when all else fails, go beat up Arthas. He won't mind respawning, and it's what he's there for: to give all of us heroes the chance to defeat evil, and all of us villains the chance to steal his sword.[12]

---

[11] "How to Be Nice", Blizzard Entertainment, WorldofWarcraft.com, <www.worldofwarcraft.com/info/basics/benice.html>.

[12] For a different take on utilitarianism and deontology with a focus on ninjas, see Chapter 10 in this volume.

2
Render Unto Caesar

KEVIN N. HAW

> Booming virtual economies in online worlds such as *Second Life* and *World of Warcraft* have drawn the attention of a U.S. congressional committee, which is investigating how virtual assets and incomes should be taxed.
>
> —Adam Pasick, reporting from the Reuter's Second Life bureau (October 15th, 2006)

Willhelmia Bloodfang Elfbane, Grand Warrior Duchess of the Troll Army, Defender of the Defiled Realms, Scourge of All Fair Creatures, shifted her seven-foot frame nervously in the too-small chair as the Tiny Man decided her fate.

"You were saying, Ms. Elfbane?" the Tiny Man prompted. He didn't look up from the thick sheaf of papers spread across the surface of his battered, government-issue metal desk.

"Er, ah, yes," Willhelmia said, her voice raspy against the quiet office noises that were the only sound in the harshly lit gray cubicle. "So I normally wait for the Meaties—"

"'Meaties'? The human subscribers of the Game?"

"Yes. They, the knights and good wizards and that ilk, they climb Doom Mountain and face off with me. They come at me and smash and fight and, er, stuff."

"And then?"

"Well, if they kill me, they complete the Troll Queen Quest— Hey! Doesn't that—"

"No, Ms. Elfbane," the Tiny Man replied as he continued to scour Willhelmia's file. "Virtual Death does not absolve taxpayers of their obligations."

"Oh."

"These subscribers, though, they pay for the privilege of logging in and fighting you in the Game?"

"Um, sure. Me and lots of other monsters."

"Well," the Tiny Man nodded, closing the folder with a note of finality. "You generate revenue. That makes you an employee."

"But that means—"

"Yes, you're subject to withholding."

"But, that's crazy! I don't even get paid!"

"Really? What happens to all the equipment of the heroes you defeat?"

"Well, er, I put it into my treasure horde."

"So you work on commission."

"But it's virtual property. It only exists inside the Game!"

"But it can be sold or auctioned on any number of Internet sites to other human players. That makes it income—taxable income." The Tiny Man paused for a moment, a frown creeping over his sallow face as he scratched his bald pate. "You know, if there're fluctuations in value, you might be subject to Capital Gains as well. Hmmm. . . ."

"But, but . . . I'm *Virtual*!"

"Ms. Elfbane, if you feel you're being singled out because of your minority status, I can assure you—"

"No, it's just . . . I just can't understand how you people think I owe $1,673—"

"It's $1,724 with interest and the fine."

"But, I don't *have* that kind of money!"

"With all due respect, I've heard *that* before," the Tiny Man snorted. "And before you start telling me about how you didn't know you were subject to income tax or you didn't think the IRS had jurisdiction in virtual worlds or any of those other excuses, I'll remind you that I've heard all of those as well. You're not the first Digital American I've audited, Ms. Elfbane."

The Trolless, whose interactions with humans were normally limited to screamed obscenities and mutual attempts at decapitation, found herself gnashing her fangs and reflexively reaching to the hip of her armored skirt. Alas, instead of finding the comforting weight of her favorite axe, the empty space brought back the humiliating memory of how the pudgy, glassy eyed security guard in the lobby had confiscated the weapon. Not that killing one little Tiny Man would have helped, of course. From what she'd heard, this whole "Death and Taxes" thing had been going on for a lot longer and was invented by people much more devious than she could even fathom.

She was out of her depth, she realized as she wiped the corner of her eye with a claw. But even as she tried to control her breathing, to count to ten as she had been advised to do before disemboweling anyone out in the Nondigital World, she felt frustrated tears streaming down the green scales of her face. Realizing it was no use, Willhelmia buried her face in her hands.

It just wasn't *fair*!

There was an awkward moment, the only noise disturbing the suddenly silent office being her gravelly sobs and the rhythmic "clang!" of her mailed fist smashing the steel plates of her skirt in frustration. Then, she saw movement in the corner of her eye and realized that the Tiny Man had left his perch behind his desk to offer a box of tissues. She accepted one and blew her nose with an echoing moose call that set the overhead fluorescent fixture swaying.

"Thanks," she whispered as faint half shadows rocked across the office.

"It's okay," the Tiny Man nodded quietly, standing on his toes to place a companionable hand on the spiked bronze plate covering the seated Willhelmia's shoulder. "I understand. After all, we here at the IRS are not without sympathy. . . ."

She nodded, dabbing at her tears with the tissue as she stared down at the Tiny Man's loafers.

". . . and I don't see any reason why we can't allow you to work off this debt—"

The words caused Willhelmia to snap her head up in surprise. He couldn't *possibly* mean . . .

A look at the Tiny Man's face, though, dashed that idea as she saw not the leer she'd been expecting (hoping for?) but instead the practiced, serious expression of a salesman making a pitch. Nevertheless, Willhelmia realized as she crumpled the tissue, if the Tiny Man had a way to square her debt with the IRS, it was worth considering.

"What," the Trolless asked with a wistful sigh that went completely unnoticed by the bureaucrat, "did you have in mind?"

"Well, Ms. Elfbane, it's a special project from the Commissioner himself. You said you commanded an entire troll *army*, is that correct?"

The Internal Revenue Service recently began outsourcing debt-collection activities to more aggressively pursue people who owe taxes. The IRS has already turned over to private agencies the names of more than 13,725 taxpayers who owe the government about $73.5 million. (Tom Herman, *Wall Street Journal*, November 15th, 2006)

3
Finding Adam Smith in Azeroth

ELI KOSMINSKY

World of Warcraft is perfect. Although it may be impossible to avoid getting ganked in Stranglethorn Vale as a lowbie, and harder still to keep up a meaningful conversation in Barrens chat, in at least one respect, *WoW* achieves perfection. Probably without even intending to, Blizzard has created an environment with a perfectly competitive market, where individual Tauren and Draenei compete for and set the prices of goods without the influence of any outside forces. While in the real economic world of government bailouts and global energy cartels it's near-impossible to find examples of Adam Smith's "invisible hand" at work, in *WoW*, its presence is hard to miss.

Since perfect competition is the theoretical foundation on which any real world free market is based, finding an example of it could be incredibly significant. Such an environment could be used to reach a number of ends, from testing economic hypotheses, to helping to build more accurate economic models. Fortunately, all those lazy days you've spent grinding Thorium or disenchanting your greens to pawn your loot in the auction house may actually have been advancing the science of economics, by helping to create a perfectly competitive market that simply couldn't exist in the real world, but flourishes in our own virtual world.

The ideal example of perfect competition must meet several basic criteria, each of which helps create a market with the lowest sustainable prices for all goods. These criteria include the existence of multitudes of sellers, homogenous goods, perfect communication among buyers and sellers, and an absence of barriers to market entry. Let's see how *WoW* stacks up against these measures.

Finding a Perfect Market: WoW Economies FTW

Innumerable Participants

The most significant factor that defines a perfectly competitive economy is that there must be an enormous number of sellers rivaling one another in the industry. If this condition doesn't exist, prices will not drop as much as possible. To better understand why, try imagining a single hobby store opening up in a small town; as the exclusive sellers of *World of Warcraft* miniatures, they have effectively created a monopoly and are able to charge a steep price for their tiny Nagas and Voidwalkers. However, if another, similar store opens up nearby, the original one must lower the prices of its miniaturized goods to stay competitive and continue making sales. If, for some unexplainable reason, ten more identical hobby stores opened in town, every shop manager would have to lower prices like mad in an effort to stay in business selling plastic Murlocs. Of course, this situation is unrealistic, as no reasonable entrepreneur would open a hobby store surrounded by eleven others.

However, these hyper-competitive circumstances are common in Azeroth. If I want to sell a stack of Mithril bars, I have to compete with scads of other players with the exact same intention. Over time, this competition has driven Mithril prices as low as they can be without forcing sellers to leave the market. Even though in putting my bars up for auction, I increase the amount of competitors in the market for Mithril, I cannot change the overall price at which Mithril is traded. This is because the market is so saturated with sellers that a single player entering the market, or leaving it for that matter, has no effect on prices at all. That is, any individual can exit the market "without any appreciable variation resulting in the price of the commodity," in the words of A.A. Cournot, who gave perhaps the first definition of perfect competition.[1] The unfathomable number of players selling Mithril serves another useful purpose: it simultaneously makes it impossible for every seller to get together and decide to raise prices collectively. This act would keep prices from settling as low as they are. There are certainly enough participants in the markets for Azerothian commodities like Mithril to create a level of perfect competition difficult to imagine in the real world.

---

[1] Augustin Coumot, *Researches into the Mathematical Principles of the Theory of Wealth*, first published in 1838 (Macmillan, 1929), p. 90.

Homogenous Goods

Another factor that defines a perfectly competitive market is that its goods are homogenous. Homogeneity of goods means that all items of a given type must be identical and indistinguishable from each other. In the real world, it's difficult to find this kind of uniformity because there usually are a number of different items that can be purchased for the exact same purpose. Let's say, for example, that for some crazy reason I wanted to spend my hard earned dollars to buy a gold farming guide. I would have a nearly endless amount of choices. I might be tempted to buy Trigma's Gold Farming Guide because I've received pestering messages from its creators in-game. Or, I might choose a guide with a good deal of positive feedback from real users. If I find one guide preferable to another, I would be willing to pay more for it, which prevents the lowest possible prices from being established.

In Azeroth, however, the rules are slightly different. If I want to craft a Spellweave Robe, I would have no preference for one piece of Spellweave cloth over another. I've never seen a piece of cloth with the message text, "The craftsmanship could be better . . ." That's because all commodities, including every piece of Spellweave, or copper ore, or Netherbloom, are identical, save perhaps its location on a mob or in your bag. Since every item of a given type is indistinguishable from the next, the only factor that determines which piece of cloth I'm going to buy is the price. Because of this, sellers must compete to offer their goods at the lowest price if they expect to make a sale. This war for low prices of completely indistinguishable goods helps establish perfect competition in a virtual world in a way that would be impossible in the real world.

Perfect Communication

Adam Smith, the Lich King of classical economics, wrote that in order for true competition to exist, "The economic units must possess tolerable knowledge of the market opportunities."[2] What this basically means is that every buyer and seller in a market knows the price at which every good is being offered: we now call this phenomenon "perfect communication." In a market with perfect

[2] Adam Smith, *The Wealth of Nations* (Modern Library, 1937).

communication, buyers are always able to find and purchase the lowest priced product in question. This is a difficult feat to accomplish in the real world.

Let's say I'm in the market for a series one Undead Warlock action figure. Clearly, I want to pay as little as possible for it, since having less money means more work, and less *WoW*. I might first compare the prices of as many internet sellers as I can. Although the Internet helps communication of prices immeasurably, it isn't quite perfect. I might still get a better price by calling around to local stores to ask if they're selling it any cheaper. Maybe it's Christmas time, though, and the phone lines are busy, so I have to drive from one store to another in search of my staff-wielding, skull-impaling figurine. All of these actions impose a cost on me. Maybe not a monetary cost if I'm only browsing the web, but certainly a time cost in that there are more valuable things I can be doing with my precious minutes, like fishing every last coin out of the Dalaran fountain. This other action that I give up is called an *opportunity cost,* and this opportunity cost might prevent me from going out of my way to find the lowest priced 'lock out there.

On the other hand, for the Orcs and Gnomes among us, opportunity costs simply aren't an issue. In *WoW*, since the majority of trades are done through the auction house, where prices are organized and reported nearly instantly, there is no cost associated with gathering the information required to make the absolute cheapest Spellweave Robe. Since all the prices from all sellers are right there for every buyer to see, sellers cannot get away with charging a higher cost, so the lowest sustainable prices prevail.

No Barriers to Market Entry

Once market knowledge is gained through the magic of perfect communication, Smith points out that there must then be freedom to act on this knowledge. This is the basis for the last aspect of perfectly competitive economies, and it is one that is the most difficult to embody in any world, be it real or virtual; that is, a total lack of barriers to market entry. Barriers exist in the form of costs that prevent sellers from moving from the production and sale of one good to another.

As an example, let's imagine Blizzard's production facilities. Most of their machines are likely devoted to manufacturing *WoW*

CDs, as it's obviously their most popular game. However, what if all of a sudden, nobody wanted to play MMORPGs anymore? Now, for whatever reason, people have become more attracted to RTSs than they are to female Night Elves. Blizzard, therefore, decides to switch their production lines in favor of *StarCraft* to take advantage of the rush of players to this less developed market. Unfortunately, this could require reprogramming their machines or perhaps buying new ones. It certainly would mean developing and investing in new marketing and advertising strategies, all of which would decrease the time and capital that they can put toward producing and selling other games they make. These costs are barriers to entry into this new market, and if those costs are too great, Blizzard may decide to just stay in the market they're already in. This leaves their competitors' games, like *Age of Empires* and *Command and Conquer*, with one less potential competitor in the marketplace, so they can charge higher prices for their games. Where we see higher prices, we see a breakdown in perfect competition.

However, in *WoW*'s world of elementals and Nether drakes, market changes can occur much more smoothly. Let's say I usually spend my time farming Crystallized Shadows to make Protoscale Leg Armors. Then, one day, a patch is released with a new dungeon that transports you to the Maelstrom to fight a horde of water-based foes. Now, frost-resist gear is in high demand. So, I decide to fly over to Wintergrasp to start farming Crystallized Fire instead, to get the mats for Superior Frost Resistance. It takes no different skills or investments than my earlier business.

Very quickly, I've been able to enter an entirely new market; a market that may be more profitable, given the circumstances. The only opportunity cost I've incurred is the Crystallized Shadow I could have been farming in my flight to Wintergrasp. Since the barriers to market entry are so small across the board in Azeroth, whenever a good like Crystallized Fire becomes particularly profitable, an influx of players will rush to compete for it simultaneously. Increased competition leads to lower prices, and, as before, these persistently low prices are an indicator of a perfectly competitive market.

Markets in *WoW* and IRL

So you can see that *World of Warcraft* is, on the face of it, a better example of a perfectly competitive market than anything we see in the real world. The question, then, is whether Azerothian markets really are anything like ones on Earth. If they are, then Blizzard and its eleven and a half million players would have helped to create a platform on which we could gather entirely new information on how free markets work.

Unfortunately, there are certainly areas where the parallels between our real and virtual worlds break down. In the real world, consumers have real needs that must be fulfilled. If our corporeal selves do not eat, we die. In *WoW*, a lack of food may be unfortunate, but not life-endingly so (and even if it were, we could always spirit rez up again). Also, the natures of real and virtual goods are somewhat different. In the real world, if Blizzard wants to make more factories to print games at a faster rate, there's only so much iron ore in the world with which to build factories. The earth's resources are finite, and supplies limited. However, there's no limit to the amount of iron that my pickaxe wielding Dwarf can find in his surroundings. Of course, his production rate is restricted by the respawn time of mining nodes, but the nodes will always respawn in the end.

Yet there are more similarities than might be apparent between real world goods we can touch and virtual world goods that we can only link to. The most essential of these similarities is that prices can be controlled by what Smith calls "the invisible hand." Smith used this principle to explain how prices are "pushed" towards optimal levels when buyers and sellers negotiate to work out prices, because what benefits one party tends to benefit everyone involved. This works even though both buyers and sellers are acting only in their own self-interest.

Although Smith probably didn't expect his concepts to be applied to virtual economies, the invisible hand does indeed work in Azeroth as well. When I put my Frostweave cloth on the auction house for the lowest price around, I don't do it because my character or I have a kind soul, but because I am looking to maximize my own profits (the offenses my toon has committed against Sickly Gazelles should be proof enough that his soul is not a saintly one). However, in posting cheap cloth prices to guarantee myself profit, the community as a whole is benefitted as they get a bargain on the goods they want. Without any efforts on the part of GMs or artificial forces, Azerothian citizens are able to keep prices where they should be.

Since prices and goods within *WoW* are so similar to those seen on Earth, we should be able to measure the value generated by

Blood Elves just like we measure the value generated by actual people. In the real world, the wealth generated by individuals and nations can be analyzed by measures like Gross National Product (GNP), which measures a country's income and output. There should be no reason why *World of Warcraft* should be lacking a theoretical GNP. Noting this, a researcher named Edward Castronova set out to determine the rate at which wealth was accumulated in, not *WoW*, but *Everquest*, which was the MMORPG du jour when his work was done.[3] Using this rate, along with conversion figures taken from currency selling websites, Castronova was able to figure out the GNP for the "country" of *Everquest*: it came out to $135 million. This number was similar to what one would expect to find in the real world; the GNP of *Everquest* per person was near that of Russia, and the annual wages of *Everquest* players (if they were to convert their platinum into dollars) would have put them above the poverty line in New York. Virtual worlds can have very real Earth-like economies.

The parallels between the traditional and virtual economies are certainly helped by currency trading websites like the ones used by the research cited above. Together, these websites make up the industry for real money trade. Despite the fact that nobody likes to see the ghost-like avatars of gold farmers hunting around, they do help bring real value to the currency we all spend so much time collecting. Regardless of whether or not the big names in RMT, like IGE,[4] are ruining the level playing field that many players seek in *WoW*, the $1.8 billion trade across the world in virtual items does show that "MMO's are just as much economies as games," as Julian Dibbell, creator of the virtual world research blog, Terra Nova, points out.[5]

More specific similarities are also evident between the goods we can touch and feel and those that exist only as pixels on a screen. In both worlds, different sets of people use different sets of items. Michael Morhaime, the president of Blizzard, most likely wears

---

[3] Edward Castronova, *Virtual Worlds: A First-Hand Account of Market and Society on the Cyberian Frontier* (2001). See also Castronova's book on the culture and economics of virtual worlds: *Synthetic Worlds: The Business and Culture of Online Games*.

[4] <http://en.wikipedia.org/wiki/IGE>.

[5] Julian Dibbell, Julian "The Life of the Chinese Gold Farmer," *New York Times Magazine* 17 (June 2007).

more expensive clothes than you or I do. Similarly, level 80 toons are equipped with more expensive armor. Goods in both worlds also take up "physical" space to a certain extent, in that (ignoring mules in *WoW*) a player must allocate space to keep track of his or her belongings. Another connection we could draw between real and virtual economies would be the existence of a number of different markets in each locale. On Earth, different countries of varying populations, preferences, and ages, have markets that function under similar rules, but with widely varying results. In *WoW*, different countries and continents are insignificant, since auction houses are linked; but, the existence of different servers with self-selected members mimics in certain ways the existence of different countries. Just as real world economists have the opportunity to study countries as small as Monaco alongside those as large as China, virtual world economists can study high population servers like Illidan with low population ones like the barely-pronounceable Jubei'Thos. Together, all of these intricacies relating Earth to Azeroth make *WoW* an appealing tool to learn about how economies work.

Buffing Our Economic Knowledge with *World of Warcraft*

The question, then, is whether the similarities between real, global markets, and virtual, Orgrimmar-based ones, outweigh the differences to the point where we can learn from this new world that we have helped to create. Fortunately, it's possible to test whether the markets of *WoW* function like real markets by making predictions about how they would act if they were, in fact, perfectly competitive, and then observing and analyzing the way the *WoW* markets actually behave.

In any perfectly competitive market, more buyers and sellers lead to more stable prices. The reason for this is clear even in Azeroth. As we all know, the drop rates of most items are random, and work off of a specific percentage. So, the amount of a given item that is listed in the auction house at any time basically depends on how lucky people are at gathering it on that day. On smaller-population servers, it would only take a small group of lucky Warlocks or Hunters to increase the supply of a good, say wool cloth, to unusually high numbers. This increase in supply would lead to temporarily lower prices for wool, and some very happy power-leveling tailors. However, on higher-population servers, it would be harder for a small group of them to change the server price of wool cloth due to the higher baseline amount of it, leading to more stable prices. So, if the *WoW* economy really functions as a market—a perfectly competitive market—higher population servers in general should demonstrate more stable prices than lower population servers.

Still, just because higher numbers of players on a server should lead to more stable prices, does not mean that it will. As has already been noted, there are aspects of virtual Azerothian goods that could make *WoW*'s markets behave differently than theory would predict regarding real world goods. My own statistical analysis of different serves, however, shows that in the case of heavily traded goods like Netherweave cloth, prices are nearly twice as stable on high population servers as low population servers, indicating that *WoW*'s virtual market does in fact behave as would be predicted in a perfectly competitive market.

Another area where the markets within *World of Warcraft* behave as expected is in price efficiency. In the real world, prices are defined as efficient when it's impossible to make money without taking on risk. Let's say I'm involved in the market for gold buying and selling for real world currency. I look online, and find a gold farming website offering 500 gold for the low, low price of eight dollars. However, my oblivious neighbor is willing to pay me twenty dollars for 500 gold because he desperately needs a Gryphon. Now I stand to make a twelve dollar profit simply by exchanging my own money to gold and then back into money. That would be an example of market inefficiency, and also an example of what economists call arbitrage. Arbitrage does not exist in a truly perfectly competitive market. If we look at the situation I profited from above, one could see how my plan would have been foiled were real-world markets perfectly competitive. Armed with perfect communication and information, my neighbor would have quickly recognized a cheaper source of the gold he craved. How does arbitrage look in *World of Warcraft*?

As would be expected, *WoW* markets display very little arbitrage. Above, the two items that were traded, real world currency and gold, were objects that were easily convertible from one into another. The same can be said for certain items in Azeroth, such as lesser and greater planar essences. Simply click on three of the former and you get one of the latter. Therefore, if the markets in

World of Warcraft are perfectly competitive, the ratio of the prices of these goods should be exactly three to one. Otherwise, I could potentially profit simply by buying greater planar essences, decomposing them, and reselling their components at a profit. Again, research shows that the most common trades for these goods occur at five gold and fifteen gold, which is exactly the ratio we would predict.[6]

But as observant *WoW* players may have noticed, there's usually some discrepancy between the prices of planar essences. The difference listed by Allakhazam is normally around five percent. How might we explain this variation? First, the prices of lesser essences likely lag behind those of their greater versions, because fewer people think to purchase lesser essences since they're used directly in fewer recipes. Secondly, some players are probably not interested enough to check what the most appropriate price for their fractional essence is. Here we may have run into one of the eternally insurmountable boundaries to forming a completely perfect market: human laziness.

Still, that doesn't mean we can't come darn close to an idealized market. *World of Warcraft* may be the best example of a perfectly competitive market we have available to us. This makes *WoW* potentially productive ground for learning about the very economic system that the free markets we know and love are based on. It's easy to conceive of using *WoW* to better understand how consumers behave when faced with goods that have genuine value in a setting more observable than the real world and more realistic than a laboratory. It might eventually tell us more about the real world economy, and ultimately something about humanity's values and beliefs. At the very least, knowing the power of *WoW*'s markets will allow you to tell your parents/boyfriend/girlfriend that all your time spent in *World of Warcraft* isn't wasted. *WoW* is more than a game. It's a fertile, flourishing economy. It's real. And it's perfect.[7]

---

[6] Eli Kosminsky, *World of Warcraft: The Viability of MMORPGs as Platforms for Modeling and Evaluating Perfect Competition* (2008). Retrieved from <http://elik.exofire.net/index.php?p=1_3_Research>.

[7] The author would like to thank the esteemed Thomas Andriello for his assistance in writing this chapter.

4
A Meaningless World . . . of *Warcraft*

LUKE CUDDY

I emerge from the vibrant Lushwater Oasis. After a quick glance back at the palm trees and Centaurs, I set my sights in front of me. It's late and I have other quests to complete, but it's night-time and the moonlight is casting a brilliant hue over the hills in the distance, cascading down to my, at this point, level 12 Troll Shaman. The curiosity hits me: I want to know what's on the other side of those hills. I know it's another territory, but what territory? Can I even get there this way? And, if so, what will the land be like? What sorts of Non-Player Characters (NPCs) will be there? Will I encounter any other Player Characters (PCs), and will any of them want to start a fight (I'm playing PvP)? A sense of adventure envelops me. Despite the dangers, I move forward . . .

I've long since passed this point in my adventures through Azeroth, but the above represents a thought process that I would repeat in different contexts throughout the course of developing my first toon. But in *this* context, here's the relevant philosophical question: what's the point of my little excursion through the Barrens' hills in the first place? I haven't completed any quests in the hills. I haven't talked to any other players. I haven't helped out my guild in any way. So what's the point? Is there a *purpose* to my actions in light of the rest of the game?

Why the Auction House and not a Battleground?

You do occasionally hear gamers talk about how some aspect of a game they're playing "has no purpose." Sometimes they'll explain it as the designers having fun with the development process—

Dancing Troll Village, for example. If you press this line of thought too far, you start wondering exactly what has a purpose and what doesn't. Do *WoW* professions have a purpose? Will failing to learn any professions prevent you from progressing in the game? What about the quests? You don't need to complete every quest to level up, so are some quests pointless? What about talking to other players? For a good portion of the leveling up process you don't *have* to talk to anyone to complete quests. And yet *WoW* is known as a social game, incorporating numerous gameplay mechanics that encourage communal play. When Stan Marsh is playing *WoW* on *South Park*, his father, Randy, wonders if he should be out socializing with his friends instead, to which Stan replies: "I *am* socializing, artard. I'm logged on to an MMORPG with people from all over the world, and getting XP with my party using teamspeak."[1]

But let's put *South Park* aside. Because gamers often use the phrase "beat the game," implying that there is some condition under which there is nothing left to do in the game—implying that it is complete—it seems to make sense that certain in-game components "have no purpose." Anything that does not go toward "beating the game" is pointless. But even this line is often blurred. What does it mean to "beat" *WoW*? When you join a respected guild? When you reach level 80? If this is true, though, then why is it that many players think the game doesn't even *begin* until you reach level 80?

The problem with labeling an in-game action as "pointless" and another as "meaningful" is that such a label presupposes an overall point to the game, the existence of which is debatable. But if it's questionable whether actions in *WoW* have meaning, what about actions in real life? Is there any overall point to everyday actions such as brushing your teeth, sending a "hi:)" text to your best friend, or throwing a banana peel in the garbage? Do *these* actions presuppose an overall point to life? *Is* there an overall point to life? For centuries, and in many different cultures, philosophers have asked the meaning of life and proposed different answers. Some have claimed that life has no meaning, a position known as *nihilism*.

Can playing *WoW* be seen as a response to nihilism? I think the answer is "yes," but a complicated "yes." The German philosopher,

[1] Taken from <http://www.southparkstuff.com/season_10/episode_1008/epi1008script/>.

Friedrich Nietzsche, penned one of the most famous responses to nihilism, which involves something called an "Overman." To find out how all these things connect, we're going to have to understand meaninglessness itself.

Meaninglessness on Earth

Think back to when you were waiting in line at the mall for your copy of *Warcraft III: Reign of Chaos* (I know, I know, we didn't all get the game at the mall, but just stick with me for the sake of the example). What was everyone around you doing? Waiting in line too? Maybe your mind started wandering at this point as you began to observe others in line—some chatting, some waiting patiently, some waiting impatiently. Maybe the situation caused you to reflect on your purchase of the original *Warcraft: Orcs and Humans* which, at the time, you may not have been too sure about. When you played it, though, chances are you had at least some fun strategizing the eventual decline of the opposing faction. Next, maybe you reflected on your purchase of *Warcraft II: Tides of Darkness*, the critically-acclaimed sequel, and the game that really showed gamers that the *Warcraft* franchise had something to offer.

But then you might have started thinking to yourself, what's next? After *Warcraft III*, that is. You buy the inevitable expansion, and then . . . well, then comes *World of Warcraft*, right? Then *Burning Crusade*, then *Wrath of the Lich King*. But the question still remains: what *then*? Scholars have sometimes asked this question in different contexts. In discussing our species' lack of an external goal (beyond an evolutionary one), the philosophically-inclined biologist, E.O. Wilson, writes:

> It could be that in the next hundred years humankind will thread the needles of technology and politics, solve the energy and materials crisis, avert nuclear war, and control reproduction. We can hope for a stable ecosystem and a well-nourished population. But what then?[2]

What then, indeed! The problem is that the question will always remain, whether we're discussing our goals as a species or personal goals. You might have played every game of the *Warcraft* franchise, bought every collectible, strategy guide, book, comic, and

---

[2] E.O. Wilson, *On Human Nature* (Harvard University Press, 1978), p. 3.

maybe even the trading card game, but when you put it all in perspective, there doesn't seem to be a point. You buy a game, you beat it. You buy the expansion, you beat it. You buy the sequel, you beat it. You read *World of Warcraft: Beyond the Dark Portal*, you buy a new *WoW* adventure book!

Are your actions in life ultimately leading anywhere? Or is your life just one game after another, one thing after another? The pessimistic German philosopher, Arthur Schopenhauer, gave the following description of the predicament of life:

> A man finds himself, to his great astonishment, suddenly existing, after thousands and thousands of years of non-existence. He lives for a little while, and then again comes an equally long period when he must exist no more.[3]

Just one of the many examples of the way Schopenhauer's writing can put things in perspective. Like a fickle flame, our existence is small and insignificant in the eyes of the universe. You buy and play game after game, but for what? You're just going to die anyway while the world goes on, just as it did before you were born.

A bit harsh, I know, but it's a good way to understand nihilism. In the existential school of philosophy, nihilism is often described as a feeling of endless pointlessness. Has your life ever felt this way? You wake up to an alarm, you go to work or school (or both), you come home, you level up your Night Elf Druid for a few hours, you go to sleep, then you wake up and do it again, and again, and again.

There are many ways to respond to nihilism, from drug addiction to religious devotion. Friedrich Nietzsche, however, saw nihilism as a stage that could be overcome. He thought that a God-based value system was, at its foundation, devoid of meaning. Famously, he introduced the "death of God," which refers to the death of the *idea* of God. He thought that the idea of an all-powerful, all-loving, and all-knowing being was not strong enough for people to sustain given the Western scientific worldview that had taken hold since the Enlightenment.

The scientific worldview tells us that humans are not so great. We are not the center of the solar system, let alone the universe.

---

[3] Arthur Schopenhauer, "On the Vanity of Existence" in *Studies in Pessimism* (Wilder, 2008).

We're one planet revolving around one star that is one of billions of others. Not even our galaxy, which is composed of over two hundred billion stars, is special. Furthermore, scientists estimate that there are two hundred billion galaxies in the universe. So where does that leave us? To the known universe, human life is considerably less significant than an ant crawling on the kitchen counter, or a measly level 3 Scorpid Worker in Durotar.[4]

Or consider a seemingly more "significant" NPC in *WoW* like King Bangalash. When you first encounter him wandering the tropics in Stranglethorn, there is a certain majesty to his appearance—the silky white fir, the proud demeanor. And yet, he's only a level 43 quest boss. And the specific Bangalash you encounter and kill to complete the quest is part of a single instance; the rest of Azeroth will not miss this one Bangalash. Furthermore, a new Bangalash will spawn eventually to replace the one you killed. On Earth, humans as a species are like a single Bangalash—short-lived and insignificant. Humans die, the universe goes on. Bangalash dies, *WoW* goes on.

Nietzsche was deeply aware of the implications of the human predicament. He also thought everyone was aware, whether they realized it or not. For Nietzsche, there are a couple of ways to respond to nihilism. One way is to take refuge in religious faith: if this life is meaningless, then God and the afterlife give life meaning. This is a fair route given the general beliefs of the American population, and one that many people take. Nietzsche, however, believed that people taking this route are desperately clinging to an idea—God—that has lost its force, meaning, and vitality, even for them. In other words, he believed that their faith is empty. In his typically colorful style, he writes:

> Before God! But now this God has died. You higher men, this god was your greatest danger. It is only since he lies in his tomb that you have been resurrected. Only now the great noon comes; only now the higher man becomes—lord . . . God died: now we want the Overman to live.[5]

---

[4] For a recent video that gives a current—and sexy!—account of the Western scientific worldview see National Geographic's *Journey to the Edge of the Universe* (2008).

[5] Friedrich Nietzsche, *Thus Spoke Zarathustra* (Penguin, 1954), p. 288.

This quote reveals Nietzsche's answer to a dead God and a nihilistic universe: the Overman, or a being that transcends the accepted value system and goes on to create his own values. More from Nietzsche:

> Let us therefore limit ourselves to the purification of our opinions and valuations and to the creation of our own new tables of what is good . . . We, however, want to become those we are—human beings who are new, unique, incomparable, who give themselves laws, who create themselves.[6]

These new human beings who "give themselves laws" and "create themselves" are Nietzschean Overmen. For Nietzsche, the Overman is to man as man is to ape. The Overman is at a higher level of evolution than man. The Overman does not conform. He does not understand himself in relation to *any* value system; he is his own value system. He loves every aspect of his existence, the good and the bad. He affirms his life in all its manifestations. But to become an Overman, a person must waft in the pit of nihilism before overcoming it (and it is a pit!).

WoW as a Response to Nihilism

Before going on with Nietzsche, let's recall the key question posed earlier: can *World of Warcraft* be a response to nihilism? We've seen Nietzsche's response, but how does *WoW* fit in? To begin to answer this question, it will help to take a look at the Magic Circle, an idea that was introduced by a Dutch thinker, Johan Huizinga.[7] Consider the following fictional scenario. You're watching professional golf on TV. Tiger Woods is about to make a long putt that, if successful, will win him the tournament. However, just as Tiger is about to putt, he stops and scratches his head. Then he picks up the golf ball, walks over to the hole, and drops the ball in. He has not technically made the putt, but he has technically transported the ball from where it was on the ground to the hole.

Has Tiger won the tournament? Naturally, the officials in this situation would disqualify Tiger since he did not follow the rules.

---

[6] Friedrich Nietzsche, *The Gay Science* (Vintage, 1974), p. 266.

[7] See Johan Huizinga, *Homo Ludens: A Study of the Play Element in Culture* (Beacon Press, 1950).

What has happened in this fictitious scenario is that Tiger has stepped out of the Magic Circle. Before playing in the tournament, Tiger and all the other players made the decision that they would be playing golf according to the rules of golf. They would use designated clubs to swing, designated balls to hit, and designated courses to play on. To be in the Magic Circle is to accept the rules and conventions of a game without question. A baseball player does not ask *why* three strikes constitute an out; he simply accepts this rule, and the others, thereby ensuring that he is inside baseball's Magic Circle.

Expanding on Huizinga's original idea, Katie Salen and Eric Zimmerman note: "Within the Magic Circle, special meanings accrue and cluster around objects and behaviors. In effect, a new reality is created, defined by the rules of the game and inhabited by its players."[8] In the example above, Tiger Woods left the Magic Circle because he did not respect these special meanings. When we decide to play a game, we respect the core rules of the game as absolute and, if we don't, we have not stepped into the Magic Circle.

How does a player step into the Magic Circle in *World of Warcraft?* Well, for one thing, he accepts the fact that there are other sentient races besides Humans—like Trolls and Orcs. He accepts the fact that the natural forces in Azeroth can be manipulated and controlled to a great extent: magic. He accepts the fact that teleportation is possible, and so on.

It's not as though the *WoW* player actually thinks that teleportation is possible or that Trolls exist. He has entered the Magic Circle, and in that circle there are Trolls and teleportation. Consider what someone might say who is *not* willing to enter *WoW*'s Magic Circle: "What? That Human Warrior just jumped off of a huge cliff that looks at least one hundred feet high. How could any human fall that far and not die, however strong? That's just not realistic." This person is unwilling to accept rules that exist in *WoW*, but do not exist in our reality. He's not in the Magic Circle.

When you step into the Magic Circle, a special thing happens: you accept the rules and order of the gameworld. This acceptance can be incredibly refreshing. If the meaninglessness of the real

---

[8] Salen and Zimmerman, *Rules of Play: Game Design Fundamentals* (MIT Press, 2005), p. 96.

world bears down on you—if you appreciate the insignificance of human life to the rest of the universe—then you can always enter *WoW*'s Magic Circle (which contains its own significance), and this is what so many players do. Salen and Zimmerman note: "The fact that the Magic Circle is just that—a circle—is an important feature of this concept. As a closed circle, the space it circumscribes is enclosed and separate from the real world" (p. 95).

The Magic Circle is significant for a discussion of nihilism because it shows exactly when meaning is created. When is life meaningful? When you decide to step within the bounds of the Magic Circle. When the weight of nihilism constricts, *WoW*'s Magic Circle awaits you. By stepping into the Magic Circle you are accepting the meanings of Azeroth as absolute, and denying the significance of the world outside (the real world). This is simultaneously an affirmation of the meaninglessness of the real world and a response to it. So the answer is, yes, *WoW* can be a response to nihilism. But, as we'll see, this is only the first step. I said it was complicated!

Dissolving *WoW's* Magic Circle

Let's return to Nietzsche and the Overman. Is there any way that we can see those in *WoW's* Magic Circle as having achieved Overman status, as having created their own values and transcended traditional humanity (or traditional Orchishness, as the case may be)? Unfortunately, there doesn't seem to be a good argument that this is true in light of Nietzsche's thought. Although players have denied the meaning of life outside of *WoW*, many have replaced those values with the ones given by the Magic Circle itself—level up, complete quests, join a guild, hate the opposing faction, and so on. This is similar to replacing the importance of this world with that of an afterlife—the route of the religious man and a no-no in Nietzsche's book. The Overman affirms *all* aspects of his life, not just those aspects connected with *WoW*.

At the beginning of this chapter I raised questions about goals within the game. When I walked through the hills in the Barrens and didn't complete quests, what was the point? (And don't tell me that it's the exploration XP, because we all know how insignificant those amounts are!) When you have lengthy conversations about the latest movie you saw through guild chat, what's the point? These sorts of actions dissolve the strength of *WoW*'s Magic Circle by showing that the circle itself doesn't always separate us from the real world.

In fact, recent theorists have denied that the Magic Circle is as strong as early theorists thought it was, particularly in relation to Massively Multiplayer Online Role Playing Games (MMORPGs). When stepping into Azeroth, for example, gamers bring their attitudes and ideals with them, especially when talking to other players in the game. Edward Castronova makes the claim that, in MMORPGs like *WoW*, the distinction between the real world and the gameworld via the Magic Circle is no longer very helpful.[9] There are a few aspects of *WoW* that seriously blur the line between the real world and Azeroth. Gold farming, for instance, is when players amass in-game currency and items and then sell them for real world currency. Is the gold farmer in the Magic Circle or not? If gold farming has real-world implications—and it seems to—then it has a serious effect on the circle's integrity.

In light of this analysis, my actions in the Barrens' hills can be seen as a dissolution of the Magic Circle; I did not accept the traditional rules and goals of the game, such as completing quests and leveling up.[10] Many gamers use guild chat as though it's an online message board—they might as well not be playing *WoW*. These actions, I think, are evidence not only that the bounds of *WoW*'s Magic Circle are unclear, but also that players often dissolve any circle that might exist. I have gamer friends who will not play *WoW* because of the very fact that the in-game goals are not as clearly defined as they are in console Role Playing Games.

One way to look at the player's dissolution of the Magic Circle is as an affirmation of the meaninglessness of the game itself. If stepping *into* the Magic Circle gives the game meaning, then dissolving the circle takes it away. Before you get mad at the idea that *WoW* is meaningless, consider the greater context. *WoW* is separated from

---

[9] Edward Castronova, *Synthetic Worlds: The Business and Culture of Online Games* (University of Chicago Press, 2005), pp. 147–161.

[10] One could wonder why there even are "traditional rules" associated with a game like *WoW* that permits so much player freedom. But I think questing, grinding, or raiding qualify. After all, some players don't even begin to step outside these traditional rules, whether consciously or unconsciously, until long past the time they reach level 80 by, for instance, flying their mount around to territories pointlessly or idly chatting with guild members. The Gnome Tea Party (discussed in Chapter 9 in this volume) is a clear example of players stepping outside of traditional gameplay.

life only superficially, by the Magic Circle. If life itself is meaningless, and *WoW* is an aspect of life, then *WoW* is meaningless too. Once the Magic Circle is seen to be an artificial boundary, then it disappears. So let's look at the possible progression of the player so far. Insofar as it connects to the question of whether playing *WoW* can be a response to nihilism, the player must follow these steps in order:

1. **Realize that life is meaningless**
2. **Enter *WoW*'s Magic Circle**
3. **Dissolve *WoW*'s Magic Circle, realize that *WoW* itself is meaningless**

Should the gamer stop here? Are there more steps besides the three above? Well, as we'll see, the gamer can stop anywhere she wants (and many gamers do). But in relation to Nietzsche there are definitely more steps. The gamer who's reached step 3 above is *not* an Overman.

Dissolving *WoW's* Magic Circle and Continuing to Play

Let's take the dissolution of the Magic Circle further. What happens when the player dissolves the bounds of the magic circle—when he steps out of the Magic Circle—and at the same time he willingly keeps playing? Well, now the player is getting into Nietzsche's territory. In the face of a meaningless Azeroth, the player continues to play. He does what *he* wants. He doesn't care that the game tells him he should complete quests, join a guild, or raid and instead he wanders, he chats with other players, he auctions off his potions.

Nietzsche's Overman, remember, sees the world as meaningless but creates his own values anyway, in the face of the uncaring universe. He rises above the nihilistic stage. In a few different places Nietzsche discusses the idea that we should create ourselves as though we (as people) are works of art, like a painting or a sculpture. Taking a look at some of his ideas about art can help us understand what this means.

Although he's never clear about the specific values the Overman would create, some of Nietzsche's writing seems to point to the idea that the Overman would see art as one of the highest values.

Nietzsche writes: "Art makes the sight of life bearable by laying over it the veil of unclear thinking."[11] Much of Nietzsche's discussion of art can be found in his first book, *The Birth of Tragedy*. In this book Nietzsche says that life finds meaning through art; art brings our lives a deeper level of experience: "Art is not merely imitation of the reality of nature but rather a metaphysical supplement to the reality of nature, placed beside it for its overcoming."[12]

Nietzsche would later admit that the ideas he presented in *The Birth of Tragedy* were a bit amateurish. Still, even his later writings make it clear that Nietzsche had a special place in his heart for art, especially insofar as he thought we need to create ourselves as art, as the Overman would. Nietzsche was fascinated with the act of, and especially the human capacity for, creation: "In man, *creature* and *creator* are united: in man there is matter, fragment, excess, clay, mud, madness, chaos; but in man there is also creator, sculptor . . ."[13]

How do these ideas about art connect to *WoW*? Can exploring Azeroth or creating a toon be considered acts of creation? For all we know, Nietzsche might have been fascinated with videogames had it ever been possible for him to play them. What if someone was to tell Nietzsche that he could not only observe the world of van Gogh painting, but that he could explore that world as well? I think the prospect would entice him.

Wouldn't exploring the painting be a bit like playing *World of Warcraft*? After all, *WoW* is an in-depth, immersive world capable of being explored (let's put aside the image of a gamer trying to show Nietzsche how to use the keyboard and mouse). And Azeroth is not boring or trivial; one of the first things critics noticed about *WoW* was the beauty of the environments, cities, and dungeons, and the seamless blending between territories. I still remember my amazement after coming across certain territories for the first time—Un'Goro Crater comes to mind.

When I first encountered the entrance in southwestern Tanaris it was night-time. As I headed down the trail into Un'Goro, I glanced back to a surreal scene of two black obelisks and a gargantuan cactus patch against the stars. Continuing, the prehistoric feel of Un'Goro gradually materialized: twisting vines hanging

---

[12] Nietzsche, *Human All Too Human*, (Cambridge University Press, 1996), p. 151.

[13] Nietzsche, *The Birth of Tragedy* (Vintage, 1967), p. 140.

[14] Nietzsche, *Beyond Good and Evil* (Penguin, 1973), p. 136.

down from the tops of wide trees, Raptors wandering the shore of a misty river flowing from a waterfall, the sounds of insects and other beasts pervading everything.

Or consider taking the flight paths. Although taking a flight path from, say, Tanaris to Orgrimmar is not always the most direct route, as your avatar flies over the ocean it's hard not to admire the view of a sunset in the distance or a pirate ship off the shore. In fact, your lack of control over the flight itself *forces* you to appreciate the sights along the way. Naturally, gamers will differ on what territory or aspect of the game they experience as enjoyable, but we can all agree on this: there is at least *something* we all find enjoyable.

*A Human Warlock flies over a river in Elwynn Forest on a flight path (*World of Warcraft*, Blizzard Entertainment, 2004).*

Creating a character can certainly be seen as artistic. Consider the pride one feels after creating a toon and reaching level 80. Clearly, there is a big difference between a noob Human Mage and a maxed out Death Knight. Creation within Azeroth can take different forms. One of them is building up experience within the game, traveling around, experiencing the surroundings as appealing, beautiful. Another is pimping out your toon, getting new armor and items through numerous raids or quests.

In a Nietzschean sense, this sort of creation within the game can be seen as the player affirming his existence in the gameworld, as breaking out of the Magic Circle and exploiting the meaninglessness of the game. The actions of the player here are the fourth step, the one that comes after the dissolution of the Magic Circle (an updated list of steps is coming up). The player is having fun. Nietzsche talked a lot about Dionysus, the Greek god of wine. One who lives as an embodiment of Dionysus is living life to its fullest and really enjoying his time on earth. The player who sees his toon and his excursions through Azeroth as art is exploring his Dionysian side within the gameworld.

Death Knight as Overman?

Still, no matter how cool a maxed-out level 80 Death Knight might be, it unfortunately isn't quite what Nietzsche has in mind with the Overman. The problem is that the player affirms her existence *through* the Death Knight in the game, and in so doing denies her existence in the real world. It's okay to identify with your avatar, but when you forget that you exist not only in Azeroth but on Earth too, then you're making an implicit statement about your real world identity. However, there's a fifth step, and it's always possible that a player will take it as a result of her experiences in Azeroth.

For instance, what if the player begins to create an analogy between his playing *WoW* and living his life outside of the gameworld? He might start to wonder about the real world equivalent of a maxed-out Death Knight. How can you max yourself out in the real world? Again, Nietzsche thought that the Overman would rise above the nihilistic stage of life and create his own values. The Overman would affirm his existence, say "Yes!" to life. He would create his life like a work of art. Another quote from Nietzsche:

> To "give style" to one's character—a great and rare art! It is practiced by those who survey all the strengths and weaknesses and then fit them into an artistic plan until every one of them appears as art… and even weaknesses delight the eye.[14]

The gamer has to use what he's learned in the gameworld back in the real world. If you can create yourself in *WoW* in the face of the meaninglessness of the game, why can't you create yourself in real

---

15 *The Gay Science*, p. 232.

life in the face of the meaninglessness of life outside of the game? Let's look at the complete steps (including the addition of the fourth and fifth) that can lead to a full affirmation of life in the Nietzschean sense.

1. **Realize that life is meaningless**
2. **Enter *WoW*'s Magic Circle**
3. **Dissolve *WoW*'s Magic Circle, realize that *WoW* itself is meaningless**
4. **Play *WoW* anyway in the face of its meaninglessness, affirm your existence within the game, create your toon as a work of art**
5. **Appreciate the analogy between *WoW* and real life, affirm your existence in reality, create *yourself* as a work of art**

This does *not* imply that *WoW* isn't worth playing once you've reached this point. On the contrary, *WoW* is part of life so a person can simply have fun playing it. Saying "Yes!" to life means saying "Yes!" to all your actions in life, including your actions through your avatar in *WoW*. You can have fun and enjoy your three hour excursion through Azeroth, just as you can enjoy your three hour excursion through Yosemite National Park.

There are some other implications. The first is that people can potentially get stuck on any step, and they do. Many people realize that life is meaningless (step one), and they simply wallow in nihilism for most of their life, never finding meaning anywhere. Many enter *WoW*'s Magic Circle to escape the meaninglessness—a fact seemingly supported by Azeroth's present eleven and a half million worldwide players. The strength and appeal of Azeroth is why so many people get stuck on this step. Probably a good deal of those who reach step two make it to step three or four eventually, whether they're conscious of it or not. But it's only the exceptional gamer who makes it to step five, who maxes herself out in life as she did with her *WoW* toon, who affirms her existence both in Azeroth and in the real world. Which step are *you* on?[15]

---

[16] I'd like to thank Donavan Muir and Mike Bruce for their very useful comments on Nietzsche. I'm also grateful to Steve Barbone for his very helpful comments in general.

5
A Mage in Motion

JUAN FERRET

"Here we go," I whisper, as the gates holding us back from the frozen peaks and canyons of Alterac Valley finally open the flood of would-be heroes ready to fight the Horde and their allies, the Frostwolf clan. I summon my nightsaber mount—I'm still amazed that this feline three times my size is able to appear from a parallel world (or wherever the hell he comes from) to carry me swiftly without protest. With a growl he leaps over the ridge alongside other Alliance heroes: there are noble Elf Warriors and terrifying Death Knights riding next to shadow Priests and demonic Warlocks. In front, a holy Paladin and a Draenei Shaman are arguing about who is the better healer, while a diminutive Rogue is pick-pocketing them (somehow I think she's just pretending). A Druid and a Dwarf Hunter ride up to me, demanding some conjured water. I shrug my shoulders in disbelief as I begrudge what is expected of me these days. "Don't you know I can't conjure drinks and ride?" I mutter tersely.

I am Admetus, a Human Mage. My personal story is short since, for some reason, I don't have much recollection of my past. I live in the world of Azeroth, although many of its denizens call it "The Server" especially when the so called "Lag" demon appears to "slow" or "crash" it. I have to admit I have never quite believed these stories, since I have never experienced the "Lag." I only know of this phenomenon from others who describe it as a momentary stoppage of all actions in the world. I have often wondered that if we all experience this lag in the same way, how could we know that there was indeed a lag?

Disappearance and Lag

Still, many believe it exists and this leads them to threats about changing "servers" and to blasphemous tirades against the mighty pantheon of the gods of Blizzard. These divinities apparently control and have the power to destroy or "shut down" our world, as some prefer to say. Many of my fellow denizens believe that once a week, to remind us of their power, the Blizzard gods "shut down" our server for a few hours. I have also never experienced this, but many claim they do, and every Tuesday after midnight cries can be heard around Azeroth lamenting the impending but momentary doom. As with the lag, I remain puzzled: if all things disappear simultaneously only to reappear a few hours later undisturbed, how can we tell that we have in fact disappeared?

We ride through the frozen canyons and valleys of Alterac with ease. No Horde in sight. From the corner of my eye I see a wildflower. I magically dismiss my mount and proceed to collect it almost without intending to, as if compelled by a force beyond my control. I'm an herbalist, you see. I collect and alchemically alter flowers into powerful potions, which then I sell, gift to friends, or drink myself. "It is strange" I whisper, for I have never seen a flower in Alterac Valley before or growing from a crusted sheet of ice for that matter. As I wonder over this strange herbal riddle, the last Alliance rider disappears over the hill. I feel something or someone staring from a distance behind me. I turn around on my heels expecting the worst but I see no one. This isn't the first time I've experienced the sensation of a towering presence behind me. I have been feeling this since I began training as a Mage, or questing as some call it, in the Northshire Abbey of Elwynn Forest over four years ago. As a matter of fact, I don't remember much of anything before that. How strange.

This feeling of being watched has grown more distinct and acute. Recently it has been accompanied with the disturbing realization that the mysterious presence may not just be observing me, but somehow affecting or attempting to control my actions. A few years ago, in one of my long walks around Stormwind (or runs, rather; I don't know why most of us always run around rather than walk; we must be in a hurry I guess) a renowned sage from Dalaran was lecturing his students, at the steps of the Cathedral of Light, about the idea that our actions are nothing more than the inevitable consequence of our ordered universe.

I remember him saying: "Our free will is just an illusion and we do not control our actions. This is a hard deterministic position—what is *is* because something distinctly caused it through and through and cannot be otherwise. Chance and possibilities are also mere illusions solely referring to our lack of knowledge and control." He mumbled something about how the thought of a universe ruled by chance was akin to the sight of the horrible motion of a mass of maggots in their carrion bed. A particularly bright student stood up and slapped the sage across the face. "There can be no judgment against me if there is no real element of chance in our universe," she said as she sat back down. I heard later that she replaced him as the head master of the academy.[1] As I reckon with this memory, I realize that of late this feeling is definitely more than the sensation of being watched, as if a foreign agency is controlling my actions. But if an external agency is behind my actions . . .

Fleeing from an Undead Rogue

Suddenly I feel a sharp pain on my neck and lose control over my limbs, dropping the herb I've just gathered. I think a Rogue has just sapped me! Maybe that was the presence I felt and it could be my undoing. After a few seconds a back stab leaves me reeling with pain. I quickly invocate a Frost Nova spell that reveals the Undead Rogue and leaves him frozen in place. This spell tends to last only a few seconds so I proceed to do what I do best in dangerous situations: run away. As I flee I cannot stop thinking about my previous recollections of the meaning of freedom and the agencies in control of my actions. I figure that since the Rogue would be chasing me for some time—for they seem more than any other class to relish the chase—I would carefully consider the possibilities.

Since my current action is running and I cannot shake off the image of the motion of the maggots, I begin by entertaining what motion entails. "A good choice" I whisper, since motion is the basis of all of our actions. Motion is to *go* from A to B, I state to myself. Yet somehow I feel that I cheated by trying to define motion this way since "to go" implies motion. So I try again: motion is to *change* space locations in a given time. I feel satisfied until I realize that I

[1] The online Stanford Encyclopedia of Philosophy is a good resource for summaries of this debate and other philosophical topics (plato.stanford.edu).

may still be cheating since change implies motion as well. Even worse, I have just introduced two concepts that may be deceptively complex: space and time. Rather than making matters simpler, I am making them worse. How can something so simple be so difficult? And that damned Rogue is still chasing me!

I consider that to go from A to B I must first pass the halfway point between them. Let's call it A'. Using the same reasoning, to go from A to A' I first need to pass the halfway point, A''. To go from A to A'' I must first pass through A'''. And . . . I shudder. I imagine this as a line in front of me.

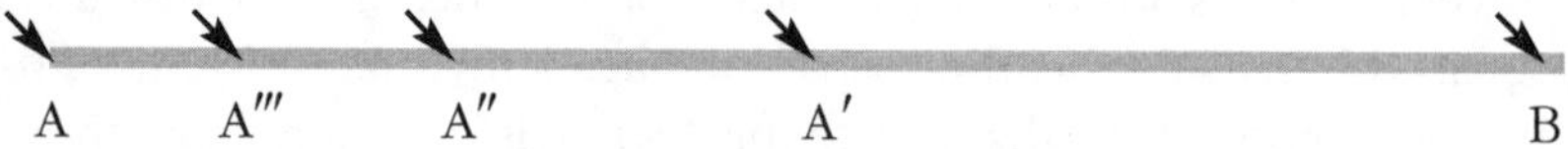

I can physically go from A to B, but from this thought experiment I can infer that motion is impossible since it would take an infinite amount of time to traverse the infinite points between A and B. I can't move from A to B, or even worse, I can't move at all since B can be any point arbitrarily close to A. "Motion is impossible," I conclude aloud. Yet here I am running away from that Rogue and he is getting closer. But how can he be getting closer if it would take an infinite amount of time to go from A, him, to B, me? This is giving me a headache.

Suddenly, a booming voice that appears to come from inside my head proclaims: "This is the well known paradox of Zeno."[2] After a startled moment I reply: "Who are you?" As I ask the question I look around nervously hoping that the sound came from the woods instead. A sardonic laugh follows my query. Distraught by this new event I try to stay focused on my other problem: the Rogue-in-chase.

A Moving and Motionless Rogue?

Noticing that the Rogue is still a good distance away, I distract myself again with this problem of motion. Obviously the problem must lie with my reasoning, since I can clearly move from A to B

---

[2] For a solid introduction to Zeno's paradoxes I recommend Huggett's article in the Stanford Encyclopedia and his edited volume, *Space from Zeno to Einstein: Classic Readings with a Contemporary Commentary* (MIT, 1999).

and the Rogue keeps getting closer. Unless I think that my reasoning is so sound that the experience of motion is illusory. I wake up from this thought by stepping on a cold creek that serpentines its way towards a crevice on the ridge I am running through. Let's substitute the letters for numbers. I consider: A is zero, B is one and I imagine adding the numbers in my head, to go from A′ to B is half the distance, to go from A″ to A′ is one fourth of the total distance and so on: $\frac{1}{2} + \frac{1}{4} + 1/8 + \ldots$ I don't have to add them all up to know that they should equal 1. But that's of course assuming that I *would* add them all up, all the infinite fractions $1/2^n$ (with n being all the positive whole numbers) between 0 and 1. "That's the answer to the problem," I declare satisfied. Since the sum of all these fractions add to 1, motion can occur.

"In the nineteenth century they called this solution the convergence of infinite series," rattles the bodiless voice. Exasperated I shout: "Who are you? How do you know what I'm thinking? And what the hell is 'the nineteenth century'?" I am not certain if I will get an answer. I haven't seen the Rogue now for some time . . . maybe I lost him.

Hmm. But if the problem is really the infinite time it takes to traverse the distance from A to B, saying that we can have an infinite time to add the infinite series, does not solve the physical problem of the paradox of motion since it would take me an infinite time to traverse the distances. The answer must be something else. What am I assuming? I assume that there are an infinite amount of points between A and B and that it takes some time to go from one to another. One of the solutions could be to postulate that between these infinite small distances, the time it takes to traverse them is practically zero, instantaneous, and I can clearly have an infinite amount of those. Immediately I recognize that, although a possible solution, I make things worse by suggesting that the essential component of time has no time in it. Oh! So maybe there is a minimum or discrete amount of time for every event.

"Dude, that's the idea behind Heisenberg's principle about energy and time. Well done."[3] This time the voice does not rattle me, but I am perplexed about the comment so without much thinking I ask: "I don't know what that means at all. Can you explain?

---

[3] For more information on quantum mechanics and Heisenberg's principle I would recommend beginning with Alaistair Rae, *Quantum Physics: Illusion or Reality* (Cambridge, 1986).

What is this principle about energy and time?" Not expecting a reply, I am surprised when I hear: "Well. The paradox of motion and Heisenberg's principle in quantum mechanics, er . . . the best scientific theory about motion of small things, are not necessarily related, well, so I thought, until you mentioned this."

Another option pops into my head. What if there aren't an infinite number of points between A and B? That is, what if between any two points in space there are a limited number of points? That would mean that there is a minimum distance. If so, we would not run into Zeno's paradox since this would not require an infinite amount of time to traverse. So space could be discrete and maybe so is time. But that is a weird thought since space appears so fluidly continuous. But appearances are deceiving, like my guild leader likes to say.

"Wanton" Mechanics

"Whoever you are," I say "Can you explain that principle of 'wanton mechanics'?"

"Quantum mechanics" says the voice with a chuckle. "It is a long story. It struck me that your reasoning was very similar to a fundamental principle of this very successful account of nature. You see, Heisenberg found that at small scales some types of properties of systems, like position and momentum or energy and time, are related in such a way that neither can be said to be fully part of the system simultaneously with a precise value. That is, if we have the position of a system fully well defined, then nothing can be said of the property of momentum; as if the system did not have it. This coincides with what the first physicist to uncover quantum mechanics, Max Planck, found about the state of black bodies. The energy or amount of stuff or amount of action a system can do, he concluded, is not formed by all possible values of energy within a certain range, but it comes in discrete amounts or chunks; 'quantum' means packet or discrete." After a pause the voice continues: "That's why I was surprised when you thought similarly to an ancient paradox."

"Are you my conscience?" I ask timidly. Before I can hear a reply the Rogue reappears, but I am able to freeze him again with a cone of cold spell right before he strikes. I am lucky. Let's keep on moving, or can I?

I attempt to run at a faster rate to get away quickly from the soon to be thawed and highly irritated Undead Rogue, but somehow I can't. I always seem to run at the same rate of speed. I realize that the only few exceptions to this fact are when I run with a Hunter or if I take a swift potion, which I inconveniently don't have with me at this time. As usual, I left it in the bank.

"Why can't I run at a faster rate, or at a slower rate for that matter?" I ask my new "friend."

"I am afraid that if I tell, you will be shocked to hear the truth," the voice utters in gloom. "Try me" I reply before really considering the consequences. After a long pause, the voice says: "Already then. You are my creation. You are a character in a virtual world and I control your actions. If I want you to run you run, if I want you to stop you stop." All of a sudden I stop running. I want to run, I will to run, but can't. I begin to tear up. What I thought had been my own free choice of action, now feels like a clear illusion. Before I can get too depressed, as if my "master" can sense it, I begin running again—which is good since the Rogue is after me again, too. A terrible feeling of void overpowers me and I feel faint. I always thought I was in control of much of my life . . .

Lack of In-game Control

"I can tell you to run, walk or stop. But the game . . . er, the world does not allow any continuity between those actions," the voice states as a matter of fact. "Ah," I exclaim, finding some way to reassert my independence, "then this fact of motion in my world is indicative of the idea that rate of motion also occurs in discrete amounts: either walk at a given pace, run, ride, or stop." After a moment of silence my new "master" slowly pronounces: "Yes, except that motion always depends on a given reference frame. One's state of rest or rate of motion depends on which point of reference is chosen."

"What?" I quickly reply back. He proceeds: "Imagine that you are traveling at 3 mph on Gold Road. Someone next to you traveling in the same direction at 3 mph will say that you are not in motion in relation to him or her."

"Well, then, according to this thinking, then no one is in motion in reference to themselves," I say smugly.

"That's right. And a great scientist, years ago, used this thinking to reveal some amazing facts and laws about our universe," the voice replies, and continues: "It turns out that the properties of systems, and not just motion, depend on the reference frame in use to determine those properties." My thoughts are now turbulently spinning out of control.

Once again the Rogue catches up with me with his speed up abilities and is near another backstab attempt. "I can't believe I forgot about this . . ." I hear the voice mumble. I turn towards the Rogue, cast a polymorph spell transforming him into a sheep. I wonder for a moment about this act of transmutation but figure that since I can't even get clear on basic motion, I should not even attempt to understand complex biological metamorphosis. I ask: "Did you do that or did I do that?"

"I did. Sorry. Well, we did since without you I can't do much." Says the voice.

Still puzzled about the last event and discussion I turn to gain some distance from the now polymorphed Rogue looking quite harmless at the moment. "I forgot about Blinking too," the voice acknowledges. "What the? . . ." before I can finish I find myself twenty or so yards ahead of where I was. "How did you do that? And why didn't you do this before?" I ask with irritation.

"I just forget to use it. My main *alt* is a Priest. Hey, I will put you on 'autorun' and be right back, I need to get some coffee. I'm thirsty." Puzzled as to the meaning of all of these assertions, I notice the Rogue dispelling my polymorph incantation and continuing his pursuit. I have gained quite a distance though, so I feel secure to come back to my thoughts (are these my thoughts? And where are they?). How is it possible to go from A to B, at an instant? Did my body travel from A to B crossing all the space in between or did I just "skip" the space in between and appear at B? Is that what happens if space is discrete for regular basic motion?

"Hey, what did that famous scientist say about all of these?" I yell, hoping for a solution. Nothing. Worst of all, I get stuck behind a tree with my arms and legs flapping in a running motion but remaining in place. "Get your damned drink and come back! The blasted Rogue is almost on me . . ." I manage to scream before the Rogue strikes and batters my defenseless body to a pulp. I try to conjure some defensive spell, but to no avail. My legs and arms, still flapping against the tree, are the only things in motion. Oh, the irony.

"I'm back," the voice cheerfully states. At that moment I let out an agonizing scream while silently cursing my creator for having forsaken me. I fall to my knees and drop down to the ground (actually I have fallen into the tree somehow, only my legs are showing).

"Oops. I'm sorry. Don't worry. I will resurrect you at the nearest graveyard," my master said confidently—as if I didn't know since I have died many times before. Now I know to blame him and not me, though. I consider what happened when I blinked. I was able to traverse a distance instantaneously or very quickly at least. This does not seem much different than hearthing back to my favorite inn once in a while. (I have this hearth-stone that I can use to return a great distance away to my favorite inn). Oh, and also similar to my abilities to teleport myself and others around "the server." Of course. But how is that possible?[4]

More Explanations from "Above"

"Let me tell you," the voice said while loudly sipping his "coffee." I wonder for a fleeting moment whether that drink is giving him a stamina or spirit buff. "The same scientist I told you about, Albert Einstein, trying to show that quantum mechanics was not a fundamental theory . . ."

"Wait. Wait," I exclaim, "You mean that the same man that did great work in science also challenged it?"

"Yes, it's a long and beautiful story, I will tell you in full some day. But let's get back to our question. Einstein and others proposed a thought experiment to show that there was something wrong with quantum mechanics. See, quantum mechanics also showed, besides properties of systems occurring in discrete amounts, that these properties only occur in the system as possibilities until the time comes when the system is measured. Then the system 'collapses' in one of its possible states."

"Hold on. Measuring a system picks one of its possible states? That's crazy. This entails that before 'measuring' something that something exists only in possibilities," I state in disbelief.

"That's what many of them working on this believed. Einstein too felt it was crazy so he thought of a way to show that a different explanation was needed. He concocted a thought experiment,

---

[4] A good resource for the conceptual puzzles that still haunt quantum mechanics is: Yakir Aharonov and Daniel Rohrlich, *Quantum Paradoxes: Quantum Theory for the Perplexed* (Wiley, 2005). It may surprise the reader to know that some of these riddles can, in fact, be tested. The best-known example of this is John Bell's inequalities that helped resolve the EPR paradox. See John Bell, *Speakable and Unspeakable in Quantum Mechanics* (Cambridge, 1987).

now referred to as the EPR experiment, where a system is composed of two entangled parts called electrons."

"Okay," I mutter in reply.

"Imagine that these electrons separate and move very far apart. Also, to make things simple imagine that the electron, when measured, can only show up to be either up or down. Then if we measure the nearest electron, and let's say that we find it up, because the system was entangled and there was conservation of momentum then the other electron will have to be down. Since we find out that the second electron is down without ever measuring it, then Einstein claimed that quantum mechanics was incomplete, because we just violated the rule that only things measured can show their actual properties."

I consider asking questions right away, but reflect instead for a moment and then ask: "Could it be possible to conceive of both electrons still as part of the same system? You said that we had a system formed of both electrons, but then it separated. Could the electrons still be entangled at a distance?" There was silence at the other end and feared that he had gone back for more "coffee."

"Well, many ascribe this as a process of non-locality, that is, that the act of measuring an electron affects the other at a distance," he says with a measured tone.

"I see. So my being measured at A could instantaneously affect, somehow, that something or I will appear at B with the blink or teleport spell. Is that right?"

"Yeah, but remember that quantum mechanics is about small things, like electrons, and humans are a different matter. You can teleport and blink because . . . eh, well, let's leave that for another day. Let me resurrect you now." A good idea I think as I begin to wonder what the difference could be between electrons and humans. "And by the way, another scientist named John Bell, years later, figured out a way to test Einstein's claims" he adds. "And?" "The experiments appears to show that what quantum mechanics teaches us is correct. The electron before measurement is in a state of both up and down possibilities. Precisely what Einstein was trying to avoid."[5]

---

[5] A good resource for Einstein's concerns with quantum mechanics is Arthur Fine, *The Shaky Game: Einstein, Realism and the Quantum Theory* (Chicago, 1996).

Which World Am I In?

"Here you go," my master states with satisfaction. "Let me go on a *bio* break and will be right back. It's the coffee." Before I can answer I sense that he has already left. A special bond is beginning to form between the two us, for sure. Does my master exist in this same world I inhabit or is the voice in a parallel yet connected world? Maybe my master resides in the same parallel universe that the mounts go when magically dismissed. But if our worlds are connected, are they part of the same world? This reminds me of Siwel Divad, a Wildhammer Dwarf friend of mine from the academy who once postulated about the existence of possible worlds, and also of T'tereve of TtiWed who argued that every time there is a choice in front of us, the world splits into two separate parallel universes, each containing one of the possible choices. Maybe this is what "the server" is, a large array of parallel universes.

My master has left me at the graveyard with little health or mana and with many questions about the nature of reality and motion. As I wait, I wonder whether there are differences between our worlds. I wonder whether the problems of motion have to do with our conceptual systems or with the very reality of experience. I wonder also whether in fact teleportation is not another word for actualization of a large system. I wonder . . . as I wonder alone in the graveyard, I notice the familiar face of the Undead Rogue appear from behind a hill. I hope to be a Mage in motion soon.

Journeyman Philosopher

The sublime experiences of *WoW*. Familiarize yourself with this topic by reading . . .

Azeroth versus the Experience Machine (SILCOX and COGBURN): 0/1
Boredom, Power, and Self-Actualization in Azeroth (BROWN): 0/1
World of Warcraft as Collector's Paradise (COMPAGNO and COPPOCK): 0/1

Description

Different people have different experiences in Azeroth. This is obviously true and yet it isn't uncommon to hear players make the assumption that their specific experience of *WoW* is the "right" or "only" one. In this section the authors consider some of the experiences to be had in *WoW*.

Is there such a thing as having too much fun? Is *WoW* an example of an activity that qualifies? On the other side of the coin, can one get bored in the *Warcraft* universe? What is boredom? Can one have peak experiences playing some previous games of the franchise, such as *Warcraft II*? Players seem to collect different things in Azeroth, from potions to toons. What is collecting anyway? Can collecting things in *WoW* be a valuable experience in itself?

Rewards

You will receive: **+3 Intellect!**

6

Azeroth versus the Experience Machine

MARK SILCOX and JON COGBURN

Still living or already playing?

—motto of the German game parts company <www.spielmaterial.de>

Everybody wants to have fun. But how much is too much? Some enjoyable activities are fleeting and ephemeral by their very nature: one expects a carnival ride to end, and too much eating, drinking, or dancing can quickly turn from pleasant to downright uncomfortable. There are, perhaps, only a very small number of genuinely fun activities that it's possible for us to imagine going on *forever*.

World of Warcraft is clearly one of these activities, for two distinct reasons. First, in order to play the game well and get the maximum amount of fun out of it, one should spend at least some time trying to imagine what it would actually be like to be a creature who has dwelt on this strange and perilous fictional planet since birth. And in the second place, *World of Warcraft* can certainly be (in at least one sense of the word) a powerfully *addictive* form of entertainment. Habitual players commonly talk about the power that the game has to completely take over their lives. Usually they are just talking about relatively short periods of intense, focused gameplay—a long weekend, say, or a few sleep-deprived nights in a row. But for better or worse, some of us do get more seriously "hooked," and except in a few rare and bizarre sorts of instances (for example, when we end up neglecting our families, or forgetting to eat regular meals) it seems perfectly possible that our lives might actually have been improved by the experience.

Our Quest

The question of whether a life devoted entirely to enjoying oneself would truly be desirable is certainly a philosophical one. In *Anarchy, State, and Utopia*, the American philosopher Robert Nozick develops a fascinating thought experiment to show that there really is something wrong with having this much fun. Nozick proposes that if we were ever faced with the realistic prospect of living such a life, most of us would choose against it. He asks his reader to imagine

> an experience machine that would give you any experience you desired. Superduper neuropsychologists could stimulate your brain so that you would think and feel you were writing a great novel, or making a friend, or reading an interesting book. All the time you would be floating in a tank, with electrodes attached to your brain. (*Anarchy State, and Utopia*, Basic Books, 1974, p. 42)

This type of science-fictional scenario is actually quite familiar nowadays, thanks to novels like William Gibson's *Neuromancer*, Neal Stephenson's *Snowcrash*, Spider Robinson's *Mindkiller* and *Vurt* by Jeff Noon, as well as films such as *The Matrix, Avalon*, and *Existenz*. Unlike the creators of these fictional works, Nozick doesn't devote much time describing what it might actually feel like to be plugged into this sort of a device. But he does argue quite forcefully that most sane, rational human beings would prefer not to be plugged into such a machine. The majority of us, Nozick suggests, would refuse such an offer even if we could somehow be reassured that the machine would never break down, malfunction, or shorten its user's natural lifespan.

Nozick gives three reasons for why the prospect of an artificially fun-filled life would not appeal to us. First of all, Nozick says, "we want to *do* certain things, and not just have the experience of doing them." Although the user of an experience machine might be tricked into thinking that she was engaging in lively activities—skydiving, acting in a play, or slaughtering Orcs with a heavy sword—there's an important sense in which she wouldn't really be *doing* anything at all.

Second, a person plugged into the experience machine would lose the ability "to *be* a certain way, to be a certain sort of person." In everyday life, we want to accomplish things that will make it appropriate for others to think of us as clever, brave, witty, self-sacrificing, or dignified. But although what happens in the experience machine might imitate events in the life of a person who has these sorts of qualities, we certainly wouldn't develop them for ourselves, since from the moment one plugs in, one becomes little more than an inert lump of human meat.

Finally, Nozick contends, we know that we could never ultimately be satisfied by living in an entirely "man-made reality, a world no deeper or more important than that which people can construct" (p. 43). Part of the charm and fascination of everyday life for human beings (or at least for the more fortunate amongst us) is that the real world is full of beauty and surprises that no amount of human ingenuity could ever anticipate or accurately reproduce. And even given the heavy price in pain and frustration that we must pay to inhabit such an environment, most of us neither would nor should be prepared to give up access to it forever.

Thanks to the designers and architects of *World of Warcraft* and other games like it, we are all in a much better position to assess the overall plausibility of Nozick's experience machine argument than anybody was back when his book was first published in 1974. The person who chooses to inhabit Azeroth for even a very substantial portion of his life would of course be in a somewhat different position from that of the hypothetical person who has "plugged in" to Nozick's imaginary machine. But it seems to us that the similarities are striking enough that, if we look at Nozick's reasoning in light of some basic facts about what it's actually like to play *World of Warcraft*, it will be possible to get a much clearer sense of the overall plausibility of his argument that there really is such a thing as having too much fun.

The Unbearable Slightness of Doing

Every *World of Warcraft* player has had an experience like this: Marshall McBride has sent your intrepid adventurer to take out an encampment of Kobold scavengers just to the north of Northshire Abbey. After dispatching the vermin with extreme prejudice, the adventurer returns to receive her award, only to be sent by McBride to dispatch Kobold mine workers further north. But when passing through the campground on the way to the mine, the adventurer finds the camp once again completely filled with scavengers.

The novice player might just suppose that another band of scavengers has moved into the previously cleared camp. But as more quests are completed, similar things happen over and over again. In addition to all of the nameless monsters that populate the game, unique individuals inevitably crop up again very soon after the player has killed them. For example, if the player's character kills Fersh the Kobold overseer, a minute later Fersh will be right back there again bidding his Kobold underlings to work harder. At some point the player is bound to realize that even though you might "kill" an individual inhabitant of Azeroth, she will soon be back and up to her old tricks. And while quest givers such as McBride won't ask you to kill Fersh a second time, they will ask millions of other players to do the exact same task.

This radical inability of characters to affect the history of Azeroth has been raised by critics of the game before.[1] It's likely to be a feature of *World of Warcraft* for a long time, given the need to provide quests for so many different player characters at once.[2] But Nozick's argument can help to explain why some gamers view this feature as a bug. In "real life" when we perform an action, some aspect of the world is always irretrievably changed. Even if I glue back together the teapot I have inadvertently broken, the teapot is still changed by my actions. Azeroth is radically unreal in just this way. Because monsters always respawn in preparation for the next adventurer, characters are completely powerless to effect change in the virtual realm.

Philosophers have come up with a bewildering array of answers to the question, "What is the meaning of life?"[3] But, with perhaps one notable exception,[4] all agree that we find meaning and value

---

[1] We first started thinking about this issue after a conversation with Billy Bryan, who critiqued the game on this very ground. On-line game critics have made similar points; see especially Chris Dahlen, "The Lameness of World of Warcraft: And What to Do about It," *Slate*, <http://www.slate.com/id/2153757/>.

[2] At the time of this writing, there are actually rumors that Bioware's forthcoming MMORPG *Star Wars: The Old Republic* will be such that players' actions permanently affect the state of the world in non-trivial ways (thanks to William Schultz for the hat tip; see Wikipedia, *Star Wars: The Old Republic* <http://en.wikipedia.org/wiki/Star_Wars:_The_Old_Republic>). It will be interesting to see the extent to which they can really do this in a way even remotely analogous to how things work in the real world. Even a partial approximation would be an enormous feat of both programming and artistry.

[3] For an excellent overview, see E.D. Klemke, *The Meaning of Life*, second edition (Oxford University Press, 1999).

[4] See Albert Camus, *The Myth of Sisyphus: And Other Essays* (Vintage, 1955).

in large part due to the effects our actions have on the shared world we inhabit. The disagreement concerns what kind of activities change one's world in a way that produces the most meaning and value. But if this is right, then *World of Warcraft* play is without meaning and value for exactly the kind of reason that Nozick raises.

Hang on a second, though; this criticism is missing something. Azeroth is not merely comprised of the repeatable quests and Non-Player Characters that make them possible. To characterize it that way is to leave out part of what makes *World of Warcraft* what it is; Azeroth without the Player Characters is not Azeroth. And a major part of the brilliance of *World of Warcraft* is that Player Characters *do* change, based on quest completion and players' choices. At the very start of the game, players pick a species, a class, a gender, and an appearance. Then, as they complete quests, they not only "level up," but also choose professions, develop skills, and acquire useful goods through discovery, building, and trade. And the *World of Warcraft* character inhabits a world where all of the other characters are constantly changing as a function of each other's behavior. In *WoW*, players co-operate with one another to complete quests, whether joining a group on the fly during one evening's playing or by becoming part of a more permanent guild. In this way, a character's actions profoundly affect how the other characters develop in the world of the game.

The massive multiplayer aspect of *WoW* is precisely why it is not an experience machine in Nozick's sense. When characters are in guilds, their players in "the real world" have formed a community to assist one another, and one's play does affect the lives of other players' characters as well as the people playing them. One rarely gets any sense of how this latter phenomenon is taking place, though, given the wide geographical distribution of *WoW's* habitual players. And this fact does make one wonder whether the users of a machine like Nozick's that merely *simulated* such indirect forms

---

Sisyphus was condemned to push a rock up a hill over and over again. Every time he gets it to the top it just rolls back down. Camus not only argues that Sisyphus's condition is analogous to ours, but that Sisyphus is happy with his lot, as should we be. It's especially sad that the great existentialists such as Camus were not able to play video games. For sustained meditations in this vein, see Jon Cogburn and Mark Silcox, *Philosophy through Video Games* (Routledge, 2008). Chapter 7 discusses Heidegger and Sartre on video games and the meaning of life.

of human contact would really be that much worse off. In particular, if the merely virtual beings in a Nozickean matrix were good enough to fool the plugged-in person, might it be rational to consider them intelligent and worthy of moral regard themselves?

Being More (and Less) than You Can Be

In order to play *World of Warcraft*, a person must pretend to be something that she is not. In the case of some of the *WoW* characteristics—like race or class—it's quite easy to explain how players are able to do this. Anyone who has read *Lord of the Rings* knows what it's like to be an Orc; anyone who has fought in a playground brawl can imagine and simulate many of the actions of a Warrior. But when it comes to a character's basic traits, it's harder to make sense of how roleplay is supposed to happen. How could a person of medium intelligence succeed at playing a character of high intellect? How is it even possible to play a character of great spirit if one is oneself shy, introverted, or naturally gloomy?

As is the case with all role playing games descended from TSR's original *Dungeons and Dragons*, characters in *World of Warcraft* are able to do things that their players cannot. And this is not just because there are far more dragons on Azeroth than on Earth or that magic does not seem to work the same way here. Characters in such games are able to accomplish tasks based on scores for basic attributes such as intellect and spirit, the same attributes that human beings on Earth possess to greater or lesser degree. And this is when weird things can happen. It's perfectly possible (and probably fairly common) for a player who is a dullard to play a character with a very high score for intellect. Of course, it would be far less fun if the game restricted the player character's intelligence, charisma, (etcetera) to the amount the *player* had (assuming this were even possible).

In light of this disconnect between a player's Earthly characteristics and her character's Azerothly attributes, it is particularly interesting to consider Nozick's claim that we should shun the experience machine because we don't really get to *be* any particular *way* in there. The character you pretend to be in a role playing game such as *World of Warcraft* clearly is not you, and in most cases that character *could not* be you, because the basic traits that dictate what she can accomplish in the game are incompatible with the basic traits that characterize you on Earth.

If this is right, then when we boast to our co-workers about what we accomplished on Azeroth last night we are being just as irrational as the person plugged into Nozick's machine who takes pride in being such a good writer. The person is not a writer, but rather just has the programmed experience of writing a book. *I* didn't kill the orcs, and should in no way feel psychologically invested in the fact that a character I was controlling did so.

Here again, the defender of the game has a good response. Consider a Navy pilot who has landed her F-14 on the deck of an aircraft carrier for the first time. This action is regarded as being one of the most difficult things a human being can do, so our pilot is right to be proud. But imagine a Nozickian challenger saying, "You didn't land. It was only because you were in a plane that you were able to do that. Moreover, the airplane can do things you systematically can't as a human being, such as fly. So it's irrational for you to be psychologically invested in what the plane does."

Why is this a bad argument? Part of what it is to *be* a pilot is to maneuver airplanes in certain ways. *Being* a pilot requires that the pilot have an intimate relationship with things that are not the pilot's body, including things that allow the pilot to do things that her human body systematically (as a function of evolution and the laws of physics) cannot do.

It is similar with computing machines. We have a friend (Alan Westcoat) who briefly owned a video arcade. During the period in the mid-1990s when first-person shooter PC games were much more advanced graphically than the old coin operated fare, he wired his arcade so that players could put on immersive goggles and pay by the hour to play *Doom*. Strangely, given the graphic violence of the game, his most steadfast repeat customer was an elderly, wheelchair-bound woman. Every week she told our friend that she'd come to "get my legs back." Though she enjoyed the gameplay as much as the other customers, the real thrill for her was how she could manipulate with her hands the controls that gave her the experience of running around and jumping on things.

Though my body is physically weak, *World of Warcraft* allows me to play a Warrior of renowned strength. And my play is something that *I* am doing.[5] It is difficult to tell from Nozick's rather

[5] In Chapter 1 of *Philosophy through Video Games* we consider the general problem of this section in light of players' tendency to speak in the first-person

hasty description whether any similar sort of opportunity is provided for the user of the experience machine. Perhaps the "player" of Nozick's machine as he understands it is only *passively* experiencing whatever the superduper neuroscientists have decided to program. But if that's the case, then the designers of games like *World of Warcraft* seem to have discovered a genuine type of gratification that, if it were added to the menu, would make the experience machine considerably more difficult to resist.

The Third Reason: Transcendent Knowledge

Nozick's complaint about being limited to a "man-made" reality is somewhat cryptic. He writes:

> There is no *actual* contact with any deeper reality, though the experience of it can be simulated. Many people desire to leave themselves open to such contact and to a plumbing of deeper significance. (p. 43)

At first blush this sounds like someone complaining about the experience of living in cities. Perhaps we need to leave the "man made" realm to get back to nature where we can discover "deeper significance." But strangely, the only example Nozick gives is the use of psychoactive drugs like opium and LSD; their defenders (according to Nozick) claim that their use can lead to the experiencing of a transcendent realm, but their critics claim that they only produce hallucinations.

Nozick provides no argument why man-made reality can't lead to the kind of transcendental contact he is gesturing at. After all, *all* of our contact with reality is already mediated by human sensory apparatus. The world looks, smells, and sounds quite different to dogs, humans, and bats, yet we humans nonetheless seem to be open to truths that transcend what our senses present us with. Our human senses do not present us with infinite totalities, but almost all of mathematics relies upon the belief that claims about infinity can be truths that transcend this limitation.

So what is it about the experience machine that might preclude this openness? We conjecture that Nozick is sensitive to the way in which the real world is able to surprise us in so many unforeseen

---

singular about the actions of their characters. We argue that there is nothing remotely irrational about considering one's characters to be a part of the self.

ways. In some sense, a movie or book—or an experience machine—is all already there. But there is a richness to the real world. A movie of falling sand is a finite thing, but a real handful of sand can be manipulated in an infinite number of different and surprising ways. The real world itself is open to our creative intervention in a way that allows unbounded discovery and manipulation. Artworks are not.

If this is what he intends, we think that Nozick is wrong here. Human beings constantly interpret even "static" art forms like novels in new ways. Was Hamlet's hatred of his stepfather justified, or was he just being a whiner? Are the Horde's inhabitants more innately disposed to evil, or was there just a series of tragic misunderstandings? Any significant work of art raises questions like this, and part of what it is to experience them is to take a stand on these sorts of interpretive issues.

For video games such as *World of Warcraft* this point has extra salience. Unlike the experience machine, videogames are interactive in the sense that the experienced artwork is in part a function of the decisions of the game's players. In no way are sophisticated videogames "closed" in the sense that Nozick seems to have in mind. In fact, large scale commercial video games like *World of Warcraft* are so enormously complicated that their design teams always end up being surprised by what happens when players actually play them.[6] At the furthest extreme, nobody foresaw the enormous growth of real-world markets for virtual items in these sorts of games. Yet it happened and changed gameplay in novel ways.

Thus, there is a sense in which videogames and other great artforms are *not* "man made." People play a role in bringing them into existence, but once here they have a life of their own, to be interpreted, manipulated, and explored in ways the artists and audiences never could have foreseen. As is certainly the case with psychoactive drugs, not all artworks necessarily allow for the obtaining of surprising, transcendent knowledge. But the fact that humans help to create artworks should not lead us to think that this possibility is foreclosed.

---

[6] The implications of this point are discussed extensively in M. Silcox and J. Cogburn, "Computability Theory and Literary Competence," *British Journal of Aesthetics*,46:5 (2006), pp. 369–386.

Forward! Into the Breach

One of the most dangerous argumentative strategies that a philosopher can ever adopt is to speculate on the significance of scientific discoveries that haven't yet actually been made. Aristotle remains infamous to this day for his claim that women had fewer teeth than men, which he obviously arrived at without having bothered to count.[7] And Immanuel Kant thought it was a consequence of the structure of human thought itself that space had to have a Euclidean, three-dimensional structure,[8] whereas physicists of the twentieth century have concluded (presumably through the use of their all-too-human minds) that this claim is empirically false.

Nozick is not the only writer to have speculated upon what it would be like to live in a permanent, simulated environment. There's already a sizeable philosophical literature on the ethical and metaphysical significance of "virtual reality"[9] even though VR technology still only exists in any meaningful sense of the term in films like *The Matrix*. Furthermore, Nozick's conclusions concerning what human beings would value if we were ever faced with the option of "plugging in" to an experience machine are certainly not as open to such straightforward refutation as the two claims described in the previous paragraph. Nonetheless it seems to us that a little reflection on the experiences that are available to the player of *World of Warcraft* should suggest that the human appetite for happiness is both more robust and more psychologically complicated than Nozick's argument represents it as being.

This conclusion all by itself is quite interesting for a couple of reasons. First, it helps to provide players of the game with at least some justification for pursuing their enthusiasm at the expense of other activities that might otherwise seem more worthwhile, on account of having more to do with the "real world." And second, it reassures us that the artists, designers, and programmers currently working to improve *World of Warcraft* (and to develop other

---

[7] See Aristotle, *History of Animals* (Adamant, 2005), p. 31.

[8] See Immanuel Kant, *Critique of Pure Reason* (Hackett, 1996), pp. 71–85.

[9] See *The Metaphysics of Virtual Reality* by Michael Heim (Oxford University Press, 1994) and *Surviving the Age of Virtual Reality* by Thomas Langan (University of Missouri Press, 1990).

games like it), building gameworlds that are even more exciting, immersive, and realistic than Azeroth as it stands today, are engaged in a genuinely valuable project, rather than some sort of a sinister plot to tempt us away from what we'd really want, if only we were a bit more rational.[10]

---

[10] We'd like to thank Billy Bryan, Emily Beck Cogburn, Luke Cuddy, Joseph Dartez, Neal Hebert, Skylar Gremillion, François Raffoul, Chris Ray, William Schultz, and the students in Mark Silcox's 2009 "Philosophy of Games" class at the University of Central Oklahoma for helpful discussions about the issues addressed in this paper.

7

Boredom, Power, and Self-Actualization in Azeroth

PAUL BROWN

World of Warcraft has been a startling success, both critically and commercially. The game finds its way into many "best of" lists. Expansion packs shoot up the bestseller charts like arrows from a Hunter's bow. This *WoW* amour is justly deserved. But what about those games that first introduced us to the lands of Azeroth? Have they been forgotten? Is something as important, and philosophically plump, as *Warcraft II*, for instance, now seen as just a museum piece gathering dust in a long forgotten corner of videogame history? I sincerely hope not. For, at the time of its release, *Warcraft II* was seen as very special indeed, receiving staggeringly high review scores and sales of over a million. Equally importantly, *Warcraft II* is a game that begins by saving the player from boredom and ends by offering eternal happiness. Lest we forget, then . . .

Even Elder Races Get Tired of Waiting

As odd as it may sound, boredom is an interesting subject. It is also a relatively recent one. According to contemporary philosopher Lars Svendsen, the word wasn't recorded in English until the 1760s and it was the nineteenth century before any philosopher—Søren Kierkegaard—discussed boredom in any real depth. Since then, however, the topic has caught the philosophical imagination and has been as much a topic for debate as the *best* way to level up has been in the *Warcraft* community. Grind, definitely. Or quest. No, grind. Aagh! Er, anyway . . . boredom is particularly applicable to a discussion of *Warcraft II*, affecting both the world of Azeroth and the world of the player. Firstly though, what exactly is "boredom"?

Give Me a Quest!

Twentieth-century philosopher Martin Heidegger allotted a considerable number of scholarly pages to the discussion of boredom. For our purposes, though, we'll settle for his following definition: "Boring—by this we mean wearisome, tedious; it does not stimulate and excite, it does not give anything, has nothing to say to us, does not concern us in any way" (*The Fundamental Concepts of Metaphysics,* p. 83).

We'll also consider Svendsen's thoughts on boredom, which he terms "one fundamental existential experience."[1] Existentialism—a theory largely defined and popularised by French philosopher Jean-Paul Sartre—has at its heart the idea that the individual is free and entirely responsible for his actions, his own morality: there is no such thing as Human Nature and we are not guided by an external moral force. Svendson is suggesting that how to fill our time meaningfully and with items of interest is entirely down to us. The question is, how? Here, Kierkegaard can help. Kierkegaard spent most of his time philosophising about the fundamental problems of human existence, of which he believed there were three; namely, boredom, anxiety, and despair. Boredom, he believed, was the worst of these, calling it "the root of all evil."

The work in which Kierkegaard's thoughts on boredom are most articulated is *Either/Or*. In it, Kierkegaard poses the question, "How should we live?" He presents the points of view of the fictional authors—"A" and "Johannes Climacus" for *Either* and "B" and "The Judge" (who are eventually revealed to be one and the same) for *Or*. Part I concerns the "aesthetic" life, the life as experienced by the individual, through the senses. "A" argues that the best way to live is by seeking out and experiencing sensual pleasures. Part II concerns the "ethical," and "B" argues that the best way to live is by choosing our own actions, motivated from within, not from the world of external stimuli. With *Either/Or* Kierkegaard allows the reader to draw his own conclusions regarding the "best way" to live. If you were thinking that these ideas seem to foreshadow those of existentialism noted above, you'd be right. Kierkegaard is often called "the father of existentialism."

The section of the book that most concerns us is *Either*, and in particular a section entitled *The Rotation of Crops*. Here, "A" sug-

---

[1] Lars Svendsen, *A Philosophy of Boredom* (Reaktion, 2005), p. 11.

gests that boredom can be avoided by a change of method, viewpoint, or attitude towards something, giving the example of a farmer "changing the method of cultivation and the kind of crops." In this way, the individual is doing something to fight boredom, for again in the words of "A," "what . . . is more natural than to seek to conquer it" (*Either/Or Part I,* p. 264).

I Got a Brain! Not

In thinking about boredom in relation to *Warcraft II*, we can apply it to both the world of Azeroth and the situation of the player. Let's take a look at Azeroth as it's first presented. The story of *Warcraft II* is obviously a continuation of that in the first game where the corrupted (well, possessed, if we're going to quibble) sage Medivh, brought war to the land of Humans. As we all know, he sells out his people for the Titans' powers and the *clearly* misguided belief that the Orcs will give him their unswerving loyalty. Orcs? Loyalty? Get away with you, Medivh. Why did Medivh want the Titans' powers? Because he was bored with his own. They were, to use some of Heidegger's words, "intrinsically boring." Boredom is also the reason the Orcs want more land, specifically the Lordaeron continent, in *Warcraft II*. They have grown bored with what they have gained in the Great War and a peaceful life and want fresh delights for the eyes . . . and the swords. This is clearly suggested by words of the gloriously overblown voiceover that opens the game: "Eager to engage in battle once again, the Orcs constructed ships of war to bear them across the Great Sea. The Orcish warriors yearned for the sounds of battle to fill the air, and looked to the far horizon for new blood to spill."

For the Orcs, then, their crop rotation involves a change from peace back to war, a change of old enemies to new (those that dwell on a different continent, with the subtle cultural and racial differences this implies) and, perhaps most importantly of all, improved means of spilling this new blood. If we look at the increased strength of the "Orcish hordes" in this second game, it's clear that they have somehow "upgraded" themselves to make the coming battle more interesting. For instance, the lowest of their units, the Peon now have the ability to cause a limited amount of damage, while entirely new, more skilled units appear in the higher ranks, replacing lesser skilled units from the earlier campaign. A good example of this is the creation of the Troll Berserker, a clear replacement for the Necrolyte of yore and drastically superior to it when judged by any criteria: Hit Points, Range, or Damage. Their cannon laden Warships are pretty impressive too. It's still fighting, but turned up to eleven.

Once their initial boredom had been relieved and the Orcs had the taste of blood on their undoubtedly hairy tongues, it is likely that an even stronger motivational force than boredom took over. This force is known as "the Will to Power" and is discussed later.

When My Work Is Finished, I'm Coming Back for You!

So, if boredom accounts for the initial motivation of Azeroth's inhabitants, what of the humans on the other side of the screen? We know that *Warcraft II* was the first and, so far, only game in the series to be ported to console, both the Playstation and the Saturn. While this was clearly a commercial move on the part of Blizzard and Electronic Arts, it's also of great importance in terms of our focus on boredom.

Roger Silverstone and Eric Hirsche[2] have described how new technology begins as something wild, unknown, and perhaps a little bit feared. But new technology eventually becomes tamed or domesticated. A technological object such as a television set is placed and used in the home, and it eventually blends in to its new environment, known and understood by its users. It's "tamed" and therefore accepted. One method of taming is through the creation of boundaries or zones: certain technological items being "roped off" within particular areas.

A recent study of how boundaries are created within the home is Katie. J Ward's "The Bald Guy Just Ate an Orange."[3] Ward observes how several families domesticate technologies through the creation of such boundaries. An obvious, and very pertinent example of such, is the PC and its positioning in the study. This is because of the PC's history as a work machine and its continuing use as a multipurpose tool, still largely skewed towards work. In the words of Ward, "the function ascribed to the technology by the user determines the way in which the technology will be displayed.

[2] Silverstone and Hirsche, eds., *Consuming Technologies: Media and Consumption in Domestic Spaces* (Routledge, 1992).

[3] In *Domestication of Media and Technology* (Open University Press, 2006).

Since one of the main uses of the computer is for work purposes, it is displayed in a study/work room that is distinct from other family space within the household in its spatial and temporal arrangement and rules." The PC, then, usually remains in the study.

But what of the game console? While the console is still undertheorised, a parallel can be drawn with the television set, something, which in Ward's research is most often placed in the living room, because of its association "with leisure and relaxation." The console can be allied to the television set in this way, not only because of their technological relationship—the television set being necessary to the console's function—but also because of their similar cultural purpose: leisure.

Work Complete

Boredom can be kept at bay relatively easily in the study: in terms of PC use alone, there is always something interesting to do. It is quite possible to expend a significant amount of time rotating the crops of the web, email, and schoolwork. Even in 1997—the year of *Warcraft II*'s console release—before the Internet became ubiquitous, this was still the case. The study also, typically, has other distractions: books and periodicals to browse through and engage the intellect. The living room however has . . . soft furnishings. It is, in short, an intellectual dead zone, a desert of the dull. No matter that we go here willingly to escape stimulation and that the living room has been designed to ease the mind of intellectual burden; often the mind doesn't want it. The games console, then, provides something of an oasis of entertainment and may, in Kierkegaardian terms, prevent the supposed evil that stems from boredom taking hold. Indeed, to return to the words of "A," "what was it that delayed the fall of Rome? It was *panis* [bread] and *circenses* [games]" (*Either/Or*, Part I, p. 258). Well, quite. That is not to say that all games played on console will stimulate or even begin to alleviate boredom—many are as coma-inducing as the curtains—but *Warcraft II* does. And it manages this in several ways.

It manages this initially through its energetic opening sequence: striking music and colourful, dynamic visuals comprised of myriad images: cannons, warships, and knights in shining armour bedazzle the brain as the game's title scrolls horizontally across the screen. A thumb of the Start button and another set of similarly vibrant visuals begin, this time overlaid with an oral history of

Azeroth, as noted above. Through this cut scene or—to use a phrase coined by games scholar Barry Atkins—piece of "gaming cinema,"[4] *Warcraft II* begins to stake its claim on the player's intellect. The player is likely to be familiar enough with gaming convention to know that he will shortly be part of this exciting action and his boredom will already be beginning to dissipate. The question posed by Svendsen—"How is one to escape from a world that is boring?"—is starting to be answered.

This exciting set-up would be wasted if the gameplay itself were humdrum. But this is far from being the case, due to both the initial novelty of the experience on console and the inherent qualities of the game itself.[5] To play such a game on console in 1997 was crop rotation in itself, an exciting new venture in a familiar place: in the living room and on the TV set. It is the deeper aspects of play, however, that are the most important. Regardless of which side he chooses, the player is immediately charged with building "four farms and a barracks."

Your Command?

In many games of the era, the player usually took control of only one element: guiding a futuristic racing car through the roller-coaster routes of *Wipeout*, say, or manipulating Mario through some unlikely looking acrobatics. By contrast, the very first level of *Warcraft II* tasks the player with control of six—three footmen and a peasant along with a town hall and a farm. This immediately challenges the player's use of Working Memory, the name given to the theory of how many elements a person can hold his head at any one time. When research started on the subject in the 1950s, the "magic number" was thought to be around seven. More recent research, however, suggests it is as low as four. Though some of the elements remain on screen, once deployed, many don't: footmen patrol the perimeter and the peasants may be in and out of the mine and forests. This increases exponentially as the game progresses, with the player having to keep in mind off-screen activities

---

[4] Barry Atkins, *More than a Game* (Manchester University Press, 2003), p. 38.

[5] *Warcraft II* was one of only nine Real Time Strategy games to appear on the Playstation, and one of only four released in 1997. For the Saturn, the RTS scene was even more arid, with only two games in the genre being released in the console's lifetime.

such as sea patrols, archers and the construction of oil platforms, with all that their successful management implies. It isn't even as if the player has been given as straightforward a mission as it first seems, with his thought processes likely to be proceed along the following lines, if a little more conceptually:

> *In order to create the buildings, I need materials and money.*
>
> *I therefore need to harvest lumber and mine for gold.*
>
> *Hmm, it seems only peasants can do this.*
>
> *As there is an ever-present threat of attack, I doubt there's time to wait for one peasant to do all the mining and chopping. I need, therefore, to concentrate on gaining more peasants.*
>
> *Ah, but now I've thought about attack, I'd better defend against it before starting to mine for gold. Got to prioritise. I'll deploy my footmen.*
>
> *Er, but where?*
>
> *Well, as I have only three, I'll triangulate the optimal positions for them to take on the map. Oh yes, always thinking . . .*
>
> *Oh, hold on, should they wait or patrol? Better patrol for more coverage.*
>
> *Where was I? Oh yes, the peasant/farm/barrack situation. I'll set my peasant to mine for gold in order to buy more peasants.*
>
> *Yes, that makes sense: the new peasants can mine for more gold and lumber so more farms and the barracks can be built.*
>
> *Job done. I am a genius.*
>
> *Hold on, what's happening with my footmen? Agghh they're being attacked! Regroup, regroup!*

And so on. All of this is before decisions need to be made regarding the placement of the said farms and barracks or thinking through the deceptively complex rock, paper, scissors gameplay. During this early stage of engagement, the player must also come to terms with the game's internal logic or reality. Some real world thinking applies—that wood is needed to construct buildings—but some doesn't: the creation of living beings from gold for a start. Is this is a further, hitherto unknown, stage of alchemy, perhaps? The above also presupposes that the player does only that which is asked of him—*Warcraft II* allows the player to go considerably off task if he chooses to do so. And this is only the first level. Add to this the aesthetic layering of backstory, music, dialogue, and a beautifully crafted map and it becomes ever more difficult to believe that anyone could find himself bored by such a scenario. Bewildered, yes. Bored, no.

I'm Very Busy

Such an intense engagement with the gameworld may well in fact lead to the player becoming immersed. The metaphor of immersion has its roots in literary theory and was appropriated and embellished by those studying digital environments. Like the literal example of being submerged in water from which it originates, immersion suggests the idea of being completely submerged in a text. Victor Nell, one of the pioneers of the study of immersion in literary forms noted that readers are sometimes said to be "lost in a book."[6] In our case, players are "lost in a game," specifically a game of *Warcraft II*.

Janet Murray, one of the first thinkers to apply the concept of immersion to the electronic arts, noted that the player entering a convincing gameworld, such as the one offered in *Warcraft II*, initially experiences this feeling of immersion, "the sense of being transported to an elaborately simulated place."[7] She continues to say that the sense is maintained and deepened by the player's actions in that world, which she terms "agency." Murray argues that the more the player sees happening as a result of his actions, the more his feeling of agency increases. The greater the feeling of agency, the greater the sense of immersion and the sense, therefore, that the Gameworld is real: "Our successful engagement with these enticing objects makes for a little feedback loop that urges us on to more engagement, which leads to more belief." Following this argument, the sense of agency and immersion through playing *Warcraft II* certainly increases. The player begins by controlling a handful of Footmen, a single Peasant, and managing a small construction job. He ends up managing an army of Dwarves, Rangers, Mages, and Paladins and is tasked with saving the world.

Say Hello to My Little Friend

So, here we have a once bored player, now absorbed into a world in which it is possible to achieve, to succeed . . . to dominate. Allow me to introduce you to the ideas of Mr. Nietzsche. Born in 1844, Nietzsche was a German philosopher who is still most com-

---

[6] Victor Nell, *Lost in a Book: The Psychology of Reading for Pleasure* (Yale University Press, 1988).

[7] Janet Murray, *Hamlet on the Holodeck* (MIT Press, 1997), p. 98.

monly—and incorrectly—linked to the nationalistic ideology of Hitler and Nazism.[8] One of his prevailing contributions to the field of philosophy was his concept of the Will to Power. The Will to Power had several influences, perhaps most notably, in the field of philosophy, the notion of the Will to Live, proposed by Arthur Schopenhauer. Schopenhauer argued that the central motivating force for all living creatures was to survive. To this end, they take all means necessary to avoid death, and ensure survival of their species by the act of procreation.

The first flowering of Nietzsche's Will to Power was evident in his earlier writings (*The Wanderer and his Shadow* and *Daybreak*) but it was first named as such in *Thus Spake Zarathustra,* one of his major works which, like Kierkegaard's *Either/Or*, is as much read as literature as philosophy. Like Schopenhauer, Nietzsche also saw "the will" as our fundamental drive, the "basic disposition manifested in all that transpires in human life, and in all other phenomena as well."[9] Unlike Schopenhauer, however, Nietzsche believed that the will to exert power was *greater* than the will to live, as individuals often sacrifice their lives (or sex lives!) in order to ally themselves to what they believe is a greater, and essentially powerful, cause. For instance, dedicated soldiers willingly die for their country and monks forego the opportunity to continue their lineage in order to maintain a connection to God. Nietzsche articulates the meaning of such sacrifices as entirely related to a desire for power: "Even if we stake our lives, as martyrs do for their church—this is a sacrifice that is offered for *our* desire for power or the purpose of preserving our feeling of power"(*The Gay Science*, p. 87).

While Nietzsche reworked and embellished his Will to Power throughout the rest of his sane life,[10] with the concept eventually allowing for an all-encompassing theory of metaphysics (what exists and what makes that existence possible), most of his published writing concerns itself with the Will to Power as it relates to Man and his relationships, both with others and, perhaps surprisingly, to

---

[8] Nietzsche's half sister, Elizabeth, worked hard to achieve this link, creating a permanent collection of Nietzsche's work (The *Nietzsche-Archiv*), which purposely misrepresented his ideas. To this collection she invited Hitler. In reality, Nietzsche was vehemently opposed to both Nationalism and anti-Semitism.

[9] Richard Schacht, *Nietzsche* (Routledge, 1983), Chapter 4.

[10] Tragically, after a collapse on a Turin street, Nietzsche was deemed insane for the final eleven years of his life (1889–1900).

himself. There are, therefore, two forms of the Will to Power: the overt and the sublimated.

With the overtly expressed Will to Power, Man aims to have dominance over others. He turns his drive outward, to "appropriation, injury, overpowering of the strange and weaker, suppression, severity, imposition of one's own forms, incorporation and, at the least and mildest, exploitation" (*Beyond Good and Evil*, p. 125). The sublimated Will to Power, on the other hand, relates not to repression (which Nietzsche believed was unhealthy), but to self-mastery, or "self overcoming"—Man's overcoming of his own weaknesses.

I Am Ironman!

For an immersed player, the overt Will to Power is manifested. In one of the aphorisms from *Daybreak*, Nietzsche speaks of "the striving for distinction." Man, he says has a desire to dominate over others, or "the next man." This domination may not necessarily be of a negative nature, but negative or not, the gratification derived is purely selfish[11]:

> . . . even when he who strives after distinction makes and wants to make a joyful, elevating, or cheerful impression he nonetheless enjoys this success not inasmuch as he has given joy to the next man or elevated or cheered him, but inasmuch as he has *impressed* himself on the soul of the other, changed its shape and ruled over it at his own sweet will. (*Daybreak*, p. 85)

The player certainly dominates over the next man—or, indeed, Orc if he so chooses—in *Warcraft II*. If he isn't ordering grunts to the goldmine, he's tasking them with building barracks. If he's not commanding ships to set sail, he's making invisible lumber smiths work round the clock and if he's not got a taskforce drilling for oil, he's rallying his troops to storm Orc defences.

---

[11] In his excellent novel, *When Nietzsche Wept*, Irvin Yalom brings several real life characters from nineteenth-century Vienna into vivid focus, none more so than Nietzsche himself. There's a particularly well-drawn scene in which the novel's protagonist—Doctor Josef Breuer—makes Nietzsche bristle by merely paying him a compliment. In Nietzsche's thinking, Breuer is exercising the Will to Power over him (Harper Collins, 2003).

There's also the feeling of power that comes from simply teasing (bullying, you say!?) the characters. For while it is necessary to click on a character to issue a command, is there any player who hasn't also prodded a peasant just for fun? Just look at how they squeal. Their responses range from the slightly miffed ("You're making me seasick") to frustrated ("Give me a quest!") to outraged disbelief ("Are you still touching me?"), this last exclamation also containing an implied accusation of somewhat sinister physical impropriety. Perhaps, though, there is no greater feeling of power-through-unnecessary-action than by clicking on a sheep: Baa Baa Boom! The player has certainly impressed his "own sweet will" on *its* soul.

With the number of Footmen, Archers, and Knights (not forgetting Critters!) growing with each new level, the satisfaction achieved through the player exercising his Will to Power continues and increases throughout. The ultimate feeling of domination, however, comes with reaching the game's final stage. Here is the result of the player's dominance over his army, the Orcs and, indeed, the entire world of Azeroth. But even for those who fail to retake the Kingdom, those who watch their Archers annihilated and Mages massacred, there is still a sense of power to be gained:

> If a war proves unsuccessful one asks who was to 'blame' for the war . . . Guilt is always sought wherever there is failure; for failure brings with it a depression of spirits against which the sole remedy is instinctively applied: a new excitation of the *feeling of power*—and this is to be discovered in the condemnation of the 'guilty'. . . . To condemn oneself can also be a means of restoring the feeling of power after a defeat. (*Daybreak*, p. 88)

In other words, everyone's a winner.

Bring It On!

As well as being immersed in the game, the player is still part of the real world, on the living room couch to be exact. As part of this reality, the player has also been exercising the sublimated variety of the Will to Power. As has been suggested, the sublimated was, for Nietzsche, the concept's highest form:

> . . . here at the end of the ladder stands the ascetic and martyr, who feels the highest enjoyment by himself enduring, as a consequence of

> his drive for distinction, precisely that which, on the first step of the ladder, his counterpart, the *barbarian* imposes on others on whom and before whom he wants to distinguish himself. (*Daybreak*, p. 85)

Although Nietzsche talks of the martyr "enduring," there is no reason not to take a broader view of this asceticism and apply it to the figure of the dedicated game player. The player is, in effect—and to appropriate a term from the First Person Shooter (FPS) genre—*dual wielding* his Will to Power and in doing so is both barbarian *and* martyr: the former in the game, the latter outside of it, on the couch. In addition to wanting to lead his army and Azeroth to glory, he wants to master the more abstract, procedural aspects of play and game-ness: he wants to *beat the game*. In order to achieve this, the player has to live something of an ascetic life, perhaps denying himself adequate amounts of rest, food, baths, and the company of friends. Moreover, he is trying to overcome his own failings as a player.

Warcraft II is a complicated game, demanding substantial intellectual engagement. It also requires some manual dexterity in manipulating the game pad. Boredom could still have been avoided by choosing a more limited game, but in choosing and continuing to play this one, the player is also choosing to suffer, choosing to make forehead ache and fingertips bleed, the equivalent of Nietzsche's man that climbs "on dangerous paths in the highest mountains so as to mock his own fearfulness and his shaking knees" (*Human, All Too Human*, p. 95).

The reward for exercising both forms of Will to Power is considerable. Nothing less than true happiness, in fact:

> What is Good? —All that heightens the feeling of power, the will to power, power itself in man.
>
> What is bad? —All that Proceeds from weakness.
>
> What is happiness? —The Feeling that power increases—that a resistance is overcome. (*The Antichrist*, p. 4)

A Noble Quest

Without wanting to stray too far from philosophy, it would be remiss of me at this point not to mention that the notion of control or "mastery" also has a parallel in more mainstream psychology, particularly the Third Force of the discipline pioneered by Abraham Maslow and Carl Rogers. Maslow, the key mover in this field, is perhaps best remembered for his hierarchy of needs, in which he ascribed numerous needs as the motivating forces behind man's behaviour. The hierarchy, often represented by—and reduced to—a triangle, is comprised of "basic" (or deficiency) and "higher" needs. The basic needs include such things as food and shelter while the higher needs take account of such things as intellectual stimulation and aesthetics. From a lifetime of refining the theory, Maslow argued that the happiest in society are motivated by what can perhaps be best viewed as a distillation of these higher needs, and these he termed growth-needs. They include such things as "self-sufficiency," "autonomy," "independence," "richness," and "complexity" (*Towards a Psychology of Being*, pp. 93–94). They also include "mastery."

These are exactly the sort of things the player experiences through his engagement with *Warcraft II*. And just like those exercising their Nietzschean Will to Power, those who manage to satisfy these growth needs, argued Maslow, are self-actualized and happy. Furthermore, those who fulfil their growth needs, regularly enjoy Peak Experiences, "transient moments of self-actualization. They are moments of ecstasy" (*The Farther Reaches of Human Nature*, p. 46).

Maslow went so far as to compare these moments of ecstasy to religious experience, noting that the moments recounted by his subjects were essentially the same as those revelations experienced by the originating prophets of all well established, organised religions. For the player of *Warcraft II*, it's highly possible that these peak experiences continue throughout the game, most likely at the end of each level. Consider the first level, and attendant thought process, discussed above. The player is given a short list of tasks to complete, but the method of tackling them is his own, (meaning he has autonomy), and the actual doing of them is complex and rich. When the level is complete he has mastered that level, his use of working memory, and any of his game-playing weaknesses—a clear recipe for one of Maslow's quasi-religious peak experiences.

Stop That Persistent Clicking

Finally, as we've hit upon this notion of religious experience, it seems only natural to return to the thoughts of the philosopher whose essay gifted this chapter its title: Søren Kierkegaard. More specifically, it seems natural to return to his theory on how we should live. Following the first two stages (or, the much more evocative "existence spheres") discussed earlier—the aesthetic and the ethical—is a third and final stage: the religious. Kierkegaard initially introduced this stage—as something separate from the ethical—in the 1845 work *Stages on Life's Way*. Here, and in several publications that followed (particularly *Concluding Unscientific Postscript* and *The Sickness unto Death*), Kierkegaard put forward the theory of the authentically religious, which, he argued, is the highest plane of man's existence.

Being the father of existentialists that he was, Kierkegaard said that this could only be achieved through an entirely subjective faith, not one determined through Christendom, by which he meant organised religion. If one achieves this faith, one becomes "contemporary with Christ" and achieves "eternal happiness" (*Concluding Unscientific Postscript*, p. 32).

While Kierkegaard was referring to religion, with a mischievous pinch of philosophical salt (well, okay, an oceanload, but it really would be impolite to keep Kierkegaard out of *our* final stage!), his theory lends itself to a wider interpretation: namely that such a higher plane of existence can be achieved by playing *Warcraft II*. The game presents an entirely subjective and particularly intense experience that can't be understood through the established institutions of gamedom, such as the Almighty Metacritic or the Holy E3. It is understood, *felt*, by the player himself when he becomes "contemporary" with the game. From this comes, if not eternal, then at the very least substantial happiness.

From boredom to power to peak experience, and from the sofa to Azeroth and beyond, the player of *Warcraft II* is involved in something very special indeed. It's time to take it out of the museum.

8
World of Warcraft as Collector's Paradise

DARIO COMPAGNO and PATRICK COPPOCK

Now, I need just to get hold of a few more claws to carry out my rite!

Collecting fictional game objects can be a risky activity for avatars in computer games. It needs some careful attention and is quite time-consuming for players too. Even in games where it doesn't look as if you're gathering much at all, you're awarded game points or credits for skillful gameplay—perhaps the simplest kind of collection. At the other end of the scale we have Massively Multiplayer Online Role Playing Games (MMORPGs) involving structured *tasks* and *quests*—like *World of Warcraft (WoW)*. These games involve players, their game characters, and the fictional objects they manipulate in the construction of complex and demanding narrative pathways, with fictional objects at the center of attention as they are sought out, collected, contested, bought, or stolen.

Collection activities in games have a primary in-game value: they allow players to advance through the game. Our level of progression in any *WoW* gameplay session may be grasped by simply looking at our avatar's weapons and other items: the copper, silver, or gold from which weapons are made are already meaningful signs. Apart from this, players conspire with other players to attribute value to aspects of gameplay, characters, fictional objects, and social activities not "officially" sanctioned by the norms and rules cooked up by game designers and programmers. In *WoW* avatars' appearances are important not so much in terms of actual game mechanics, but in terms of ludic (playful) experience—turning into a bear or walking through the woods next to your very own wolf is *cool*, all other factors excluded. Playing for the sake of playing is often something *else*, not specifically *in the* game. "Subversive" player practices of this kind seek, then, to establish alternative value systems, often related to quite specific types of "collectables" and collection activities that we shall look into here.

The Philosophy of Computer Game Objects

Fictional computer game objects, including player avatars, are probably best conceived of as *intangible* cultural artifacts, since they are essentially immaterial. However, from a philosophical—or, more specifically, phenomenological and semiotic—perspective, fictional game objects must also be considered *experientially real* for players who relate enactively (through environmental interaction) to them and use them to fulfill their own gameplay goals. Players take game objects so seriously as "collectibles" that they're prepared to invest considerable time, energy, and even economic resources to acquire them, and to negotiate, cooperate, and compete with other players for their possession, conservation, or destruction.

How many hours have we spent trying to get to a Journey's End? These hours of playing together with others are what construct the ludic value and concrete *reality* of *World of Warcraft*. If that staff, or some other valuable weapon can also be bought on eBay, then that's another sign of something else *real* going on in Azeroth. You can't usually use money to buy things that don't exist—but the very fact that we *do* purchase them makes them real for us anyway.

Ludwig Wittgenstein speaks of "seeing as" as a fundamental component of our everyday interpretations and understandings of the world.[1] We have a *habit* of perceiving things in a certain way, and they tend to end up *being* that way for us. But there is no objective *need* to relate to things in that particular way. We probably all recall Hans Christian Andersen's fable of the young child and the emperor's new clothes. There, the fresh gaze of the child acts as a perspectival shift that cuts through a socially generated haze of illusion and hypocrisy, allowing him (or her) see how things actually are. So, how can collection practices in *WoW* be characterized and categorized philosophically, and thus re-conceptual-

[1] *Philosophical Investigations*, Part 1, paragraph 74 and Part 2, Chapter IX.

ized? What kinds of collection practices are explicitly and implicitly presupposed by *WoW*'s systems of rules, norms, and values?

Five Root Metaphors for Collecting

One very general thing that collecting does do, is to *make or create sense*; it gives a place, a role, a value, not only to each single object that makes up the collection, but also to other potential collectibles that as yet have to be discovered. Collectors constantly *desire* something more. They are *in need* of something, and this something else must be sought out elsewhere. This *tension*, this drive for people to act, is the true value of collecting. In "Glorious Obsessions, Passionate Lovers, and Hidden Treasures: Collecting, Metaphor, and the Romantic Ethic," Brenda Danet and Tamar Katriel[2] discuss five root metaphors of collecting: 1) collecting as *hunting*; 2) collecting as *therapy*; 3) collecting as *passion*, *desire*; 4) collecting as a *disease* and 5) collecting as *supernatural experience*. Let's see how these metaphors might link up with what goes on in *World of Warcraft*.

ONE, *Hunting and Gathering*: Accomplishing your Goals

What might "collecting as hunting" have to do with *World of Warcraft*? The term "hunter-gatherer" is generally used to refer to societies that subsist through hunting animals, fishing, and gathering edible plants. In most hunter-gatherer societies, subsistence involves direct procurement of edible plants and animals from the wild, and foraging and hunting without recourse to domestication. Now, these are clearly activities that not only humans take part in on a day to day basis. Animals and insects also need to eat and raise their young, so some form of hunting and gathering behavior is common to all living creatures.

In *WoW*, we are real hunters-gathers because we don't seek to cultivate fields or manage shops like some of the in-game creatures and beings do: there isn't much time for us to sow seeds, exploit land, and domesticate animals while following *quests*. The sense of

---

[2] In Stephen Harold Diggins, ed., *The Socialness of Things: Essays on the Social Semiotics of Things* (Mouton de Gruyter, 1994)

living the "warrior" life we feel while playing *WoW* is probably grounded in the fact that it gives us an immediate sense of *achievement*: you seek out your prey (your "collectables"), and then obtain your reward, in the form of experience points (XP) or other kinds of "valuable" fictional objects.

In completing sequences of quests, players experience a particular kind of *structured time*. Quest items are connected both to what you *have done* in the past, what you *have not yet done* in the present, and to *objects* you may receive as rewards in the future. At the very beginning of your career as a Tauren Druid, for example, it is the fact of being accepted in the Thunder Bluff community that moves you on towards your first quests. But already after a few hours of gameplay, you have plenty of active, but unfinished quests, linked to previous ones you carried out for your mentors (as Mull Thunderhorn, or Baine Bloodhoof), and to the next ones in line for you. All these steps and the various objects related to them act as time "markers" making our own playing time intelligible—like a kind of metronome governing the basic rhythm of our play.

If we focus on collecting in terms of this first metaphor, we find in *WoW* a number of players involved in short-term hunting and gathering activities, propelled through time and space by requirements of objects that must be collected. These rewards do not have to be virtual *things*. In higher level quests, as in "A Donation of Wool" (reading: "A donation of sixty pieces of wool cloth will net you full recognition by the Undercity for your generous actions", that is, 350 in reputation in the Undercity), rewards are valuable but unwearable. This leads us to our second metaphor.

TWO, *Hoarding:* Nuts, Gold, XP, and Compulsion

A further extension of simple hunting and gathering activities is *hoarding* (especially of food). This is a natural behavior also in certain animal species. In the real world, hoarding takes place mainly in two specific forms: *larder hoarding*, collection of large amounts of food in a single place (a larder) which usually also serves as the nest where the animal lives (hamsters are famous larder hoarders); and *scatter hoarding*, the formation of a large number of small hoards or caches of nuts and other seeds (many squirrel species, including the eastern gray squirrel and the fox squirrel, are well known scatter hoarders).

If we go now back to Danet and Katriel's list of collecting metaphors, we quickly realize that, also in our contemporary cultures, hoarding is often connected with their negatively toned, fourth, metaphor: "collecting as a disease." Some of you will recall the two well-known fictional characters—Shylock in Shakespeare's *Merchant of Venice* and Fagin in Dickens' *Oliver Twist*—used to exemplify this kind of social malaise in two different cultural settings. Might obsessive hoarding behavior also be seen as an aspect of the inner life of *World of Warcraft*?

To hoard is to *accumulate*. It is also accumulation over *time*: gaining experience is one such temporal process of gradual accumulation. All players to some extent hoard phases of their own experience and the objects and things connected with these. Time, which under the hunting-gathering perspective was a matter of knowing what to do next, under the sign of the hoarding metaphor becomes a form of linear progression. Quests lose their specificity (except regarding some epic items) as our avatar "puts all our eggs into one basket." Initially, quite different kinds of collectibles may merge into one and the same kind, as they become monetarized into XP. I can kill wild wolves, or sell self-tailored robes and vests, purge the Winterhoof Water Well outside Mulgore of wandering beasts, or a nearby neighborhood of nasty Palemanes. In the end all this is summed up as XP, a sort of *counter* that keeps no trace of the particular means by which we have incremented it.

Collectors *appear* to desire highly distinctive individual objects (a certain sword, a particular pet like a raptor or a chimaera, and so on), but in collections the whole is generally more important than each single element: even a wonderful piece on its own, without its larger circle of "friends," will have little, if any, value for a collector. At least from the point of view this particular metaphor. Still such long-lasting gathering activities can't really be called "obsessive," if they are positively linked with other aspects of collecting we are taking into consideration, building up an organic gameplay experience.

But in *WoW* we also find the curious phenomenon of "gold farming." Players are said to be "farming" when they begin hunting again and again in the same game region infested by low-level creatures, so as to gain as many XP and virtual gold nuggets as possible, with as little effort as possible (but with commensurate loss of time, if not by means of cheating). When "farming" in this way we are certainly *hoarding* both XP and virtual gold. But as the verb "farm" suggests, in this way we are also losing the most profound sense of hunting and gathering activities: a sense of honest, meritocratic achievement! This phenomenon becomes even more apparent when gold farmers begin to exchange (against the EULA: the "real" rules of computer games) virtual gold they have earned for *real money*.[3] In a sense, then, compulsive hoarding can be linked to people who *buy* virtual gold in this way: they collect what ought to (according to good game practice) be a *reward*, but without any in-game merit, without any kind of *real* accomplishment. (I guess this depends on how important to you the achievement feature is. There are achievements for lots of things, including keeping track of looted money. But then, isn't this endorsing an end-justifies-the-means attitude?) Of course, in doing so, they may well manage to accomplish even wider personal goals with this particular strategy, but they are missing what is the main point for me, and I assume many other players: *playing the game*. Non-specific accumulation is bypassing some of the specificity of the hunting and gathering phase.

Seen from the particular viewpoint of the hoarding metaphor, then, players of *WoW* are passionately involved in accumulation of gold, XP, and other game items, building an experiential memory of a past history whose details are not immediately "visible" in the present moment, but that nonetheless are grounding our avatars' present (and future) existential conditions.

THREE, *Mating*: Collecting to Seduce Significant Others

Another example of collection behavior in nature is represented by the male bower bird, an accomplished avian architect that has long fascinated us with its complex courting behavior. Instead of using just showy plumes or a romantic melody to attract mates, the bower bird constructs an elaborate structure (a bower) on the forest floor from twigs, leaves, and moss. It decorates its bower with colorful baubles, feathers, pebbles, berries, and shells. Bowers aren't just nests for raising baby bower birds; they are bachelor pads designed to attract and seduce one or more mates. Each bird builds its own shape of bower and prefers a different decorating

---

[3] Ge Jin, a PhD student at UC San Diego, has produced a documentary on this phenomenon: <http://chinesegoldfarmers.com>.

scheme. Some surround bowers with carefully planted moss lawns. Others have been known to steal shiny coins, spoons, bits of aluminum foil (even a glass eye) in an effort to create the perfect romantic mood.

So, do player collection activities in *World of Warcraft* display any of this kind of mate-seeking oriented function? Well, here it seems that we need to know more about the actual social dynamics between players as individuals and members of a wider gaming community to say anything very concrete about this. But it does seem possible (if we are to judge from the elaborately clad, muscularly, or in other ways corporally well developed forms of *avatars*, both male and female) that some kind of other-oriented, "bower-birdlike" collection and decoration activities play some kind of central role in *WoW* culture. Avatar personalization is certainly a specific kind of collection activity in itself. You can display only one armor at any given time, but having a very cool one also means that you can *afford* it, and also that you may *have had* other, perhaps less cool, armors before this one. The collection is in some sense *invisible*, hidden in the past but implicitly signified by the actual armor you now have.

This phenomenon is linked to Danet and Katriel's metaphor of "collecting as desire, passion." This may happen both in a direct way (we play *WoW* in order to meet, and play with, others), and in an indirect way (while playing we desire to be recognized and esteemed by others). In fact, all our desires and passions are oriented to, and dependent on, other people: even if we do not actually want to be seen as "showing off," we still need the attention of the other, of our society or guild, of our peers, to attribute *real* value to our objects (especially our collections). We *learn* to desire together with others.

The specific aspect of collecting activities made explicit through use of the mating metaphor is the fact that our (virtual) life is a shared process of co-construction of relationships with others. MMORPGs tend to stress this relational experiential component in order to create a "more real" fictional world for us to move and act in. There we live in a *socialized time zone* where we may take active part in constituting and elaborating each other's selves. Here, our real lives and our real Earth-time insidiously permeate the fictional *World of Warcraft*, since people we enter into relationships with "there" through our interactions with them and their avatars are real, live people inhabiting the very same actual world as we do.

FOUR, *Nurturing*: Playing with others

A complementary aspect of having an *illness or disease* is taking part in some kind of *therapy* (Danet and Katriel's second metaphor); and a complementary aspect of *accumulation* is *distribution*. In nature, many species nurture their offspring for quite some time. Lion cubs, for example, are born blind and completely defenseless, so their mothers look after them away from the pride for up to two months. When they move back into the pride, lionesses cooperate with, and help, one another, often thanks to a synchronization of their respective reproductive cycles.

Today, there probably couldn't be a more provoking assertion than conceiving of, and talking about *World of Warcraft* in terms of therapy! But as we all know, playing is just one of the ways we have of temporarily decoupling ourselves from the world and just having fun, getting to know people, and "testing" new character types and personalities (which is *also* a form of collection, considered in experiential terms). By *immersing* ourselves in a virtual world we can happily experiment with the pleasure of concealment behind a personality-protecting avatar. In *WoW*, we not only live another life, but we also *take care* of this second life and our own gameworld creatures that live there. Often, this "taking care" involves offering help, advice and attention to other players, and also taking care of Non-Player Characters (NPCs) and even objects.

As was the case with our previous mating/passion metaphor, the nurturing metaphor highlights social aspects of *WoW*, rather than those connected with hunting, gathering, or hoarding activities. If winning a battle against another player gives us a strong sense of achievement (since it has been a "real" victory, with a "real" loser on the other side), our sense of satisfaction is even greater if we manage to complete a task or defeat a foe *together with other players*. It is no mere coincidence that some experienced players say that *WoW* first begins after we pass level 60, where all quests *require* the participation of *groups* of players to be successfully carried out (though others claim it doesn't begin until level 80). Not to mention the *endgame* itself, which is based on efficient coordination of groups of highly experienced, and thus particularly well qualified, players.

Simple collecting activities may become a type of "therapy" when carried out together with others, especially if what we most desire to collect and take care of are shared memories of past and present events, experiences, and relationships. It is far too simple to say that virtual experiences together with others aren't sufficiently real to be cared about. Time used for collection activities (marked out solely by way of sequences of acquisitions and accidental, or other forms of loss of objects) is linked to the existential timelines of our individual and shared life stories as persons and players, and the complex chains of *significant events* that work to entangle all these stories with each other.

If in our mating metaphor some kind of common time frame existed, driven by the slow but unremitting percolation of actual Earth-time into the fictional realm of *World of Warcraft*, here the reverse occurs. The *WoW* time frame, as played out through coordinated actions of organized groups of players, acquires new levels of breadth and depth. There is more intensive attunement of many different types of individual experience: group quests may take hours or days to be completed. This requires involved players to pledge to reset their own clocks to the game time frame, sacrificing portions of their own Earth-time to that of the game. A quest becomes a real event, which may create a need for players to, for example, renounce their real life meetings or dinner parties in order to immerse themselves together with others in the in-world gameplay.

FIVE, *Dying*: Linking to Transcendence

It appears that animals do not have supernatural experiences. We sometimes notice them performing repetitive acts, or "rites," but we tend to interpret such activities in terms of their utility. None are seen to be useless, and if some may look that way, it's either just that we haven't yet discovered their "innate" purpose (as in the case of our appendix and pineal gland), or that they are merely behaviors that once had an objective function which present day habitats have rendered useless. Still, there is one kind of rite that to our eyes still has a "sacred" aspect to it: the intentional choice of a place in which to die.

Maybe this is because a core aspect of our human cultures is the embalming and burying of corpses, decoration of urns, digging of catacombs, and erection of monuments like the pyramids. But whenever whales or elephants show they care about ensuring a "right place" to die, they look to us as though they are linking with transcendency, or "having a supernatural experience" (Danet and

Katriel's last metaphor for collecting). These animals seem as though they might care about what happens to their bodies after death, or even about what may become of the places on Earth they inhabited after they are not here anymore.

Humans perform many kinds of rites attuned to (and to atone) their own deities, and to divine time too (often seen as eternity, or as a cyclical loop). This is also the case when collecting for us becomes a means to communicate with the gods, as in doing so, we emphasize the relationship between earthly, human collecting time and divine, "transcendent" time. This is of particular interest in our present context, since in a humanly *created world* like the *World of Warcraft*, transcendent time is actually *our own real time*. We have already broached the issue of blending *game time* and *play time* in relation to the last two metaphors we mentioned. But if so far we have been discussing different means of *attunement*, we shall conclude by looking at a *decoupling* of these two time frames.

Martin Heidegger, in "Being and Time"[4] once wrote that we live for our own deaths: we are "being-toward-death." The *global objective* of our great life-game is to manage to cope with "the" one *unavoidable end*. Indeed, *time* itself is strictly linked to death (and to transcendence): for Heidegger *being* (what *really* exists, but hides itself from us) is ultimately *time*. Philosophically speaking, we are most alive when we are actually confronting our own finiteness—our *time-life* (as in "time-bomb")—since this is actually "the cure." It is what helps us decouple ourselves from the *illusion of life* we inevitably find ourselves trapped in.

Looked at in this way, both playing and collecting are activities oriented towards their own ends (or "death"). Collectors may, or may not, have an authentic desire to actually *complete* their collections: the "hunt," like the title of Michael Ende's story, is often a *never-ending* one, since other, as yet undiscovered, objects will always be capable of being desired and quested for. As Italian dramatist Luigi Pirandello puts it: "Life can't conclude. If it concludes, it's finished."[5] Still, the end, even if not consciously present for us, is in there somewhere, giving some kind of sense, *à rebours*, to all the rest.

---

[4] Martin Heidegger, *Being and Time* (Harper and Row, 1962).

[5] *One, No One, and One Hundred Thousand* (Marsilio, 1992).

Is the *endgame*, then, the authentic *global goal* of *World of Warcraft*? Well, probably, the principal goal for players is just to have fun—but also this is simply a question of giving oneself over to appreciating and enjoying the essentially *transitional* character of play, the fact that all play ends sometime, and we will have to leave the "magic circle" of the game for a while. The *endgame*, if, and when, we desire and manage to engage in it, perhaps does offer us some sense of completion. Afterwards, players may well want to start playing again, aiming towards yet another end, but this time with a brand new character they can add to their growing character collection!

Expert Philosopher

Your skills are improving! Your next task is to heighten you understanding of ethics by reading . . .

A Flourishing Revolt (SICART): 0/1
Ninja Ethics and the Virtual Theft of Virtual Goods (SERCHUK): 0/1
Remaking Azeroth (DUNCAN): 0/1

Description

Venture deeper into the ethical domain, Reader! You won't be surprised to find another discussion of utilitarianism and deontology—they're important ethical theories! But we think you'll find that the conclusion reached concerning those theories is a bit different than the one reached in the apprentice section.

In ethics we often ask questions about moral values. What sorts of models do WoW designers use to facilitate communication between designers and players? Are any of these models ethically harmful? Most of us have basic ideas of right and wrong, but in what ways are these ideas complicated by the virtual world? Do the infamous ninjas of WoW deserve ethical consideration? Are they even doing anything wrong? You may not be happy with the answers the author provides to these questions, Reader! But then, no one ever accused philosophy of avoiding controversy. Should ethical considerations be different in Azeroth than in the real world? In what ways can the design process of games benefit from a dialogue between designers and players? Is there a right or wrong way to design MMORPGs?

Rewards

You will receive: **+3 Intellect!**

9
A Flourishing Revolt

MIGUEL SICART

A Warrior fights. A Warrior fends off the enemies that populate every corner of Azeroth. A Warrior ensures that others can survive, that monsters will focus only on him, the Warrior, the first line of defence, the first line of hope. A Warrior is a hero from the beginning—through sacrifice, strength, and diligence a Warrior saves his mates one monster at a time.

But for Warriors to become the heroes they aspire to be, they need to have power. And Warriors feel underpowered. The might behind their names, behind the appearance of their powerful weapons, is only decorative, a myth. Warriors need more power, and someone, the gods, need to hear this claim.

Warriors unite! This war cry spreads through Internet forums, from warrior to warrior, from player to player: the meeting will take place in the Argent Dawn server, in the city of Ironforge. Players will create a Gnome Warrior, they will take off their clothes, they will parade—the developers need to know that the Warriors' humiliation will not prevail, that they need to be respected, that Warriors need to live up to their epic lore.

A revolt takes place. Dozens, maybe even hundreds, of Gnome Warriors parade, attracting the attention of other players who sympathize, mock, or just ignore the protest. The developers are also aware of the event. Their reaction? They threaten to temporarily ban the accounts of those protesting players if they don't desist. Some don't yield. Their accounts are banned. The developers win.

This is an account of an event that took place in *World of Warcraft* in the early days of the game, and that is now known as the "Gnome Tea Party." It was a player revolt against what they believed was a design flaw. What makes the event memorable is the consequences, the banning of player accounts by developers, under the argument that players were disrupting the "spirit of the game."

One has to wonder what an in-game event like the Gnome Tea Party says about ethics and morality, issues of right and wrong, even the reminiscence of Thoreau and Gandhi's philosophy of non-violent protest. Should the game developers be the ones to lay down the law? Or should the players themselves have a say? Is there such a thing as too much authority when it comes to Massively Multiplayer Online Role Playing Games (MMORPGs) such as *WoW*?

A History of Many Players

At the moment of writing, any reference to online computer games is illustrated by *World of Warcraft*, the incredible success story that has gathered over eleven million players around a fictional world of Orcs, Zombies, Gnomes, and Dwarves. Its popularity has made *WoW* a synonym both of economic success and of the very genre of games of which it's a part. And given its success, we can only predict that in the future, all MMORPGs will look like *WoW*.

However, the story of this genre and these games does not start, and will not end, with *World of Warcraft*. In fact, just to be purists, *WoW* is the direct culmination of a design history that was made popular with *Ultima Online* (Origin Systems, 1997), a game that was "just" an evolution of the early Multi-User Dungeons, or MUDs. Role playing over the internet has a long and rich history.

Play is an activity better practiced with others. Playing alone, like in single-player games, can be considered a historical anomaly. Yet early computers afforded the perfect "other player": ruthless, determined to win, and, best of all, easily designed by the creator of the game. Hence, most early computer games were single-player, from *Adventure* to *Asteroids*.

However, a computer is seldom a worthy opponent. It can probably match, or even beat, our skills, but it will do so without wit or soul, as the machine it is. And for games like role-playing games, that's all there is, more or less. In the late 1970s this problem was solved with the development of Multi-User Dungeons, mostly text-based environments connected through computer networks in which a number of players could meet and role play different kinds of adventures. The future of multiplayer was born.

Most Multi-User Dungeons had two crucial differences with regards to contemporary MMOs: 1. players of certain experience and skills could actually create content for the game; 2. the game had an end for players—once they reached the highest level, they became administrators too. These two design choices implied that MUD communities were highly empowered, as both users and creators of the content they were enjoying. In this sense, MUDs gave powers and tools to players to participate in the game beyond the limits afforded by the developers. Furthermore, on those MUDs, the boundaries between developers and players, producers and consumers, were either nonexistent or irrelevant.

With the advent of graphical user interfaces, some of this freedom was lost. MUDs became online adventure games, produced by larger corporations that wanted to produce revenue as well as to engage a customer base in the lavish virtual worlds they created. As noted above, the current trend of MMORPG design can be traced back to *Ultima Online*, a game that set the trend in terms of technical architecture, graphical metaphors, gameplay and community management. All current MMORPGs are some kind of offspring of *Ultima Online*.

It was not that game, though, that made the genre famous. Sony Online's *EverQuest* (1999) was yesteryears' *World of Warcraft*. Academics, the press, game developers, we were all astonished by the 250,000 players that gathered in Norrath to play a game that foreshadowed the future of PC gaming. Built on the tradition of *Ultima*, but focusing on creating a pleasant and challenging experience for as many players as possible, *EverQuest* also symbolizes the success of a way of establishing player-developer relations.

Essentially, developers saw players as consumers, engaged with a product over which they had absolute control. Phenomena like the trading of in-game assets for real money, or the extension of real communities into virtual communities were often harshly regulated by the developers, who wanted to keep strict control over the contents, products, and interactions they had designed for players. Developers used their absolute, omniscient power over the game to control behaviors, convinced that *EverQuest* was a business more than a game or a place for communities to gather.

World of Warcraft, the hugely popular game based on the *Warcraft* franchise, has only expanded these policies. In fact, *WoW* is a game controlled by the developers to a very large extent, expanding on the policies of control and the architectures of power created for *EverQuest*. These practices, and the way they relate to players, are what make *WoW* an interesting game to analyze from an ethical perspective, since it illuminates issues on player values, virtual-world ethics, and developer responsibilities.

What this history shows us, however, is a conflict between a player model imposed by developers and the actual behaviour of these worlds' denizens. As T.L. Taylor has argued, designers embed an image of a user, an "ideal" user in the products they create.[1] This means that games are designed to be played in specific ways pre-determined by the game developers. In fact, designing is not only creating interesting games, but also identifying what appeals to a core audience of players. Designing is, then, imagining players and catering to their needs, while limiting their possible behaviors.

Taylor has argued that the models that game developers tend to embed in MMORPGs fall into two categories: players-as-consumers, and players-as-troublemakers. The players-as-consumers model implies that the users of these online worlds do not have rights as citizens or producers of content, but should merely be interacting with a product in the prescribed ways. This model understands players as unproductive button-mashers who will obey the rules and comply with the decisions of the developers, regardless of how arbitrary those may be.

The second model, players-as-troublemakers, explains the reaction of *World of Warcraft*'s developers after the Gnome Tea Party. In this approach, players are seen as disruptors of a specific vision of the game imposed by the designers. Since that vision is somewhat sacred, any action that threatens the status quo, be that creating their own rules or content or publicly complaining about imbalances, will yield punishing responses, such as banning accounts. Developers are zealous over their designs, to the extent that they have even included a clause in the End-User License Agreement that allows them to act in case a player acts against "the spirit of the game." The vagueness of this phrasing, seemingly, is just an umbrella to justify interventionism in case any player tries to play in a different way as that plotted by the designers.

These two models are very troublesome. Players are not necessarily either consumers or troublemakers. In fact, players of online

---

[1] Taylor, T.L., "Beyond Management: Considering Participatory Design and Governance in Player Culture," *First Monday* (October 2006).

game worlds tend to build large social networks, contributing to the life on those worlds as much as any system of rules does. For instance, players form guilds that, on occasions, compete to be the first in accomplishing a particular feat and thus become famous. Guilds are institutionalized social networks that involve both the game world and social relations outside of it. Players may not own the world, but they certainly inhabit it, and produce social, cultural, and personal content by merely being there and playing the game. In this sense, players are more than just button-mashers: players are creative beings with the capacity of incorporating their values into their experience of the game, as well as their culture and history as players and as human beings. The Gnome Tea Party in itself is an example of this creative capacity: by appealing to the tradition of non-violent protest, Warriors united against a superior authority with righteous claims. The rest is (this) history.

This capacity of players to make these worlds "theirs" is the heart of the complex relations between players and developers, and it is also relevant when understanding some of the ethical issues generated by online game worlds. The values of such worlds should be mapped first and foremost as the values that the designers have embedded in the game world, and how those affect the creative capacities of players. Being a player of *World of Warcraft* means playing by some community-values, but also creating ethical discourses they want to live by.

Be the Player You Can Be

The idea of players as customers is so pervasive that we tend to apply it when analyzing situations that take place in games. A reader could claim that what Blizzard did, banning those players that publicly complained, was enforcing the implicit contract between two parties: players should play, and developers should make sure that they do so, without any more complaints.

Nevertheless, the nature of online worlds as places where we play, but where we socialize too, seems to demand a more nuanced approach to issues of play. Some game designers like Raph Koster have even claimed that we should think about a bill of rights for players[2]: being a denizen of *World of Warcraft* is

---

[2] Ralph Koster, "Declaring the Rights of Players" (2000), at <www.raphkoster.com/gaming/playerrights.shtml>.

much more than just being a player, in its political, cultural, and ethical implications.

Playing is much more than delegating (refereeing) responsibility to the game developers. We're not just players of *World of Warcraft*, we are somewhat citizens of Azeroth, and as such we have duties, and rights, that ought to be respected. It's not a matter of ownership, nor is it a matter of customer-producer relations. Being in a game-world like Azeroth is being an ethical and political entity that is interested in playing, but also in creating social networks and upholding those values that, as players, we want to live by.

Let's return to the Gnome Tea Party: if we analyze the event from the model of players as customers, what we see is players using the "wrong" means to complain about the product. Instead of using the channels sanctioned by the developers, they appropriate the game and "misuse" it: in order to protest for a game design imbalance through the approved means, the official forums, players staged a peaceful revolt in one server, in fact appropriating the space for other means than the designed play. This means breaking the contract between both parties, and hence justifying the actions taken by the developers.

Seeing the event from the perspective of "players as troublemakers," the picture is even bleaker: the developers considered that this protest constituted not a legitimate complaint, but an act of conspiracy against the game itself. Players did not want to criticize, they wanted to break the spirit of the game, and therefore they deserved the banning of their accounts.

However, we can see the Gnome Tea Party from a totally different perspective, one that involves understanding players as ethical beings capable of creating the values they play by. When players of *World of Warcraft* considered that the design of the Warrior class was imperfect to the extent of harming their experience of the game, they acted upon that belief. They did so by applying their agency in the game world to express their concerns. What the Gnome Tea Party shows us is that players of *World of Warcraft* have a deep sense of belonging to a world and ownership of the game, and that translates to the ethical capacity and duty, of contributing with value-based choices and actions to the game world.

In other words, players of *WoW* see the world as partially theirs, and in doing so, they develop a set of principles, values, and ethical codes by which they live. The use of the space to complain about design issues is an ethical action, understood as their duty to report what harms them and act to prevent harm. Players not only play, they also create values by which they play, and act upon them.

In philosophical terms, this capacity for players to create values and live by them can be explained by applying the general framework of Flourishing Ethics. This framework is a rather contemporary take on two ethical theories: Aristotle's Virtue Ethics and Wiener's early Information Ethics.[3] In the Western world, Virtue Ethics has enjoyed a long history, influencing many different strains of ethical thinking. Wiener's ethical theories have not been so popular, but they critically contribute to the Flourishing Ethics framework, an ethical theory for the information age.

Flourishing Ethics is based on the idea that it is good that humans flourish, that is, that they become the best they can become in moral terms. They can only do so by being *autonomous*, that is, by being in charge of their own lives, creating values and taking decisions as well as responsibility for their actions and their meaning. Humans can chose what to be, and should create their lives according to this wish of fulfilment. Flourishing Ethics, then, is the ethics of becoming the best we can become by creating our lives, and taking responsibility in doing so.

Human beings are seldom alone: in this sense, Flourishing Ethics also recognises that we are essentially social beings, and that to flourish, we need to develop good societies. The ethical development is both personal and interpersonal: we develop our values and the values of our communities. This process means that what is good in each of us, what we must strive to develop, has to be respected by the larger setting in which we live. Laws, and traditions, should then act as frames and reinforcements of the process of flourishing.

Finally, Flourishing Ethics has to be seen as a wide-scoped ethical theory: the ethical demand of becoming the best we can become should not stop on a human or societal level. Flourishing can also take place in ecosystems, informational systems, artificial agents, and even civilizations. In other words, machines can also flourish, as well as artificial environments. Translated to *World of*

---

[3] T.W. Bynum, "Flourishing Ethics," in *Ethics and Information Technology* 8:4 (2007), pp. 157–173.

Warcraft? Players, computer-controlled agents, and the very world of Azeroth—they are all subject to ethical duties regarding their development to fulfil their potential.

If we go back to the Gnome Tea Party again, we can frame it as an ethical act. Players developed a number of values that made protesting the right action to take: as players, they believed that they were being harmed, and that the same world in which they were living should stage the protest. Similarly, we can claim that their complaint was aimed at an ethical flaw in the world: the game was poorly designed, which meant that the experience was damaging their capacity to flourish. Players did not just complain: the Gnome Tea Party is an enactment of their ethical duties towards themselves, the player community, and the game world in which they inhabit. Blizzard's response damaged the ethical coherence of the game and the being of their players.

We need to move on from developer-created player models to a model that takes into consideration not only what players can do to win the game, but also what players *do* when they live in that gameworld.

Simple Harassment and Who We Are

In January 2006, a new polemic affected *World of Warcraft*. A game master, the developers' authority in the game world, issued a warning to a player who was recruiting other players for her GLBT (Gay-Lesbian-Bisexual-Transexual)-friendly guild. Interpreting the game's harassment policy in a rather particular way, the game master understood that such recruiting efforts should be taken outside of the game since they cause those recruited players to be harassed for their sexual orientation.

While this is just an example of the particular community management ideas that drive *WoW*, it shows once again that for the developers of this game, there should be not only a strict difference between real life and in-game life, but also that in-game life should follow strict observation of the rules they have laid out, regardless of community practices or values.

This policy is a misunderstanding of players. Players are creative beings. When we enter a gameworld, we not only want to create an avatar that will be our body in that game; we also want to be a part of a community of players. Being a part of this community requires acting according to the rules and values that other players deem crucial for being a productive member of the game. Playing is never a lonely activity; it is always positioning oneself in a history, tradition, and social network to which, by virtue of the game, we belong.

Since players are social, ethical beings capable of creating values and principles they want to play by, we need to articulate a model that encompasses the Flourishing Ethics framework with the actual behaviors we engage in when playing *World of Warcraft*, or any other online game. This model comes from something called "Information Ethics," and defines agents as *Homo poieticus*.[4]

This Latin expression, which can basically translate as "the creative human," defines a model of being that places ethical responsibility in participation as well as in self-development of our values in the environments we live in. In this sense, the creative human is the model that answers to the theoretical requirements of the Flourishing Ethics framework, and it can be applied to understand the processes that take place when players enter a gameworld and play within it together with others.

A player is a *Homo poieticus* because playing means adopting the rules of a world, but also committing to live by values that can be adopted and evolved so they match the requirements of personal, social, and informational flourishing. Players of *WoW* who decided to complain about the Warrior class limitations are creative humans: they decided to take their presence in the world one step further from the conventional "consumer" approach, and took the responsibility of identifying and developing a complaint to improve their life conditions.

This ethical capacity is summarized in the concept of creative stewardship. A player is given the right of inhabiting a world. That right involves the management and enjoyment of a game system as developed by the game designers. But it is not a passive position: to be a player also involves a creative aspect, an appropriation of what is given in order to improve it. To play is to become the best player you can be.

Being a player in an online world like *World of Warcraft* means participating in the shared experience of a game, as facilitated by the developers. But it also means being a citizen of Azeroth, caring

---

[4] Luciano Floridi and Jeff Sanders, "Internet Ethics: The Constructionist Values of Homo Poieticus," in *The Impact of the Internet in Our Moral Lives* (SUNY Press, 2005), at <www.philosophyofinformation.net/pdf/iecvhp.pdf>.

for other players as well as for the balance and well-being of the world you've been given and you have to inhabit. Being a player is the responsibility of being a creative human, capable of playing by the rules, but also of adapting those rules to the principle of human flourishing. If that means a revolt then so be it.

The idea of players as creative beings proposes an alternative understanding of players that includes ethical duties, and the principles of Flourishing Ethics, in the definition of what players are and how they should be treated. Events like the Gnome Tea Party show that we can define players as creative beings since they already behave that way. However, the model becomes relevant when we compare it to the developers' implicit player models, and how the clash between both determines the values of *WoW*.

Play Beyond Labor

The two models, player-as-customer and player-as-troublemaker, heavily influence the design of *WoW* and the community management policies.

In order to understand the conceptual roots of these models, we should return to one of the dominant cultural explanations of play and games in western culture: Huizinga's *Homo Ludens*, or the man-player. In his research on play, this Dutch theorist came up with a definition of players as cultural beings. It was never Huizinga's idea to develop a coherent model of mankind; however, his insights on the role of play and its experience in culture allow us to extract a plausible idea of what *Homo Ludens* means.

Given Huizinga's understanding of play, *Homo Ludens* describes how humans engage in a separate, free, and creative action called play with the goal of enjoying the benefits of this activity. However, the *Homo Ludens*, while creative within the game, does not have any kind of duty or right regarding the game itself: the player plays, and that's the extent of her involvement with the game. *Homo Ludens* explains why we like playing, the pleasures we extract out of this activity. But it's a very limited model that cannot account for the values in the game or for the complex relations between players and game creators, or even for the values of players within the game and those external to it.

The *Homo Ludens* model is the origin of both the player-as-customer and player-as-troublemaker paradigms previously presented. For a player to be understood as either/or, their creative capacities need to be ignored. There is pleasure in play, and that's what developers and players should focus on achieving. Focusing on pleasing the *Homo Ludens* radically improves the gameplay experience, and allows for a tighter control of actions and events by the developer. On the downside, it severely limits player moral agency, which can be seen as a form of ethical harm. In fact, games developed with the intention of upholding the *Homo Ludens* model tend to end up equalising play and labor: as long as we follow the rules, countless hours of play will be ensured.

The *Homo Poieticus* model proposes a much more interesting and rich understanding of players—one that is actually already present in their behaviors. Players create the values they play by, and by doing so, they keep the world together and give it a life, a sense of place. The Gnome Tea Party protesters were not trying to break the game, but to fix it. The intrinsic mistrust that developers have of players and their influence in the game is an example of an historic misunderstanding.

Furthermore, not respecting the *Homo Poieticus* means, as I said, limiting the moral agency of players. These policies of control can be therefore seen as unethical: for players to flourish, they need to implement their values in the game world, as a part of their process to become the best being they can be. Any action taken against these capacities ought to be considered unethical.

World of Warcraft is a prominent example of the tensions between the two models: the game is developed with a *Homo Ludens* paradigm in mind, and as such is hardwired with architectures and policies of control that the developers don't hesitate to apply. However, players engaging in creative actions, such as the Gnome Tea Party, shows a deeper sense of belonging and creativity. In that tension, *WoW* so often defaults to a control paradigm by which developers always have supreme power over players, whose actions and behaviors are subject to close scrutiny and punishment, even though they are just expressing who they are and what kind of world they want to live in. Punishing them for their expressive actions is a sign of the questionable values behind the design and management of *WoW*.

This Is Our World

I have written hard words against one of the most polished, well designed, and popular computer games of all time. I have done so both with the analytic intention of the philosopher, trying to explain what playing means from an ethical perspective, and with the playful goal of the *provocateur*, who wants to shake up some of our assumed conventions on games and play. As both, I want to make my claim clear: *World of Warcraft*, and any online game similarly designed and managed, presents a number of ethically questionable models that may be considered harmful for the morals of players as creative beings. *WoW*, within the boundaries I have described in this chapter, can be defined as an unethical game design.

How can an online world, then, ensure its ethical soundness? By encouraging player creativity in their game design; by giving tools to players to express themselves and become who they can become in that world. The values of a game are found in the dialogue between developers and players through the game world as a living space. It's time to move beyond the dated *Homo Ludens* model and remember that Azeroth, like any other world, is also our world.

10

Ninja Ethics and the Virtual Theft of Virtual Goods

PHIL SERCHUK

Although many dangerous creatures inhabit the lands of Azeroth, Outland, and Northrend, none are more reviled than ninjas. For those readers who have been fortunate enough to never encounter one, ninjas are characters that loot items which were awarded to other players, or have not yet been awarded to anyone. The easiest way to ninja is to just take items and hope your party doesn't notice. Five-person groups typically run dungeons using Group Loot, a setting that randomly distributes high-quality items among interested players. But at any time the group leader can change to Master Loot, a setting that gives the group leader complete control over the loot's distribution. Although the group is notified, the notification is easy to miss. Once the setting has been changed the group leader can help herself to whatever items she likes—until the rest of the group notices and leaves. Guilds usually run twenty-five-person raids on Master Loot because raid loot is too valuable to be distributed randomly. This leaves the raid vulnerable. It's not unheard of for a raid leader to ninja a rare or important drop, such as Kael'thas Sunstrider's [Ashes of Al'ar] or Illidan Stormrage's [Warglaive of Azzinoth]. Of course, the ninja is immediately kicked from the guild—but the loot is theirs to keep.

A ninja who isn't the group leader must employ different techniques. Although most bosses drop their loot directly, some drop treasure chests that contain their loot. Usually this makes no difference to a player's experience. But prior to patch 2.10 (released two and a half years after launch), items looted from chests were not subject to the game's loot rules. Honest players would inspect these chests and inform the group of its contents; the group would then decide who would collect the loot. But even on Group Loot a ninja could take items from a chest without the group's consent. These valuable (and vulnerable) treasure chests were dropped in high-level and endgame instances. In Azeroth's Blackrock Depths the Chest of the Seven was dropped after the party defeated seven Dark Iron ghosts in rapid succession. The Black Coffer, also in Blackrock Depths, was accessible only after players defeated Watchman Doomgrip and his four golems. In Outland's Hellfire Ramparts, Vazruden and Nazan left a Reinforced Fel Iron Chest for players to find. And in Karazhan, *Burning Crusade*'s most popular endgame raid, a quick ninja could take epic-level items from the Dust Covered Chest that dropped after the Chess Event.

I will CRUSH and DESTROY and . . . Oohh . . . Shiny —Why Orcs (and the Rest of Us) Hate Ninjas

Although most players have a dim view of ninjas—a quick look at Blizzard's forums will confirm this—it's quite a bit of work to enact any meaningful in-game sanctions against one. There's no way to unilaterally blacklist a player from a server's guilds, and players can always transfer to a different server or change their name. This is why ninjas continue to respawn and infuriate. Players invest countless hours running the same instance over and over again in an effort to gear up; because item drops are randomized, some groups run the same instance a dozen times and never see a particular piece of loot. It's frustrating to have a rare item ninja'd after weeks of effort. Nobody likes ninjas, wants to play with ninjas, or wants anyone to be a ninja. But does this make ninjaing immoral?

Moral philosophers aren't interested in what's popular—we're interested in what's morally right and morally wrong. And for all the trouble they cause, it's very difficult to say exactly what it is that ninjas are doing morally wrong. At first glance, it may look as though ninjas are no different than real-world thieves. And since stealing in the real world is immoral, it might seem as though ninjaing in *World of Warcraft (WoW)* is immoral too. This is an argument by analogy, and it certainly seems strong enough: since it is immoral to steal in the real world, and *if* stealing in the real world is analogous to ninjaing loot in *WoW*, then it will also be immoral to ninja loot. But it isn't obvious that real world stealing is analogous to ninjaing, at least not in a morally relevant way.

How can anyone steal a [Warglaive of Azzinoth] when [Warglaive of Azzinoth]s *don't even exist*? Clearly you cannot steal something without taking it, and *we* can no more take [Warglaive of Azzinoth]s than we can clone [Swift Purple Hawkstrider]s or shake hands with Warchief Thrall. There is a parallel problem about the ninja: how can the level 70 Rogue, Mrstabby, ninja anything, let alone the non-existent [Warglaive of Azzinoth]? I realize that some readers may find this approach chauvinistic. In my view, such objections can only be taken seriously if accompanied by an explanation of how virtual and fictional entities exist in the physical world. In the absence of such an explanation, it's reasonable to assume that thieves are real people who take real items that belong to other real people, and ninjas are virtual characters (played by real people) who virtually take virtual items from other virtual characters (played by other real people). At issue is whether these activities are analogous in a morally relevant way. To answer this question we must first see what parts of real world theft are morally relevant. We can then determine if the morally relevant components of stealing are present in ninjaing.

We Will Have Justice!—If the Blood Elves Have It, Why Can't We?

Any credible moral theory must tell us why immoral acts like murder and stealing are usually (or always) wrong: most philosophers would not regard a theory that licensed casual murder as a plausible ethical theory. Our challenge is to see if any major ethical theories license the additional claim that ninjaing is usually (or always) wrong. To answer this challenge we're going to look at two of the major ethical theories that philosophers study: utilitarianism and deontology.

If Cannibalism Be Wrong, I Don't Want to Be Right!—Was Medivh a Utilitarian?

There are two main kinds of utilitarianism: act utilitarianism and rule utilitarianism. Each stems from the work of nineteenth-century British philosopher John Stuart Mill.[1] The act utilitarian holds that

[1] John Stuart Mill, *Utilitarianism* (Hackett, 2002).

the morality of an action depends solely on its consequences. An action is morally good when it maximizes everyone's happiness relative to the potential happiness of the other available options, where happiness is typically construed in terms of pleasure and pain. You can then tell if an act is moral by looking at its consequences. Let's *temporarily* set aside the fact that the *WoW* is entirely fictional and consider the characters and events as if they were real.

Consider Medivh's effort to open the Dark Portal. The act utilitarian doesn't care if Medivh wanted to start a war or bring about a new era of peace. To see if Medivh acted morally, we must determine whether the Dark Portal's opening maximized happiness. When the Dark Portal opened the First War began. Both the Alliance and the Horde suffered countless casualties; the Kingdom of Azeroth was destroyed and humanity was pushed back to Lordaeron. Although most Orcs enjoy battle, they do not enjoy pain, suffering, or death (after all, a dead Orc can't fight). In sum: immeasurable pain and suffering were felt by both sides of the conflict. The Alliance lost a great deal of territory to the Horde, giving the Horde pleasure and causing the Alliance pain. Overall, the First War led to far more pain than pleasure. To the act utilitarian, Medivh acted immorally by opening the Dark Portal. Happiness would have been maximized had he kept the Horde on Draenor.

The act utilitarian makes no general claims about real world stealing. Suppose you find yourself wandering alone through Les Invalides. You come across Napoleon's Tomb and decide to take the sarcophagus as decoration for your personal library. Adding the sarcophagus to your collection gives you some pleasure but causes everyone else pain, since everyone else would feel as though Napoleon's memory had been defiled. Since the pain grossly outweighs the pleasure, the act utilitarian claims the theft is immoral. But now suppose you replaced the sarcophagus with a well-crafted fake, one so good that nobody would ever notice. You would still gain pleasure from stealing the sarcophagus but nobody would feel pain, since nobody would know that the sarcophagus was gone and thus never feel as though Napoleon's memory had been defiled. In this case the act utilitarian must concede that the theft is morally justified. Most philosophers think this conclusion is counterintuitive. We want to say that it's wrong to steal the sarcophagus, irrespective of whether anyone notices.

Some utilitarians address this problem by considering the happiness generated by general rules instead of specific acts. These are called rule utilitarians. Like act utilitarians, rule utilitarians associate morality with pleasure and immorality with pain. But instead of considering the pain and pleasure generated by any particular act, like stealing Napoleon's sarcophagus, the rule utilitarian considers the happiness generated by a rule that would license particular acts, like a rule allowing theft. If it were morally permissible to steal sarcophaguses then people would worry that their loved ones' sarcophaguses would be stolen. This would create a great deal of pain since everyone would have something to worry about. The rule would only create a small amount of pleasure because very few people would actually steal sarcophaguses and get pleasure from it. So rule utilitarians can easily explain why stealing is wrong: because the pain outweighs the pleasure, happiness is maximized by rules preventing theft.

The Naaru Frown on Such Behavior— Kil'jaeden Was No Deontologist

Deontological ethics takes the view that actions are good or bad regardless of the consequences. There are many varieties of deontological ethics, most of them based on the work of eighteenth-century German philosopher Immanuel Kant.[2] Kant believed that an act's consequences were irrelevant when assessing its morality.

To Kant, all that mattered was an agent's underlying good will. That's not to say good intentions make an action moral; Kant had very strict rules concerning what it took for a will to be good. These rules comprise what he calls the Categorical Imperative. The Categorical Imperative requires that we 1. only act in such a way that it is logically possible for universal laws to be formed from our acts, and 2. never use a moral agent merely to achieve some goal. A moral agent is a person capable of making and being held accountable for moral decisions. For example, rational human adults are moral agents; babies and toaster ovens are not.

As before, let's *temporarily* set aside the fact that *WoW* is entirely fictional and consider the characters and events as if they were real. Suppose Kil'jaeden the Deceiver wants to know if he was right to deceive Ner'zhul. Constraint 1. of the Categorical

[2] Immanuel Kant, *Groundwork for the Metaphysics of Morals* (Broadview, 2005).

Imperative requires that the act, in this case lying, could be willed to become a universal law. Kil'jaeden must now conduct a thought experiment to see if this is possible. Suppose there was a moral law which stated *demons may lie when necessary to secure their goals.* If this were a moral law, then regular Orcs like Ner'zhul would know that demons like Kil'jaeden were free to lie whenever they pleased. But if Ner'zhul knew this he would have no reason to ever trust Kil'jaeden, since he'd know that Kil'jaeden was free to lie. But Kil'jaeden couldn't lie to Ner'zhul if Ner'zhul didn't trust him—a lie can only be told under the pretext of trust.

So a moral law licensing lying is logically impossible; such a law would undermine the presumption of truth that is essential for lying. Kil'jaeden's actions also violate constraint 2., since he is only using Ner'zhul to realize the goal of unifying the Orcs. Even if this is a worthy or moral goal, Kil'jaeden's actions are immoral because he fails to treat Ner'zhul as a moral agent capable of deciding for himself if he wants to unify the Horde. To satisfy constraint 2., Kil'jaeden would need to treat Ner'zhul as a moral agent. To do this he'd have to tell Ner'zhul the truth; Ner'zhul could then decide for himself if he wants to help Kil'jaeden.

It should be no surprise that the deontologist claims stealing is immoral. A moral law licensing theft cannot be universalized. If stealing were morally permissible then there could be no principled notion of private property. Because the act of stealing requires the notion of private property, a moral law allowing theft is inconsistent. Theft also violates constraint 2. When you steal Napoleon's sarcophagus, you use the French taxpayer as a means to decorate your library; you are not treating the French as moral agents capable of deciding for themselves if they want to pay for your decorations.

May I Show You My Wares?—Can Goblins (and WoW's Other Inhabitants) Own Property?

We've seen how two major ethical theories treat real-world theft. Let's now see what they say about the theft of intangible items. We can distinguish between two kinds of intangible goods: digital goods and virtual goods. Let's start with digital goods. *WoW* accounts are digital goods: there is no physical file folder that contains all of your character's information. When someone hacks Blizzard's servers and accesses your account data, they are "stealing" a digital item that belongs to Blizzard. Similarly, music pirates who download the *WoW* soundtrack are taking a digital good: the soundtrack itself is not a physical item. It is debatable whether digital goods can be stolen *per se*: if I download a pirated copy of the soundtrack I do not "take" it from anyone; I make a copy of a digital item that I may or may not have otherwise purchased. Nonetheless, piracy and the "theft" of digital goods will be immoral on at least two of the theories considered earlier, rule utilitarianism and deontology.

The rule utilitarian will claim the following: if it were moral to pirate digital goods, then producers of digital goods would no longer be guaranteed an income. This would create a great deal of anxiety. Consumers of digital goods would gain some immediate happiness, but they too would be caused pain as producers would soon stop making virtual goods (on account of its unprofitability). Because piracy creates more pain than pleasure, it is immoral to the rule utilitarian. The deontologist also holds that piracy is immoral. We cannot have a moral law that licenses piracy: if everyone pirated digital goods then nobody would produce them, and so there would be no digital goods to pirate. On this view, pirates use content producers merely as a means to produce digital goods: the pirate fails to treat the content producer as a moral agent. The act utilitarian has nothing generalized to say about digital piracy: a particular illegal download is moral if it maximizes happiness and immoral if it doesn't.

In contrast to digital goods, virtual goods do not have any real-world function. Virtual goods include in-game gold and items, such as [Seth's Graphite Fishing Pole] and the [Warglaive of Azzinoth]. Virtual items typically have no real-world value, though real people do sometimes spend real money on virtual goods. Real-world gold farmers make a living selling virtual gold in this way. But unlike digital goods, virtual goods cannot be used outside of their virtual worlds: their value is conditional on the virtual world's existence. In contrast, a digital MP3 of the *WoW* soundtrack can be played on any computer or MP3 player in the real world: it does not require that a game be active or configured a certain way. Players who use real-world money on virtual goods circumvent the game's rules; philosophers typically describe such behavior as *cheating*. It is crucial that we keep this in mind when considering the (apparent) theft of virtual goods.

Unlike digital goods, which can be bought and sold by anybody, virtual items cannot be acquired by real people. You or I can own a digital copy of the *WoW* soundtrack, but neither of us can own the [Warglaive of Azzinoth]. Items like this are wielded by virtual characters like Mrstabby. But Mrstabby can't own the [Warglaive of Azzinoth] because Mrstabby isn't real. I don't think anybody owns the [Warglaive of Azzinoth] because it, along with other in-game items, simply aren't the sorts of things that can be owned. This may seem counterintuitive, so let me make the point with a *reductio ad absurdum* (proof by contradiction). This technique works by assuming that the claim I'm trying to disprove is true, and then showing that this assumption leads to an absurd conclusion.

Suppose you (a real person) own the [Warglaive of Azzinoth]. It would follow that you could use it as you please. For example, you could sell it to another player or put it on your wall. But you can do neither of these things. Blizzard prohibits players from selling virtual items.[3] Clearly you cannot put the [Warglaive of Azzinoth] on your wall since it cannot leave the game. But you also can't put it on some virtual wall—that is, until Blizzard decides to give you that in-game ability. Blizzard can also change or remove *your* item at their whim: they may decide the item is unbalanced or that you acquired it unfairly. This contradicts what seems to be a basic principle of property ownership, that (in normal circumstances) you maintain exclusive control over your property. As a potential owner, Mrstabby fares no better. If he owned the [Warglaive of Azzinoth] then it would be he who, for example, has to claim it on his tax returns and go to court if he fails to pay. But this is absurd: only real people pay taxes and go to court. So neither you nor Mrstabby can be said to own virtual items in *WoW*.[4]

Although Mrstabby cannot own items, perhaps he can virtually own items. This is not the place to offer a robust theory of virtual people and virtual property, but it's likely that any such account will treat Mrstabby as a virtual person and the [Warglaive of Azzinoth] as his virtual property. So when Mrstabby ninjas (the level 70 Rogue) Mcstabsalot's [Warglaive of Azzinoth], there won't

---

[3] Their terms of service state: "you agree that you have no right or title in or to any such content, including without limitation the virtual goods or currency appearing or originating in the Game . . . Blizzard does not recognize any purported transfers of virtual property executed outside of the Game."

[4] The situation may be different in games like *Second Life* (if it can be called a game), which are explicitly designed to facilitate real-world ownership of virtual items.

be any real world or digital theft taking place. At best there will be virtual theft. Does it then follow that there is *no* moral dilemma? I think so.

Embrace the Shadow!—There Is No Moral Dilemma

Recall that the utilitarian takes an action to be moral when it maximizes happiness. What can the utilitarian say about Mrstabby's ninjaing? Well, the utilitarian can say that ninjaing is unfortunate because it creates pain: the small pleasure generated by the player controlling the ninja is easily outweighed by the very real pain and frustration real people feel when they encounter him. But, I will argue, there is no moral agent to evaluate. As such, the utilitarian can't say that anyone is doing anything wrong when a ninjaing occurs.

The deontologist faces a similar problem. Ninjaing, if real, would violate both versions of the Categorical Imperative. It's not universalizable because nobody would run instances if ninjaing were morally permissible, and there would be no loot to ninja if nobody ran instances. The ninja, if he was a moral agent, would be using the other group members merely as a means to collect an item: this would wrong them by denying their moral autonomy. But as was the case with utilitarianism, there is simply no moral agent for the deontologist to target. And if we cannot find a moral agent then neither theory will be able to treat ninjaing as immoral, not because it doesn't seem wrong, but because there is no entity to hold morally liable. Ninjaing will be as morally benign as a natural disaster.

Let me now defend the claim that there is no moral agent for these theories to evaluate. There are only two plausible candidates for moral agency: the real person playing Mrstabby, and Mrstabby himself. Suppose the person playing Mrstabby were morally responsible for everything done by Mrstabby. The player would then be morally responsible for all the creatures Mrstabby has killed while questing, from the Kobolds slaughtered for their precious candles to the lovable fawns and squirrels he was once dared to massacre in Elwynn Forest. My critic might distinguish between Non-Player Characters (NPCs) and Player Characters (PCs), and hold that players are only morally responsible for actions against PCs. But I don't think this is a principled distinction to use when considering questions of existence or morality. The PC Mcstabsalot (Mrstabby's victim) is no more real than the NPC Warchief Thrall: they both "exist" in the same virtual world and are subject to the same limitations thereof. NPCs are indirectly controlled by Blizzard's (human) programmers; PCs are directly controlled by other (human) players and sometimes by (non-human) bots. I just don't see how this relatively minor difference could motivate such a substantial moral distinction. Moreover, treating players as moral agents yields conclusions counterintuitive to the spirit of the game. For example, PCs regularly kill one another in battlegrounds like Arathi Basin, in contested zones like Shadowmoon Valley, outside instances like Karazhan, and in major cities like Ironforge. It would be absurd to hold players morally or criminally liable for the thousands of PCs they've killed.

Mrstabby is no more viable as a moral agent. It doesn't make sense to talk about holding Mrstabby accountable for his actions because Mrstabby isn't the kind of person, virtual or otherwise, that makes decisions. If you ninja your friend's sword it's no defense to claim that it was Mrstabby, not you, who took it: your friend won't simply insist that you play as a different character, but rather he will refuse to play with you altogether. But he won't hold you *morally* culpable—it would be unreasonable for your friends to worry that you'd steal items from their real world homes. It would be quite understandable if they stopped playing with you or thought you were a lousy friend, perhaps claiming that you take the game too seriously or ruin others' fun. But they could not (and would not) accuse you of being an immoral thief who should be locked away. Neither you nor Mrstabby is a viable candidate as a moral agent. As such, there is nobody to hold morally liable for ninjaing. Therefore, ninjaing cannot be immoral. In-game ninjas can do no wrong because there is no moral agent to hold morally accountable. Perhaps our only hope is to do as (the NPC) Mekgineer Thermaplugg does: surround ourselves with Alarm-a-bomb 2600s and hope they keep the looters away.

11
Remaking Azeroth

SEAN C. DUNCAN

In just a few short years, *World of Warcraft* has become one of the most dominant computer games, eclipsing all other fantasy Massively-Multiplayer Online Role Playing Games (MMORPGs) as the most popular in the world, with over eleven and a half million subscribers at the time of this chapter's writing. As many of the other chapters in this book have attested to, the popularity of this particular game and the overall genre of MMORPGs is due to a number of factors: the complexity of the activities one needs to engage in to play the game successfully (should I put my new talent points into the Subtlety or Combat trees?), developing an understanding the game's lore (who killed that Old God in Darkshore?), learning how to work with others for raids and group play (are you geared for Naxxramas?). And, as with many MMORPGs, this complexity has historically required a degree of sheer gaming endurance to reach the level cap (why is leveling from 50 to 60 so boring?).

But, what of the broader context *around* the game? That is, diving into Azeroth and battling for the Horde or the Alliance can be quite exciting, but does the social and philosophical significance of the game begin and end at the game's login screen? "Gaming" isn't just the practice of playing a game; to understand what a game like *World of Warcraft* (*WoW*) means, we also need to wrestle with what gamers do when they're doing things other than playing.

"Everyday" players of *WoW* increasingly engage with each other and the game's developers in online discussions about the game and around the game. The panoply of websites, blogs, and Wikis focused on gaming indicate that there are resources and active communities outside of *WoW* which often help new players find their way around the game's virtual world, allow guilds of players to organize and plan, and, increasingly, feature ongoing discussions about what players believe the game *should be*. Discussions over the "state of the game" and the ways in which players believe the game should change are found in a variety of contexts, from the occasional intelligible discussion in-between Chuck Norris jokes on an in-game Trade Chat channel to arguments on private guild forums, through the more public and openly-accessible virtual locales such as blogs, Wikis, and online discussion forums.

Perhaps we need to take a peek at how some *WoW* players become "informal designers.". What kinds of design activities are *WoW* players engaging in online? Do they have consequences for players or for the game? Do they help us to consider the ways that *meaning* is made in communities such as this—in a game where players are increasingly in conversation with other players and game designers via the Internet?

WTB [New Rogue Talents] PST: Proposing *WoW* Redesigns

The official *WoW* forums (http://forums.worldofwarcraft.com) have been some of the most prominent and, judging by the sheer amount of traffic to the site, most popular places for the discussion of the game. Featuring subforums organized to handle issues on specific servers, guild recruitment, server status, and a variety of other discussions that occur around the game, they show a healthy mix of passionate, serious argument and goofy social banter (unsurprisingly including varying degrees of offensiveness, as many Internet communities do). It is within the suggestions and, often, the class forums—discussion forums tailored for specific character classes and roles within *World of Warcraft* — that many of the most complex discussions occur, sometimes involving mathematical modeling, systems-based reasoning, and intricate argumentation. *WoW*'s ten character classes (Warriors, Rogues, Paladins, Hunters, Mages, Priests, Druids, Shamans, Warlocks, and Death Knights) each feature their own unique sets of abilities, duties and responsibilities within a group, as well as issues that are wrestled with by the community of players, reflected in the unique online discussions revolving around them.

In order to understand how to play a specific class, many players attempt to better understand potential character "builds," or configurations of character talents—points allocated to the player as one levels, which can be spent to customize a character class to a player's desired way of playing. For example, one can "spec" a Druid character to serve primarily as a healer, a tank, or a damage-dealer. As Steinkuehler and Duncan showed[1], the nature of these discussions often mirrors the complex argumentative and reasoning practices found in the sciences and other privileged intellectual pursuits. Yet, another major concern for many of the long-term players in the game is simply how to keep the game interesting and to continue to make their significant investments of time and subscription fees worthwhile—after all, players spend countless hours first leveling a character, then working to make their character viable to "raid" (participate in complex, high-level group dungeon fights) or "PvP" (player versus player combat, or competing in organized battles against other players in the game, contrasted with player versus environment, or "PvE").

So, it's perhaps not too surprising that discussions on the class forums are also where much of the most interesting, detailed *design* activities take place. Or, put a slightly different way, we see in many of these threads the public iteration of arguments among players of common classes and employees of Blizzard on where to take the game, featuring what we might describe as the *co-construction of knowledge* (revisions to spells and abilities, new talent builds, and so on). Here, for example, is a selection of a post to the Rogue class forum in which a player, Dismalstrike (in February, 2007), proposed changes to how the Rogue class should work in relation to other classes in the game. In this post, Dismalstrike summarized a number of common problems with the way Rogues were configured, and proposed a set of specific changes:

> The thing that most raid leaders look at is, "What do we need to kill X boss." It isn't the trash, it isn't anything leading up to the boss. It is the boss. The utility that mages and warlocks offer ("polly," banish, health stones, soul stones, imp buffs, curses for more DPS, decurse, AI,

---

[1] Constance Steinkuehler and Sean Duncan, "Scientific Habits of Mind in Virtual Worlds," *Journal of Science Education and Technology* 17:6 (2008), pp. 530–543.

> food, water, etc etc etc). Far far exceed the utility that rogues bring to the table. ... More and more raid slots [are] given up for other classes instead of rogues.
>
> We need all, some, or at least one of the following:
>
> 1) Removal of the aggro dump for mages, and warlocks
>
> 2) Going back to the old weapon skill. Basically removing glancing blows from the game
>
> 3) A form of utility that we DESPERATELY need. We asked for a to hit aura—looks good on those dreani shaman/warriors/hunters/etc etc etc. We asked for an ability to trasnfer our aggro to another player—were told that could cause some abuse. Now we can see that on hunters—the ONE class that didn't need more aggro control - but hey.
>
> The best answer would be #2 and #3. Get weapon skill back, and give us SOMETHING to give to a raid. And don't say - CC becuase 1) raid mobs are GENERALLY immune to it, 2) Sap is the worst PvE CC since we have to be next to the mob, and 3) don't confuse a stun locking—no DPS—rogue for a combat DPS built rogue.

So, yes, even in this abbreviated form, there's a great deal of detailed, dense, specific gaming lingo here, encapsulating the detail of MMORPG-specific terminology (raid, PvP, PvE, aggro, DPS) and *WoW*-specific/Rogue-specific vocabulary (Sap, "stun locking," decurse, banish). Both earlier and later in the thread, Dismalstrike took pains to elaborate why changes such as these were necessary to balance the Rogue class versus other damage-dealing classes in the game who featured other useful raiding abilities (the "CC" or crowd control abilities of Mages and Hunters), by the subtraction of abilities from some of these other classes and the addition of abilities to the Rogue class. But, in the simplest terms, Dismalstrike's argument boils down to this: *Due to changes in the game over time, we, as Rogues, no longer have a meaningful role in the game, and here's what I think Blizzard should do to fix that.* Dismalstrike sums up a number of problems other Rogues have faced in relation to their role in the game, and takes his or her complaints a step further, developing specific recommendations on how to fix the class.

zomg blue post FTW: The Co-Construction of Knowledge

But where do informal game redesign proposals like this "go"? The official *WoW* forums feature a number of these kinds of discussions, some clearly more viable than others, and varying widely in terms of specificity (some suggesting specific talent/spell/ability changes, some serving, basically, as unfocused rants by angry gamers). In this example's case, several of the first responses to Dismalstrike's post indicated that the community was going to "pick up" the points from Dismalstrike's original post and wrestle with the ideas in them. The following are selections from the same thread:

Poster: Taertlet —

A big part of the problem at this point seems to be with the nature of melee vs ranged damage and our inability to continue DPSing when we need to run away from AOE's, cleaves (despite standing behind the mob) etc., while ranged classes just sit 30 yards out and continue to nuke. I do enjoy boss fights that go beyond the normal tank & spank but it's tough when the design of most new encounters seems to put us at a disadvantage right from the start.

> Poster: Dismalstrike —
>
> I actually han't thought about that. But you are 100% correct. Our inability to do anything in AoE heavy fights is a huge drain, or better a lack of, DPS. We just can't stand in there and pound away without taking too much mana up.
>
> Poster: Novathar (a "blue post" from a Blizzard employee) —
>
> I'll forward this thread on if you all want to put more feedback in it on things. Please keep in mind I'm not making promises of answers or anything at this point, but thought I'd let you know we're watching and still forwarding feedback.
>
> Poster: Vancitti —
>
> Posting in an epic thread. Blue posts are just rare as hens teeth in this forum, thank you for taking the time to stop in and forward our concerns Novathar. I agree with most of the previous posters. The issue at hand is not PvP. It's PvE.

That is, the discussion very quickly turned to broader issues of how Rogues, as a class, were configured to play in the game, the roles they should have in group play, as well as what specific game mechanics were at fault ("inability to do anything in AoE heavy fights" or problems fighting against "area of effect" spells which can damage combatants in a radius around the caster). The context of the discussion also shifted from PvP-centered to PvE-centered—

and that was fine! A number of posters took the original post by Dismalstrike as the beginning of a discussion which evolved organically, working beyond Dismalstrike's original suggestions and adding their own revisions to his or her proposals by bringing their own experiences to the debate.

Also, very important was the early appearance of a "blue post" by a Blizzard representative (Novathar, indicated by its blue text on the forum). The rare appearance of a Blizzard poster and his or her comments about the design team indicated to some (Vancitti, at least) that this discussion might have broader significance. If, after all, the game's designers or their representatives were paying heed to the complaints and redesign suggestions in this discussion thread, might these idle debates actually turn into an "epic thread" and help to shape the way that the game developed in future patches and expansions? This is, obviously, the hope of many of the players who engage in discussions online. Not only are players able to discuss and iterate ideas with each other about what should be changed about the game, they might just possibly actually *influence* someone to make those changes. They could, after all, have a role in the design process for the game itself.

Perhaps as a consequence, this single thread grew to encompass at least four linked threads and hundreds of individual posts on the topic of the "future of the Rogue class." These early posts kicked off a productive and often contentious debate involving the co-construction of knowledge (how do we determine what the right course of action is for "fixing" the Rogue class, anyway?) and the iteration of new game redesigns (what specific spells and abilities should be changed?). Though the consequences for these kinds of discussions are not always clear due to our only being able to see one side of the story (the player's debates and not what the community managers and game designers actually do with these suggestions, if anything), the potential philosophical implications of knowledge-building communities such as this help us to understand the ways that online cultures around games illustrate implicit epistemological stances and the ways that knowledge is constructed through practice.

Don't Just QQ, Reflect: Donald Schön and Design

That is to say, the importance of *design* becomes salient for understanding the larger context of how *WoW* players think about their gameplay, as well as for understanding the shared experience of play in this virtual space. Some players are content to simply play the game that they have been presented, but how do we understand those who devote energies to developing complex models of gameplay and enter into dialogues to further shape the course of the game?

Though the development of a "philosophy of design" is a newfound concern, it has a long history in the pragmatism of William James, C.S. Peirce, and John Dewey (the influential American "Metaphysical Club" philosophers[2]). These thinkers had a great influence on understanding how theory relates to practice, and their conceptions of thought and action shaped many early educational and psychological theories. Can we describe how people think without also describing what people *do*? The "metaphysical club" set the stage by pointedly describing the ways that action plays a role in the development of knowledge. This has come under increased scrutiny and has implications beyond the theory of understanding thinking itself, to the practice of how we can best foster the development of knowledge through how we teach, and how we learn in less formal settings.

Additionally, since the last several decades have seen an increased emphasis upon prominent design professions (from architecture through computer game design), attention has turned to the ways that design skills are learned (in groups, in professions), as well as to what this tells us about how knowledge is generated. As a consequence of the "social turn" in a number of academic fields, understanding how people collaborate and iteratively build artifacts has seen renewed interest in a number of academic disciplines—for example, literacy scholars such as the New London Group[3] have taken seriously the importance of design, positing that it is not only a handy way of talking about productive, collaborative, iterative activities in which physical artifacts are created, but should serve as *the* central metaphor for how meaning is made.

Design philosopher and design education scholar Donald Schön emerged from both pragmatist traditions and professional practice,

---

[2] For an excellent introduction, see Louis Menand, *The Metaphysical Club: A Story of Ideas In America* (Farrar, Straus, and Giroux, 2002).

[3] New London Group, "A pedagogy of Multiliteracies: Designing Social Futures," *Harvard Educational Review* 66:1 (1996), pp. 60–92.

concerned with how we think about design and epistemology. He wrestled with the philosophical implications of notions of design that were important both to academic discourses as well as professional practice. In his later work, including *The Reflective Practitioner*,[4] Schön advanced a critical argument against the antiquated epistemological stances that still pervade much of the common conceptions of what learning requires—the conception that learning best occurs after building a basis in the knowledge of some form of rational, scientific fact, then the enacting of this knowledge in practice. He saw the folly in the notion that there needed to be a *rational foundation to practice*—the epistemological stance that, in the development of knowledge, one must collect rational, scientific knowledge in a content area, and only afterwards apply it to real-world concerns.

This is a huge critique of a long-standing and central assumption that undergirds much of how we think about teaching, learning, and modern University curricula (at the very least, Schön argued, present within the German, then American University models). In fields such as the sciences, we have historically often focused on first teaching "hard facts" before teaching the everyday practice of being a scientist—to become a physicist, for example, learning Newton's laws often precedes learning how to construct an experiment, analyze it, and produce a document with its results. While these pedagogical approaches have been challenged in recent years, we can see the practice of design and the use of Schön's concept of *reflection-in-action* as a means of illustrating how learning new knowledge need not rely on rational justifications, but can be couched in the terms and practices of the meaningful activity being learned.

Schön's view of design and knowledge runs against long-standing epistemological traditions, to put it mildly. Emphasizing that the practice of *doing* need not be predicated upon knowing (learning how to, say, construct an experiment may be a valuable early practice to learn before, say, Newton's laws), Schön moved beyond Dewey's emphasis on scientific rationality while also tying these stances to critiques of educational systems. This perspective helps us the most to understand how fans of *World of Warcraft* engage in design activities online and what they get out of them—a phi-

[4] Donald A. Schön, *The Reflective Practitioner* (Basic Books, 1983).

losophy of design applied to games means analyzing the ways that fan activities around *WoW* illustrate sophisticated kinds of design practices that are hallmarks of professional practices. In other words, we have to dig a little deeper, into what *WoW* players are doing, and *why*.

L2Design, n00b: Knowledge As Design

So, let's go back to Dismalstrike's thread again and see what sense we can make of what's going on in the discussion. In his or her post, Dismalstrike presented a perspective on playing a Rogue that was based upon his or her practice—the practice of playing *World of Warcraft*, but also the practice of engaging with others in discussions on the forums. This isn't achieved by simply reading prescriptive or descriptive text about Rogues; one develops these concerns through the activities of playing a Rogue, and playing the character through a variety of complex group situations (raids, in this case). Determining that something about the class even needs "fixing" is borne out of the practice of playing a character that has meaningful activities within Azeroth, reading and replying to other Rogue players' responses within the forums, and interacting with the game's designers (or their representatives, as with the case of Novathar). In this view, any form of complex knowledge construction—be it learning how to be a molecular biologist or learning how to avoid pulling aggro off the main tank in a raid—is more than just the swallowing of facts and always involves learning through *action* and *reflecting* on that action.

Therefore, if Dismalstrike and his or her peers are engaging in meaningful practices within the game and around the game, how do we best characterize the kinds of change that goes on within a player's knowledge of the game over time? How can someone learn to play *World of Warcraft* without engaging, at least on a small level, in something we can describe as *design*? To develop a character through level 80, one needs to manage the individual design tasks of allocating talent points to "build" a character, while at the same time negotiating what one's role should be (or needs to be) in group play with a guild or other players, and understanding what parts of the high-end game one wants to eventually focus on (raid progression, PvP, and so on). As Schön argued for in other contexts, we can see that improving one's play as a Rogue involves learning how to design one's character through practice, iteration, and reflection. Becoming an expert *World of Warcraft* player means not only leveling and acquiring better gear, but the active practices of creating, revising, and shaping a character, developing opinions on what to change about one's class, and even adjusting one's expectations for the kinds of gameplay possible in such a space over time.

Therefore, we can see that, in at least one way, knowledge construction *is* design—in the sense that, in both real and virtual contexts, we often shape our understandings of the world through dynamic processes of creation, iteration, debate with others, and revision. It's a disservice to characterize an individual's knowledge when learning to play *World of Warcraft* as simply being "in flux"; in many cases, knowledge is in the process of being shaped through intentional design. Yet, the implications are more significant than just individual knowledge, because if we view knowledge as design, it implies new ways of thinking about social action, political engagement, and civic responsibility. Why should gaming, learning how to be a scientist, or any other social learning be different in this regard?

As Schön indicated, the metaphor of "design" aids not only the learning of content, but also the active, professional practices that are increasingly commonplace in everyday life. And, as the New London Group suggested, emphasizing design is no less than a call to shift what it means to be "literate" from forms tied to rationalist epistemological stances toward those that match the practices and needs of those eleven and a half million players (and counting) who have grown up immersed in these kinds of digital learning environments. That is, the stakes here are larger than just gaming, but point us to think in new ways about what learning might be in a world in which lines are increasingly blurred between recreation and education, work and play, and knowledge and action.

In the online communities around a game environment such as *World of Warcraft*, developing a sense of one's identity as a "designer" becomes a palpably powerful tool toward shaping one's character and, potentially, shaping the larger game. This implies that we can't passively view this game as a static "text" or as an ontologically fixed "virtual world" but as an actively changing, negotiated network of designed *systems*. The class discussions started by Dismalstrike were only one chain of many hundreds of threads in one of the ten class forums—for the players who have invested a great deal of their time and mental effort into the crafting of their characters, the development of a designer identity is not simply just a fun thing to do; it's a necessary next step to ensure that the game evolves in ways that will allow them to enjoy the work they've put into the game to that point. To play *World of Warcraft* is to dive into the messy activities of designing one's own character and the game itself; believe it or not, shaping knowledge is what the game is all about.

The contingent, negotiated nature of these games' systems is often overlooked—as it is, arguably, with many social enterprises. It's the way that these design practices mirror engagement in "real world" systems that speaks the most to not only what *World of Warcraft* tells us about how we construct knowledge, but how the communities around the game might point us toward better ways of working and living together. Proposing redesigns of one's character class in this game need not be an insular affair; these practices can reflect the ways that we need to re-conceptualize what knowledge and meaning-making can be in the broader world in contrast to the limited, simplistically rationalist epistemologies of the past.[5]

[5] All character names presented in this chapter are pseudonyms.

Artisan Philosopher

Justice, Role Play, and Identity. Familiarize yourself with this topic by reading . . .

Utopian Fantasy and the Politics of Difference (JACKSON): 0/1
Role Playing in *WoW* as Cathartic Social Performance (CHAN, WHITMAN, and BAUMER): 0/1
He's the Kind of Girl Who Wants Matching Daggers (ALEXANDER): 0/1
In-game Identities and Meatspace Mistakes (CHRISTOPHER): 0/1

Description

Is *WoW* racist or sexist? This claim is heard often, but to what extent is it true or false? One of the most famous theories of justice to be created in the twentieth century is that of the late American philosopher, John Rawls. Does *WoW* achieve the sort of equality envisioned by Rawls? Can *WoW* tell us anything about the positives and negatives of theories of justice in general?

What sorts of gender issues come up as a result of men playing as women and vice versa? Does *WoW* erase gender inequality from the real world or increase it? Or is it impossible to entirely eradicate gender bias even in *WoW*? When people role play in *WoW*, in what way does the lore influence their virtual identity? If players agree to the conditions of the gamespace (for example, PvP) why do they still complain about the consequences? Although you learned about ethics as an expert philosopher, the ability to create an in-game identity (a toon) brings some other ethical concerns to the table. Is your identity in *WoW* a false identity? If so, what are the implications? What do a person's anonymous in-game actions say about their morals?

Rewards

You will receive: **+4 Intellect!**

12

Utopian Fantasy and the Politics of Difference

DEBRA JACKSON

The frequent charge in gaming forums and blogs that *World of Warcraft* is sexist and racist is easily justified by a cursory examination of the game's use of a variety of all too familiar ethnic and gender stereotypes. Several of the playable races are designed with stereotypical ethnic characteristics: the "stoic" Dwarves have Scottish accents, stocky builds, hairy bodies, and drink heavily; the "vicious" Trolls have Jamaican accents, lanky builds, live in jungles, and practice voodoo and cannibalism; and the "huge, bestial" Tauren are shamanistic nature-worshipers, have a bovine appearance, and live in grassland huts next to totem-poles.

Characters also embody various gendered physical and behavioral traits: females, even among the monstrous Horde races, are beautified and feminized with prominent breasts and expressive facial features; most male characters are significantly larger and have steroidically muscular upper bodies; and, emotes such as "/dance" and "/silly" are more sexualized for females than for males, and "/silly" and "/flirt" emotes explicitly identify over half of the playable characters as heterosexual.

World of Warcraft as Utopian Fantasy

Despite its use of ethnic and gender stereotypes such as these, the *Warcraft* universe is not an inherently sexist and racist universe, but rather a liberal, egalitarian one. The game creators at Blizzard Entertainment provide players with a modest utopian vision of a world that is structurally just, maximizing both liberty and equality among participants. The principles operative in the *Warcraft* universe resemble those of John Rawls, the twentieth-century's most prominent American political philosopher.

Choose Your Identity

In his book, A *Theory of Justice* (1971), Rawls details a justification for a liberal, egalitarian ideal society founded upon principles of "justice as fairness." The core principles informing the basic structure of this society are ones that would be widely accepted because they are fair to everyone. The Rawlsian social structure is utopian insofar as it envisions the most ideal society we can hope for given what he calls the "circumstances of justice," namely a moderate scarcity of resources (enough to go around but not so much that everyone gets everything they want) and a wide diversity of participants (with their correspondingly diverse conceptions of the good life). This understanding of justice aims to resolve the long-standing tension between liberty and equality, namely that a commitment to liberty results in dramatic inequities among citizens while a commitment to equality compromises individual freedoms.

Like Rawls, the game designers at Blizzard Entertainment aim to create a social environment with mass appeal. Hence, the *Warcraft* universe is an idealized society, one that provides opportunities for fair, co-operative gaming. One feature that makes Massively Multiplayer Online Role Playing Games (MMORPGs) like *WoW* unique among videogames is the role playing aspect of players' engagement in an alternate universe. The "circumstances of gaming" include not only a moderate scarcity of goods with a corresponding competition among players to acquire them, but also that the *Warcraft* universe is pluralist, inhabited by a diversity of characters with a variety of different gameplay styles and goals. This allows players to not only imagine themselves as occupying a very different kind of world, but also of imagining themselves as very different kinds of people.

Engagement in the fantasy begins at the character creation stage. To enter into the game, one must construct a game identity by choosing a class, race, and gender for one's character, and this identity need not replicate one's real world identity. Such choices are not trivial, since these choices affect what abilities and kinds of roles one may assume within a group as well as how the character expresses him or herself in game.

How Do You Role?

Rawls's method for identifying the principles structuring the ideal society is grounded upon what he calls the "original position." Those occupying the hypothetical "original position" are entrusted to ensure that the society is fair for all of its citizens. They do not know what kind of lives the members of the society would want to live, so they assume only that people value those "primary goods" necessary for achieving whatever life plans they may have.

Most importantly, in order to envision an ideal that would not favor nor disfavor any social group over others, the theorist must imagine him or herself behind a "veil of ignorance," that is, not knowing any of the arbitrary facts about oneself such as class, race, gender, or age. These are features of a person's identity that are a matter of luck, and thus, are no grounds for any social institution conferring advantages or disadvantages. Since any theorist taking up the "original position" is equally or symmetrically situated to any other, the resulting principles of justice underlying the ideal society will be fair and, hence, acceptable to all its members.

In order for each of its 124 different playable characters to be appealing, Blizzard must assume a standpoint similar to Rawls's "original position," functioning as trustees responsible for ensuring that the gaming environment is fair to all players regardless of what kind of character they choose to role. They must place themselves behind a "veil of ignorance," that is, ignorant of which class, race, and gender will be chosen by any given player. At most, game creators know only that, whatever a player's gameplay style (PvE, PvP, RP) or goals (PvP, questing, raiding), all value the "primary goods" necessary for fulfilling those goals. To this end, the structure of the *Warcraft* universe is designed so that all characters are equally situated.

Each of the ten different classes possesses different abilities, but these differences combine strengths and weaknesses in ways that are balanced out overall across the various classes. Further, whenever one class becomes overpowered or underpowered with respect to the others, Blizzard releases a patch to re-establish the equilibrium among them. There are also slight variations in racial traits in that each race has a collection of bonuses to the characters' offensive and defensive skills, and occasionally also to their professional and healing skills; however these bonuses are also symmetrically distributed.

Playing Fair

From the "original position," Rawls identifies two principles of justice that maximize both liberty and equality for all citizens. First, every citizen should be guaranteed basic rights and liberties. These include, for example, freedom of thought and conscience, freedom of association, and equal access to political office. The second principle of justice regulates socio-economic inequalities and is expressed in two parts. The first part states that every citizen should be guaranteed an equal opportunity to obtain those positions and jobs that differentially reward people. This ensures that inequalities of income or social status are the result of personal achievement rather than arbitrary facts about the person such as class, race, and gender.

The second part of the second principle of justice, called "the difference principle," addresses the fact that natural endowments are a matter of good or bad fortune, and that the resulting rewards are also a matter of luck. It states that any socio-economic inequalities must make everyone better off than they would have been otherwise, particularly those most disadvantaged. This protects those who are born with few or no natural talents by ensuring that even if those unfortunate disadvantages make them worse off than other people, they will nonetheless have a fair chance at a reasonably good life, indeed one better than they would have if inequalities were not allowed.

The "principles of fair gaming" structuring the *Warcraft* universe are similar to Rawls's principles underlying "justice as fairness." First, as in Rawls's ideal society, players in the *Warcraft* universe are granted basic rights and liberties regarding, for example, speech, association, and office-holding. Freedom of speech is restricted only by Blizzard's harassment policy, which limits illegal, discriminatory, threatening, or otherwise disruptive language that interferes with the gaming experience. Players also associate freely in temporary PUGs (pick-up groups) as well as more long-term associations in guilds.

Secondly, and also similar to Rawls's equal opportunity and difference principles, the *Warcraft* universe regulates inequalities by ensuring that advancement is a result of personal achievement and that those most disadvantaged have a reasonable chance at a good gaming experience. All professions are open to all characters, regardless of class, race, and gender, and advancement to higher levels requires the same quantity of experience points regardless of the differences in quest sets given the different starting zones for each race. Moreover, although wealth acquisition can be massive among the most industrious players, all players have rather easy access to money and goods by looting the bodies of NPCs (non-player characters), taking advantage of the gathering professions, and selling looted or crafted items to vendors and other players. Further, once a character reaches level 80, gold can be acquired easily and quickly by completing daily quests.

The Politics of Difference in Azeroth

The politics of difference are of special interest to philosophers because, put simply, difference makes a difference. Particularly when considering class, race, and gender, differences are not simply a matter of human variety; they affect how we understand and experience ourselves, and how we are understood and treated by both those who do and by those who do not share our group membership. Moreover, these differences often affect a person's socio-economic status, professional opportunities, interpersonal relationships, and self-esteem. Like the real world, the *Warcraft* universe categorizes its occupants by class, race, and gender, and what categories a player chooses affect the character's abilities, role possibilities in group settings, and in-game self-expression. However, the meanings of class, race, and gender in game aren't exactly the same as the meanings of these terms in our everyday lives.

That Takes Class

Although class defines your social role in game, it's very different from the concept of class in the real world. In our everyday lives, class is a sociological concept describing the hierarchical division of people in a society. We generally differentiate between the "upper," "middle," and "lower" classes, and we understand "upper" as better, and "lower" as worse. What class you are a member of is determined mainly by your occupation and wealth, and your class often determines how much social power you have. Class is also often associated with certain cultural traits such as grooming, manners, and language, and people usually socialize only with members of their own class.

In *WoW*, however, class is neither an economic nor a hierarchical term; neither one's wealth nor social power nor reputation are determined by one's class. Although there are ten different classes, there are, practically speaking, only three roles that are played—tank, DPS, and healer—all of which are essential for group success. No class is privileged over others. For this reason, characters nearly always interact in diverse class settings, especially when raiding.

In some ways, profession is more closely aligned to our everyday notion of class. Each character can choose two of eleven primary professions, and all of the three secondary professions. While looting dead mobs and completing quests are decent ways to earn gold, gathering or crafting items to sell in the auction house or in trade chat is the real source of accumulated wealth. But even then, professions aren't really like our everyday notion of class. No profession is economically advantaged or disadvantaged, players interact with all varieties of professionals, and characters can change professions at any time. Thus, professions may carry the economic element of class, but they lack the hierarchical division of people into social groups as well as the cultural traits often associated with classes.

Know Thine Enemy

Unlike class, the concept of race in the *Warcraft* universe bears many similarities to the concept of race in the real world. Beginning in the Seventeenth Century, European and American scientists began classifying human populations into races based upon geographical origin and various physical attributes including skin color, facial features, hair texture, and skull shape. By the nineteenth century, racial differences were also believed to reflect differences in moral character, personality type, and intelligence level. The resulting ranking of races from superior to inferior functioned as justification for race-based slavery, colonization, and conquest.

Similarly, in *WoW*, races are divided into recognizable groups, each of which has its own homeland, physical characteristics, and language. Further, *Warcraft* lore identifies each race with specific moral characteristics and behavioral traits. In addition to the examples given at the start of this chapter, Humans are "resilient" and "resolute in their courage to maintain the honor and might of humanity," Draenei are "noble" and "armed with courage and their unshakable faith in the Light," and Blood Elves are "grim survivors [who] are committed to regaining the vast powers they once commanded." *Warcraft* lore also suggests a history of race-based slavery, colonialism, and conquest, as well as widespread attitudes of racial superiority. For example, Night Elves are described as "distrusting of the lesser races," Orcs as "possessing no humanity or empathy for other races," and Trolls as having "seething hatred for other races."

On the other hand, there are some important differences between the real world concept of race and that of the *Warcraft* world. Contemporary science rejects a biological basis for race, instead understanding race as a social construct. The association of races with moral character, personality type, and intelligence level has also been eroded, although the prevalence of racial stereotypes in popular imagination suggests the resilience of those historically claimed associations. A more remarkable difference concerns the legacy of racial differentiation. Even when contemporary political and legal institutions eliminate the differential treatment of people on the basis of race, there still remain many socio-economic advantages and disadvantages resulting from historical race-based privilege and oppression. But in the *Warcraft* universe, history strangely does not affect the present when it comes to gameplay, at least not beyond the uniting of races under two factions—Alliance and Horde. Racial differences, like class differences, mark varieties, but without doing so in a hierarchical fashion.

Shave and a Haircut

The *Warcraft* concept of gender shares many features with our real world notion of gender. While the term "gender" is commonly conflated with the term "sex," both in the real world and in *WoW*, the two terms are not the same. "Sex" refers to the biological differentiation of males and females with regard to reproductive function and identifiable physical characteristics such as sexual organs. "Gender," on the other hand, refers to the socio-cultural meanings attributed to sex differences, and these often vary according to race and class membership. It proscribes for males and females appropriate forms of self-expression and defines which social roles they should fulfill.

Gendered self-expression appears in terms of masculine and feminine styles of bodily comportment and movement, intellectual and moral orientation, and sexual expression. Gendered social roles, although varying across different historical periods and cultures, distinguish between "men's work" and "women's work," with the for-

A female Orc Warrior at the character selection screen (World of Warcraft, *Blizzard Entertainment, 2004*)

mer valued more highly. Most importantly, gender is a binary system that strictly prohibits gender crossing, especially for males exhibiting feminine characteristics, and ensures heterosexual pairings.

Like in the real world, gender in the *Warcraft* universe differentiates between characters by not only designing avatars displaying physical dimorphism, the male and female characters also display recognizably masculine and feminine forms of self-expression: the strides of the male characters are proportionately longer than that of females; when they stand, male characters' feet point outward, while the females' point forward or inward; and, male characters' dancing takes up proportionately more space and is noticeably less sexualized than that of females.

Differences in intellectual and moral orientation are expressed through the gender and racially differentiated emotes such as "/flirt" and "/silly," and gender crossing is represented as deviant and laughable. For example, female Orcs' violations of the norms of femininity are highlighted by their "/silly" emotes: "Darn, I need my chest waxed again;" "I'm very feminine. And I'll beat the crap out of anyone who disagrees;" and "What's estrogen? Can you eat it?"

Newly-Created Male and Female Blood Elf Warlocks in Eversong Woods (World of Warcraft, *Blizzard Entertainment, 2004*)

Male Blood Elves' violations of gender norms are also reflected in their "/flirt" and "/silly" emotes, which characterize them as feminine and narcissistic: "I could use a scrunchy . . . yeah, you heard me"; "You look almost as good as I do"; and "Hey, why don't you come over here and . . . Watch the hair!" Moreover, while many of the male dances are funny, the male Bloof Elf's elicits a different kind of humor. The Night Elf's "Billie Jean," the Human's "Saturday Night Fever," and the Tauren's "Peanut Butter Jelly Time" were at one point cool, sexy, or charming, while the Blood Elf's "Napoleon Dynamite" was never anything but embarrassingly dorky.

Despite the gendering of characters in terms of appearance and self-expression, gender differences have absolutely no impact on gameplay. There's no differentiation between "men's work" and "women's work;" all classes are open to both genders and the stats for any given race-class combination are identical for male and female characters. This lack of gendered social roles is reminiscent of the argument offered by the ancient philosopher Plato in the *Republic*. When determining who would make a good ruler or warrior, the only issue to consider is whether the person, male or female, possesses the right kind of soul, or personality; differences in reproductive function are irrelevant.

Similarly, the *Warcraft* universe does not restrict certain social roles to one gender, and given that there is no procreation in *WoW*, there is not even a difference with regard to reproductive function. Instead, gender differences are a matter of appearance, not job performance. In this way, the *Warcraft* universe achieves a level of gender-neutrality the real world has yet to achieve. Like class and race, gender differences are a matter of human variety rather than the hierarchical division of men of women.

WoW's Utopian Promise Broken

As we have seen, the social structure of Azeroth significantly diverges from the real world in that it is radically egalitarian. Class, race, and gender are much more a matter of human (or, perhaps better, humanoid) variety, rather than ways of hierarchically differentiating people. Additionally, race and gender differences in the *Warcraft* universe may provide flavor or interest that enhances game *feel*, but in terms of gameplay, they have little impact in the case of race, and no impact in the case of gender. While there are limitations on which classes are available for a particular race, the stats are exactly the same for any given class regardless of the character's race. And for any given race-class combination, the stats are exactly the same regardless of the character's gender. Nevertheless, in players' engagement with the game, class, race, and gender differences take on meaning well beyond the structure of the *Warcraft* universe. As we participate in the utopian fantasy that is *World of Warcraft*, we bring our real world values into play.

LFM Full on Mages/Hunters/Locks

Class, the character difference that makes the most difference to gameplay and the one least like its real world counterpart, is the least subject to discriminatory treatment. Nevertheless, players occasionally target certain classes for prejudice because they are deemed overpowered or "easymode." Most consistently, Hunters and Warlocks are mocked. Hunters, for example, are refered to as "huntards." The operative assumption is that because Hunters and Warlocks have pets that assist them in combat, playing them requires less skill.

BRB Got Gnomes in the Oven

More often, players target certain races for prejudice, especially Gnomes. Despite the fact that a Gnome Warrior has nearly identical stats as any other race of Warrior, Gnomes are rarely played as tanks. The small size of Gnomes has no affect on their combative skills, and yet they are consistently regarded as if size matters. Gnomes are also targets of racial hatred revealed in the form of snide comments and anti-Gnome violence, perhaps equivalent to hate speech and hate crimes. Arguably, some racial animosity is built into the game's social structure in terms of expressions of racial animosity or derision—Gnomes are the butt of jokes expressed in "/silly" emotes more than any other race. Nevertheless, anti-Gnome sentiment in role playing (RP) as well as non-RP servers extends beyond these scripts.

WTS Lapdance 1G

Despite the fact that gender has absolutely no impact on gameplay, players treat characters in a discriminatory fashion in terms of gender. While *WoW* allows for gender crossing insofar as male players can play female characters and female players can play male characters, doing so is often regarded with suspicion. Male players with female characters are often teased, and they are expected to reassert their heterosexuality by defending their choice to play a female character. Most often this defense comes in the form of "I'd rather look at a sexy female toon than a male one."

Additionally, male players are harshly mocked for playing male Blood Elves, presumably because these characters are coded as effeminate, hence potentially gay; and, female Orcs are rarely played, presumably because they are not appropriately feminine. Even more interestingly, the structure of the game denies the identification of certain roles with one gender, and yet players reassert gender roles in the choices they make at the character creation stage. Female characters, whether played by male or female players, are almost always healers or ranged DPS; only rarely does a female character fulfill the tank or melee combat roles. Like in the case of Gnomes with respect to other races, female characters are treated as if their difference from male characters mattered despite the fact that, in terms of combat performance, it does not.

The Politics of Difference

In the end, Blizzard's egalitarian vision is compromised by the importation of real world values into gameplay. This is likely due to the fact that the terms "class," "race," and "gender" are familiar ways of categorizing people and determining a person's social role and status. The differences that matter in the real world become differences that matter in the game. Perhaps this demonstrates the inherent limitations of theories of justice, namely that structural equality cannot achieve substantial equality. Perhaps it demonstrates the impossibility of human diversity without hierarchical differentiation. Perhaps it demonstrates a failure of readiness to accept genuine gender and racial equality. Regardless, the ways that real world values infuse the *Warcraft* world show how deeply these values infect our imagination. Is *World of Warcraft* a racist and sexist game? Yes. Because *we* are, not because Blizzard designed it that way.[1]

[1] I want to give a big TYVM to Liora, Senem, and Nick for their helpful feedback on my chapter, and a special shout out to Chris and Michele for talking me into playing *WoW*, even if they prefer to role Horde.

13

Role Playing in *World of Warcraft* as Cathartic Social Performance

PAULINE CHAN, AUDREY WHITMAN, and ALLAN BAUMER

The impression of reality fostered by performance is a delicate, fragile thing that can be shattered by very minor mishaps.

—ERVING GOFFMAN, *The Presentation of Self in Everyday Life*

Reshka nodded in thanks to the Troll Priest. A nonchalant "Don't mention it, mon" and a smirk met her gesture.

"Something funny, is there?" Reshka asked, arching an eyebrow. He shook his head and explained that he was just doing his duty to the Horde. She agreed that all must do their duty to the Horde.

"Hard to believe a Warlock's words, mon," the Priest said, eyeing her dubiously. A tired discussion she had heard and taken part in so many times, but it would be revisited upon Razor Hill. Reshka sighed long-sufferingly.

"You don't believe I can serve the Warchief? You're a priest of the Loa, aren't you?"

The troll raised his arms plaintively, "I am, mon. Don't get me wrong, demons are powerful allies. But it was Warlocks that nearly destroyed your race."

Reshka snorted, showing her tusks proudly. "Being a Priest, you know all about powerful allies, then. I can't pretend to know as much as you do about your gods, but you can't tell me that the Loa are all innocent—" The troll raised his arms in objection, but Reshka continued, gesturing to the imp by her side, "—besides, I'd rather have control over these powers than be a servant to forces unfathomable. You choose the power that people are blind to, rather than terrified of."

The priest nodded with far more understanding than Reshka had anticipated.

Virtual spaces like *World of Warcraft* are arenas for social narrative experience, and the development of strong factional affiliation. Players conduct their role play activities within a gameworld (rather than in-person, or through a chat interface) for generally the particular digital affordances of Massively Multiplayer Online Role Playing Games (MMORPGs): immersion, mechanics, context, and anonymity. Because of the immersive environment that the game offers, players have a "physical" space in which to act that reveals only the character and not the player. This physical space comes with its own mechanics, and a system of rules for governing behavior in that space. The mechanics in turn are supported by lore, which players can draw from to build their own narratives. And since role playing in digital environments provides both an added layer of anonymity and access to a broader, more casually connected community, a player has the opportunity to shed as much or as little of their "real-world" personas as they choose. *World of Warcraft*'s environment isn't consequence-free in a literal sense. It nonetheless provides a space for players to act out behaviors, emotions, or methods of communication that they cannot or will not in the real world.

In the scene between Reshka and the troll priest above, these factors influenced and contributed to the narrative that occurred between the two players. The scene takes place at Razor Hill, a low-level Horde military outpost. Palisades surround the perimeter of the town, while two rough-hewn stone structures are placed next to the roads, overshadowing the makeshift tents and soldiers that make up the rest of this outpost. Periodically, Orc soldiers ride in and out of the town on wolves, adding additional flavor.

Taken as a whole, the outpost affirms the characteristics of the mainstream Horde. And this influences the players whose avatars are standing within this environment, talking about loyalty to the Horde. The environment can add context to a scene, or be deliberately chosen as the premise for a scene. Player-run taverns, for example, are reliant on the gamespace (in this case, the various in-game taverns and inns) for the context, but then use the space to create a new tavern. This generates a narrative layer that overlays the physical tavern space, which is complete with players filling both the staff and patron roles for the scene. When Kogan walks into the tavern in Ratchet it becomes *Kogan's Fine Spirits and Milk*. He entertains guests with stories and songs, creating a new fictional context on top of the Blizzard-established content. This becomes a form of expression and a creative outlet for the player.

Role playing is constrained by three spheres of behavior: real world social codes ("Do not break character"), gameworld mechanics ("I cast Prayer of Healing") and gameworld narrative ("Reshka the warlock sharply scolds her imp for dropping a soul shard"). Each of these codes influences the embodied performance of a character. Role play overlaps those three spheres of behavior. Thus, it has elements of unstructured make-believe and structured games (which have clear win and loss conditions). The act of role playing within a game world unites narrative, player culture, and the politics of social identity. A player's identity, we contend, is shaped by the context in which that identity is developed; Horde and Alliance role players have vastly different cultures of play as a result.

Compare the following guild names: *Anathema* and *Harbingers of War* (Horde guilds) with *Legion of Heroes* and *Lux Aeterna* (Alliance guilds). By role playing in a world with a pre-existing narrative, players engage with that established lore. This lore is integrated into their play experience intentionally and unintentionally. By navigating this world through an avatar, the player has a marionette that can portray her ideas. If it cannot give the full substance of thought, it can at least give the shape of the concept via role play. This publicity allows role players in gameworlds the chance to both see other players and be seen by them. This gives pleasure without overt voyeurism or threatening exposure. The social dynamics that emerge from this boundary play strongly influence the formation of online role playing communities.

WoW role players are often marginalized (even on role playing servers), and the role playing communities that emerge are highly insular and cliquish. Because of this, dramatic social politics develop in these small groups such as scapegoating and ritual expulsion. This can happen if a player breaks the real world social codes, or their character expresses an unpopular opinion.

"Did you hear what she told Vul'na?" Pistus whispered to Kogan. The massive Tauren shook his head. The Undead's eternal grin stretched thin with glee.

"It wasn't the usual warlock drivel about redeeming themselves and understanding their own darkness—she chose the power others fear."

The Druid could feel a small chill meet his spine. Pistus smiled as her guildmate's eyes showed his full comprehension.

"Can he testify to this?"

Pistus's smile only dampened briefly. "Kogan, no one has seen Vul'na since then. His cousin said he has gone off to do some soul searching."

The Tauren stared into space for a moment, "But you think he has been lured by the call of power held in the Burning Legion?"

The poisonmaster nodded and let out a snakelike, "Yessss . . ."

"This is a serious matter. If she has betrayed us, Warcaller Gurntha must know."

Reshka sauntered into the tavern, leveling her eyes on her supposed friends. Funny what a few small words out of context could do . . .

A Mask for All Occasions

Directed role playing consists of collections of performative ritual acts. Players construct both the gamespace and their identities within that space, creating a scene's narrative within the chat window, while the environment and the objects within it provide the locational context for the scene. All ritual is performative with an implied audience of participants, recipients, and observers. A guild meeting in the throne room of Stormwind Castle spoken in public chat is a formal discussion of affairs, but also a performance for themselves and anyone who happens to be in the room. Even when alone, role play exhibits a necessarily social performance aspect.

A lone Blood Elf bows to the Warchief during his first visit to Orgrimmar. The newcomer is playing as a character, but performing for himself since no other player characters witness this event. While some of the default emotes, such as bowing, will trigger special animations on the avatar, they all appear in the chat log. Custom emotes, which also appear in the chat log, are used to freely create specific or complex actions, or to add modifiers to speech (for example, "/emote lowers her voice. 'I wouldn't go inside if I were you.'" displays as "Reshka lowers her voice. 'I wouldn't go inside if I were you'"). Yet, the game also offers various objects that can be used to aid role play in the virtual space. For example, the outfits that both Reshka and the Troll Priest wear in the initial scene indicate their relative status and experience within Horde society. Their outfits are never discussed, but from the poor quality of their clothing and their location, both of the characters seem to be average at best. As a result, neither character feels compelled to show more deference than they would to a stranger. This control over appearance allows for the "other I" to more accurately reflect the identity associated with the avatar.

What the Soul Sees

Successful social performance balances between speaking and physical body language. The first is readily controllable by a user, but the second generates a potential ambiguity. Body language is normally performed unconsciously—a series of signals given off without intention. But in digital environments, each physical action must be deliberately chosen, and so can never be truly unconscious or unpremeditated. So, unlike analogue role playing, the player is completely subsumed by the avatar.

By embracing the contradiction of this association, avatar play gives role players a pronounced sense of "I" and "other I." The "other I" can allow for the player to slay dragons and ride wyverns, impossible in the real world, without sacrificing suspension of disbelief. The avatar allows the player to accomplish more than he would be able to by himself. Similarly, this fissure in identity allows an exploration of one's self in multiple contexts. Following a verbal conflict with a friend you might feel embarrassed or disappointment; your actions do not meet your perception of yourself. In order to maintain your social identity (Goffman describes this as "face" in *Interaction Ritual*), you must bring your actions in line with that face. Players unable to express their anger constructively in "real world" social interactions might create a proud and aggressive character, such as an Orc or Dwarf in order to feel "right face" (confidence, assurance, and security), bringing their actions in line with their perception of themselves.

I Grew Up Running Rum off of Booty Bay

While some role players start role playing in *World of Warcraft*, many role players bring their prior experiences with one of these systems. This helps us understand the way in which role players conduct their role play both in and out of the game. By varying the degree to which they "invest" in their social performance, players may begin to treat that performance as a "real" expression of themselves, playing from "disbelief to belief." This enables players to explore aspects of themselves which are not fully integrated into their self-image.

Since a role played character is essentially a homunculus conjured up from our own thoughts, feelings, and experiential knowledge, we use them as dramatic agents to explore ourselves narratively. Through the course of role play, a player may eventually be able to perform the facework necessary to reconcile the disparities between their desired self and their presented self, while learning how those selves are created and maintained. Being able to identify these nearly archetypal qualities in yourself allows you to discover your own identity by separating yourself from behaviors you do not practice, and people whom you are not.

Self, Self, on the Wall . . .

Children, when first discovering their reflection, associate their own identity with both the image and themselves. It is through experimentation that they realize that they have mastery over the image. Similarly, when a player first sees her character running through the starting zones, she begins to form an impression of that character's identity as part of herself. As with the child's experience, there is both a sense of unity with the image through manipulation, and a sense of discord through not being the same body. As the avatar runs through fields, slays monsters, and dances on mailboxes, the player moves the avatar as an extension of herself, without ever physically performing those actions. The disembodiment between this alternate identity and the primary identity (the actor and the object which is acted through), represents both the gulf between ego and body, and between imaginary and real. The visual identification given by the mirror-self allows the player to attribute imaginary "wholeness" to the physical experience of a fragmented "real."

Victory or Death, Honor or Treason

The average player relates to the digital terrain and factional fiction through a playable procedure that is guided by the game mechanics, which are themselves based in lore. However, the relationship between the role player, gameworld, and narrative is much more direct and complex because of an increased investment in the narrative. If role playing in a world is engaging and interacting with that environment, then it becomes more pertinent for role-players to be familiar with the underlying narrative in order to craft appropriate personas and participate within the world in a meaningful fashion. This is particularly important when role playing in *WoW*, where players coexist within a shared space and a unifying dominant narrative. The game introduces and articulates its lore through visual cues, allowing players to identify with certain ideals. It is with those ideals that Reshka confronts in the initial dialogue, which then causes dramatic personal conflict in her guild.

I Am

The tensions between the Alliance and Horde, though implied from the premise of the game, are fleshed out in more detail for the player in the first zones. Everything in these encounters—from the contrasting architecture to the structure of the quests themselves—has been laid out to provide a guideline for factional identity to new players between the Horde and Alliance. While both character creation and *Warcraft* lore contribute to a player's formation of character identity, it is these experiences in-game that most influence players' perception of their characters' race and faction; which in turn contributes to their view of the other races and factions within the game.

Since players are only able to communicate through gestures across factions, and have no context in which to interpret those gestures, they are socially isolated from the opposite side, and must necessarily depend on their own faction as an outlet for narrative social interaction. The combination of narrative impetus and personal experience is designed to encourage players to associate more strongly with the side they are playing, building factional loyalty. This loyalty extends also to role players, though it can manifest as both a pride in the faction community's narrative and an interest in exploring and developing identities within their faction's framework.

The Spirit of the Nation

The avatar creation process provides a visual interpretation of the nation's identity. This implies the character's place as a member of their society, and what the nation's ideals are. The Human avatar is shown at daybreak in the Human's capital city, Stormwind. The "other I" being created stands on a cobblestone street that recalls the heroes of the fantasy genre. Narrative power is drawn from this nostalgia, creating a faux-medieval atmosphere reminiscent of a more chivalrous era. In using daybreak as the setting, the visual representation connects the Humans' society with one of potential, a hope for progress. This is doubly emphasized for the role player who considers that Stormwind is forced to rise to the challenge of the main human nation being brought to ruin by the undead.

In contrast, the Orc avatar is shown at sunset in the aftermath of a battle. Surrounded by various weapons that have been jammed haphazardly into the ground, the avatar stands near a tattered Horde standard. The implied philosophy behind these symbols emphasizes strength, honor, and glory in battle. The post-war scene also alludes to the Orcs' close ties of unity and military camaraderie. The dusk in the background alludes to the struggles the society has been through and will see in the future. This visual representation abets their image as the noble savages.

Hated or Exalted

The conflict between the Alliance and Horde races is also built upon a series of racial misconceptions, as can be seen in the treatment of the Frostmane Trolls in Dun Morogh, the Dwarf and Gnome starting zone. The Trolls here reside in small huts and within caves; compared to the industrial stone structures of the Alliance structures in the area, the Trolls' living situation appears savage and primitive in comparison. This is particularly noticeable in one of the first quests that players receive in the area, where little attention is paid to the Trolls besides their presence as an environmental threat, along the same lines as Gnolls or aggressive animals in the area.

From this, the player can infer that Trolls are equivalent to beasts, and similarly lack the same kind of intellect and consideration that other Alliance races would be afforded; thus, the divide between the factions becomes a perception of racial superiority rather than merely a series of unfortunate misunderstandings. For the Orcs and Trolls, Tiragarde Keep in Durotar provides this contrast. Situated close to Razor Hill, an established Horde town, this damaged white stone structure stands out clearly against the ragged palisades and red rocky terrain that surrounds it, and thus against the visual aesthetics that define the rest of the zone. The broken keep is particularly interesting as a symbol of the conventional perception of civilization, but one that has not successfully survived in this harsh environment, while its Horde equivalent remains whole and fortified; this feedback helps orient the player's sense of character identity to a more Horde-friendly approach. When players are first asked to go here upon completing their training, this quest series is carefully phrased to emphasize the honor of the new Horde by citing the betrayal and lack of "diplomacy" of the Human intruders as the reason to attack the keep. In detailing the violation of the ceasefire, the quest series emphasizes the reason for the distrust and even hostility between the two factions. Players are also led to feel more justified in being a part of the Horde, since the violence is then enacted with altruistic intentions.

The Cache of Innovation

Role players create characters, events, and narratives, referencing game elements designed by the *World of Warcraft* development team. Similarly, the game's own mechanics can also be used as tools to enhance and contextualize role playing narratives. For example, the scene at the start of the chapter follows Power Word: Fortitude being cast on Reshka. Because classes can cast beneficial spells on each other, this has developed into a buffing culture, the ritual of moral support via game mechanics. This friendly gesture is commonly done and reciprocated when possible as a way to support fellow players of the same faction. The scene actually emerges as a byproduct of this ritualized behavior (which is itself an emergent behavior from the availability of such spells) when the player stops and—as Reshka—thanks the Troll for the buff. The troll priest's subsequent reactions are based on the presence of an imp next to Reshka, signifying her status as a warlock. Though both characters do not introduce themselves verbally as a warlock or a priest (which is itself a construct of the game mechanics) they both are aware of it and react accordingly, as is played out in the rest of the scene.

> *"Come in, Reshka," Gurntha invited.*
>
> *Reshka's face held little emotion, outside of her eyes. They looked everywhere but towards the Warcaller. She found something to stare into. Pistus's glowing dead eyes. "Reshka, I have heard some . . . troubling news."*

"Hearsay is what it is. Gossip, sir."

Gurntha let out a long sigh. His face, however, revealed much. Weariness. Worry. Genuine concern lines learned through making hard choices. Another was being made.

"Warcaller," Pistus invited. Reshka simply stared.

"Here is the thing, Reshka . . . I am uncertain if we can trust you, right now. We are not removing you from the unit, but you are on probation."

Her eyes blazed with rage, but when she spoke, her voice remained calm. Barely. "What you mean to say is that I have to suffer the misconceptions and judgments of others. Sir."

"Now look here, Reshka, you know the war we're fighting with the Lich King as well as anyone. To defend arguments held highly by the Burning Legion is not something we can risk turning a blind eye to."

Reshka turned and left. Her resignation from the unit was complete. Pistus had begrudged the warlock ever since Kogan had begun spending time with her. Whatever. The rot could keep her cattle. Reshka would go to Warsong Gulch to restore some measure of honor at her humiliation.

As allied forces came together, Reshka considered what demon would aid her most in the upcoming battle. As her mind was testing strategies, she felt fortitude flow through her veins. "It's been a while, mon."

14
He's the Kind of Girl Who Wants Matching Daggers

PHILL ALEXANDER

> The biological and social sciences no longer admit the existence of unchangeably fixed entities that determine given characteristics, such as those ascribed to woman . . . Science regards any characteristic as a reaction dependent in part upon a *situation*. If today femininity no longer exists, then it never existed. But does the word *woman*, then, have no specific content?
>
> —SIMONE DE BEAUVOIR, *The Second Sex*

It started out innocently enough.

As a life-long gamer, I was overjoyed when my girlfriend showed an interest in playing *World of Warcraft* (*WoW*). I dashed out and bought her the game, then waited anxiously as it installed on her Macbook. Between gaming for fun and the hours I spend gaming for research, this gave me a chance to share a significant part of my life.

There was only one slight problem: with her first character—Jamie—my girlfriend chose to join a "ladies only" guild. That guild, however, was also in need of players, particularly experienced ones, so they were willing to make an exception and admit my female character knowing that I was a man in real life (IRL).

We played, and still do, on a role-play (RP) server, so our circumstances allowed me to take on an RP persona that was significantly different from my "real" identity and a welcome gaming challenge. It also allowed me, as a curious researcher, to test the theoretical work of another scholar. In her book *Cybertypes*,[1] Lisa Nakamura coins a new term:

---

[1] Lisa Nakamura, *Cybertypes: Race, Ethnicity, and Identity on the Internet* (Routledge, 2002), pp. 13–14.

> The term identity tourism . . . describe[s] a disturbing thing . . . the afterimages of identity that users were creating by adopting personae other than their own online as often as not participated in stereotyped notions of gender and race . . . their performances online used race and gender as amusing prostheses to be donned or shed without "real life" consequences. (pp. 13–14)

When I initially encountered Nakamura's work, I questioned how accurate her claim was that a user in virtual space could actually role-play another gender or race without feeling "real life" consequences. Nakamura's theory asserts that cyberspace can essentially be a vacation destination for users, where:

> Like tourists who become convinced that their travels have shown them real "native" life, these identity tourists often took their virtual experiences as other-gendered and other-raced avatars as a kind of lived truth. (p. 14)

I contend that while elements of Nakamura's claim are true, there most certainly are still consequences based on gender biases exhibited toward an online avatar, or in this case a *WoW* toon, and I am also fairly certain that a user/gamer's relationship with "real native life" and "lived truth" would differ significantly from what might generally be considered "lived" and "true." The scenario with my girlfriend and her guild provided me with a small-scale opportunity to test my own theory and to see first hand what it would mean to "play" female as a blood elf toon named "Sasha."

Turn and Face the Strange: Changes

But as things go in an ever-evolving Massively Multiplayer Online Role Playing Game (MMORPG), the guild situation rapidly devolved. In spite of our best efforts to play every weekend and at least one or two nights during the week, over the course of a few months the guild disintegrated into a core of three players: me, my girlfriend, and the guild mistress, Sophie. One Saturday afternoon when I logged in to play, Sophie told me she was "fed up" with no one else participating and that she was disbanding the guild. While I was saying my goodbyes and obtaining an item from the soon-to-be-defunct guild bank, Jamie found and joined a new guild, Hemlock. I followed her, joining just minutes after saying goodbye to Sophie.

With the guild change came complications, some of which wouldn't come to light until much, much later. The server where we played at the time was designated RP and Player-vs.-Player (PvP), and as such we played in character, though at times it was clear that some others among the server's population leaned more heavily toward PvP without regard for storytelling. Our previous guild utilized all non-private in-game chat as in-character (IC) discussion space, so when I met Hemlock, I did so as a woman, playing Sasha and continuing a discussion with Jamie about my desire to find two daggers that matched. The first question I fielded from the new guild was rhetorical, "the lady would want her gear to match, wouldn't she?" We then shared the story of the previous guild, which many members of Hemlock knew by reputation and realized was women-only, and over the course of several hours got to know many of our new guildmates, including our new guild master Janet.

A few days later I was online alone, checking my in-game mail when Janet struck up a conversation with me about my life, how I knew Jaime, and so forth. At the time I was under the impression we were in RP mode, so I talked for a bit about our in-game lives and how we'd come to work together as a team. It was a somewhat typical "getting to know you" sort of RP chat, the type that seasoned pen-and-paper RPGers, Multi-User Dungeon (MUD) users, and MMORPG gamers are all-too-familiar with.

The next time we all played together, Janet invited us into a clearly labeled out-of-character (OOC) chat channel. We talked a bit about our normal lives, but I only realize now, in retrospect, that nothing relating to my gender came up in that discussion. We told our new friends that we lived in Michigan, that we met as students in the same program, and that we both study rhetoric at a Big Ten school, that she had a cat I was allergic to, that I had a fascination with *Buffy the Vampire Slayer*, *Adult Swim* cartoons and all things pop culture.

As is so often pointed out by scholars and commentators, in many cases it's not particularly clear how a person intends to be read on the Internet and most must resort to letting names serve as gender indicators in the absence of other data. The only thing that the members of Hemlock knew was that the words coming from Jamie and Sasha appeared above the heads of a pair of super-model proportioned elven women in black armor with glowing green eyes who laughed a little too much and preferred to explore as a duo.

Can a Tourist Make a Home?

A week or two passed, and as a player I was swept into *WoW* euphoria because while I'd been playing for years, I finally had a toon that was approaching the (then) level cap of seventy and we happened to be on a long semester break. As a result, I found myself playing more often. Janet and her roommate, Lily were both level seventy, as was a male friend of theirs from outside of the guild. They frequently invited me to join them for dungeon instance runs and high level quests. I was always willing to tag along, noting from time to time that while I certainly didn't feel like an authentic "woman," it was clear that I behaved differently when RPing as Sasha, as the creative writing training came in handy solidifying and maintaining her character and voice. I even engaged in IC "girl talk" with Janet and Lily. They were both happy to have someone with a solid grasp of the game in the guild, and they invited me, after a few weeks of playing together for several hours a night, to be a guild officer and to serve as "third in command," responsible for helping new members of the guild and mediating when problems might arise. They placed a high level of trust in me, and I thought I was placing a high level of trust in them in return.

I'm Just a Girl

Then one evening someone asked about my girlfriend, and since the guild knew us as our characters, they asked by username. I mentioned that Jamie was busy with some end of semester work. The response took me a second to process: "I hope he can login soon."

Maybe it was a typo. It's only one letter.

"We miss him," another said.

And in that moment I realized that our RP and OOC lives had augured in a strange way. The guild knew we were in a real-life romantic relationship, and applied social norms in assuming that we were male-female, but they had looked at our two female blood elf toons, listened to our two blood elves virtually chatter away, and had spent time watching the two of us interact textually as a couple and assumed I was the woman.

My knee-jerk reaction was to correct them, so on the OOC channel I typed "Jamie is a woman." The conversation shifted away seconds later as there was some guild business involving a member quibble, and we launched into a long IC discussion handling it. I meant to talk specifically to Janet about the misunderstanding that night, but she logged off, and I logged off, and nothing more was said.

The next time I saw Janet online, a week or so later, she told me that she and Lily were going to be taking a trip for the New Year's holiday, and she wanted to know if I was willing to take control of the guild during their three-week vacation. I accepted, but because she was packing and trying to give me all the information that I would need, I didn't get a chance to revisit the misunderstanding from before, though looking back I'm not sure I considered it to be of major consequence. If anything, it was more of a *Seinfeld*-episode sort of moment that my girlfriend and I would chuckle about when discussing with others. "Our guild thought Phill was the girl!" we'd share, and our friends would giggle and make some comment about how I like to cook and look better in pink.

Truths and Consequences

Those three weeks passed, and I handled guild business without incident. Janet and Lily returned and we resumed our routine of all playing, chatting and generally enjoying our *WoW* lives away from our real lives—or so I thought. It wasn't until several months later, when Lily suffered a problem in real life (IRL), that I realized just how much assuming and projecting was taking place and how I might actually be a tourist in my own virtual life. I spent a few hours talking to Janet and Lily about her IRL problem, and I would like to think that I was at least a little bit of help and could provide some support. But the exchange revealed two things I hadn't been at all aware of, things that were lurking below the conversations. The revelation that Jamie was female hadn't corrected the Hemlock perception of me; they still thought I was a woman, too, and they now thought that Jamie and I were lesbians, and the guild in general hadn't been interpreting RP in the way that we had been interpreting RP, as they'd basically created an amalgam where they spoke both IC and OOC without any indication of a switch, which meant that for them while there was no Phill, whatever Phill they had gotten was completely interwoven into Sasha.

James Gee writes in *What Video Games Have to Teach Us About Learning and Literacy* about his own experience of the sensation of being at once both his character and himself,[2] but my experience turned that dynamic inside out: I did, indeed, experience a sort of strange sensation "playing" Sasha, but in this moment of revelation during conversation it became clear that I had been socially reconstructed. I was part of a group, and viewed as having specific traits, responsibilities, and skills, that I wasn't aware of, and in as much as it could be "real" in a virtual space, I'd been granted, or perhaps assigned, a new gender and sexuality.

Realizing all of this while engaged in a discussion about someone's real, tangible life problems, I didn't think of blurting out "Oh, no!" "You've got my gender wrong and the person you think I am is the product of my years of creative writing training" was the best option. Still, it started to weigh on me ethically, and once I told the real woman behind Jamie what our virtual friends thought our life was like, it seemed clear that we had a bit of a problem. The scenario placed me in a particularly difficult situation for two reasons: one reason was that one of my areas of study is ethics, specifically research ethics in virtual spaces, and to essentially "practice what I preach" I would need to correct the misunderstanding, and the other reason was that I have a number of homosexual friends whom I support in their desire to have recognized marriage rights, so it felt somehow "dirty" to be thought of as in any way mocking the sanctity of their relationships with what was meant to be our hobby. Now that what for months had seemed like fun, particularly well practiced RP had become an accidental deception, I couldn't continue. Something had to be done.

And I Will Try to Fix You

The instinct here, of course, was to come clean. It was simply a misunderstanding. But the ethicist in me felt like I should carefully weigh the potential outcomes of such an act, particularly given that I'd fallen into such an odd situation. I first went to an old mentor, and my mentor confirmed my belief that I needed to end anything that might be deceptive. Another mentor, however, reminded me of my own concerns for the integrity of online social networks and while he didn't specifically ask me this question, he prompted me

[2] James Paul Gee, *What Video Games Have to Tell Us about Learning and Literacy* (Palgrave, 2003), pp. 45–70.

to ponder a second issue: in the weird relationship that had developed between me and Hemlock, I'd been both given agency I didn't have and had taken away agency I thought was inherently mine. As such, my revealing that I'd accidentally masqueraded as a woman for months, becoming a close friend and sort of confidant to a number of players, might have much more far reaching ramifications than I would have thought.

I took this question to a few of my colleagues—a cultural anthropologist, a sociologist, a philosopher and a clinical psychologist. They confirmed my fears that my revelation of this complex but innocent oversight might do damage to the community in different ways: it might cause the others who had bonded as part of Hemlock to question each other, it would almost certainly alienate me and my girlfriend in any one of a number of ways, and it might damage the guild's ability to recruit and trust new users. After this conversation, I felt absolutely no confidence in telling the guild that we'd just experienced a little misunderstanding. We were clearly outside of the "oops" period in which this could be easily resolved.

As my girlfriend and I discussed the situation, we tried to figure out a "fair" solution to what had now become a significant problem. We talked about telling the truth, about how it might work better if she told them the truth and I essentially allowed everyone to come to me, and we talked about cutting our losses and just leaving. While I certainly didn't want to abandon Sasha, who had become an intellectual and emotional investment for me,[3] the best solution did appear to be to simply migrate out of the game world. Toon retention on any given *WoW* server is relatively low, so we assumed that simply leaving would present much less potential trauma to the other members of Hemlock. It wouldn't be that extraordinary for a pair of players to just leave. It happened all the time.

Make Me Over

Deleting our toons, however, wouldn't be fair to me and my girlfriend. Luckily, she'd grown tired of Jamie, who was quite literally her first toon, but she'd still earned a great deal of *WoW* wealth

---

[3] *World of Warcraft's* login script informs players each session how many days and hours they have spent playing. At the time when we "left" Hemlock, Sasha had logged almost thirty days of in-game time. She represented a month of my time and energy.

(gold and items). And I didn't want to lose the time and effort invested in Sasha, whom I'd become particularly adept at playing. In a moment of serendipity, during the week that we deliberated leaving the server entirely Blizzard offered a new service called "character recustomization." This meant I could change the name, gender, and basic appearance of my toon for a nominal fee. For another fee, I could move the toon to another server. So Jamie and Sasha met in game to say their goodbyes, Jamie passed her gold and items to Sasha, and we logged out. A quick charge to my account and a few keystrokes later and Sasha, the female blood elf became Soren, the male blood elf and moved to a new server in what my girlfriend still refers to as "*WoW* witness relocation." Jamie started over as an undead character and reclaimed her belongings and gold, and Soren began refashioning his in-game RP back story. We said "goodbye," but didn't explain that we were leaving that world forever, and while it still might seem ethically dubious, in the end we took the path that seemed the most viable and equitable.

Touring Azeroth, or Walking in the Hyperreal

What does this story, this misunderstanding and complex web of social discourse, have to say about the nature of "identity tourism?" This one example, in its way, proves Nakamura both correct and incorrect. Online I was able to "play" female, and in fact I apparently played female so well that I was read as female by a number of authentic females. There was risk, however, and there was trauma suffered by the "tourist" in my case. Philosophically, the one major issue that arises from the narrative and demands consideration is what is "real."

In "The Procession of Simulacra," Jean Baudrillard[4] argues that there is no longer a "real," that whatever was once real is now replaced by a linguistic or symbolic sign, which points to another sign, which points in turn to another sign in a potentially endless chain of signs that separate whatever things would have once been conceived as "real." While I would never argue with anyone that I'd been a "real" woman, I would certainly assert that at least in the Baudrillardian sense what I experienced emotionally while interacting regularly with the members of Hemlock was "real." I would

[4] Jean Baudrillard, *Simulations* (Foreign Agents) (Semio(text)e, 1983).

also venture so far as to argue that while "I," that is to say Phill Alexander the thirty-something gamer sitting in his apartment in Michigan, was not a "real" woman in his "real" life, Sasha was as much a real girl, at least within *WoW*, as Janet or Jamie or Lily or Sophie. She was a signifying machine, and a sign herself, which generated and pointed toward female. And in the moments where our senses of reality were incorrectly aligned, and my RP world was the "real" world for Hemlock, Sasha's agency replaced my own.

Without leaning too dangerously close to the *Matrix* films, which Nakamura herself references in her research as well, I believe that at least one valid reading of virtual space is that much like the Baudrillardian chain-of-signs it replaces the real with what Baudrillard calls a "hyperreal," a situation where the human mind can no longer, either through the complexity of the web of signifying chains or due to a simple desire not to, distinguish the "real" from the "fantasy." In other words, there are distinct times when I look back at conversations and interactions with Hemlock and realize that what we were all doing together was being experienced and interpreted as "real," and that the impact of such things was real. If one senses that a thing is real, it is real in its effect. Sasha was able to offer advice and comfort, to share stories and provide companionship during lonely moments.

The Ghost in the Machine Is You

What is of increasing importance here, then, is how we define "identity" in a digital world or digital space. Much like the infant seeing himself for the first time in the mirror, humanity now sees itself reflected by screen after screen, distorted and revised, hyperreal and counterfeit-fake.

To return to James Gee, he pondered while playing *Arcanum* if he was *James Gee* (the man) as Bead-Bead (the character), James Gee as *Bead-Bead* or James Gee *as* Bead-Bead, placing emphasis on himself first, on the character second, and on the dynamic between third. While I think the final option, the gamer as "as," is probably the closest to accurate, I don't think that in this situation I was Phill Alexander *as* Sasha. Sasha had an identity, and that identity belonged to me, in as much as anything I create belongs to me, but it is not any more accurate to claim that I am (or was) Sasha than it is to claim that Lawrence Fishburne *is* Morpheus or that Sarah Michelle Gellar *is* Buffy Summers.

There are many differences between Phill Alexander as Sasha and Sarah Michelle Gellar as Buffy Summers which are significant, however. Visually, Buffy is idealized Sarah, made up and edited, well-lit and expertly wardrobed, but both women have the same face. Sasha's face was not cast in flesh, and it certainly didn't resemble Phill even if Phill was pixilated and idealized. It is a foregone cultural conclusion that Sarah is "playing" Buffy, a skilled professional contracted to behave as an other. It's not entirely clear what cultural understanding Americans share about videogame toons or avatars, and I paid to play Sasha, not the other way around. Finally, and most important, Sarah was told by other people how to be Buffy, from how to move and how to speak to what to hit and what she thought.

To play a toon, then, is like acting and not, like projecting oneself into the digital world and not. And Sasha was me but Sasha was not me. I will never be Sasha again, but I will continue to be Phill, and for at least the relative future I will play Soren, the new body in Sasha's clothes, carrying Sasha's things, riding Sasha's horse, sharpening Sasha's matching daggers. And in some manner or another eleven and a half million (this number has surely increased since this chapter's writing) other *WoW* gamers engage daily in the same sort of identity interplay, each with what is no doubt a unique interpretation of exactly how much "self" is being projected into the screen.

Accidental Tourist, Native Speaker

This strikes at the heart of my problem with the concept of "identity tourist." A tourist consumes. The tourist takes a vacation to some other land and interlopes. At their best, tourists bring money, fuel economies, and manage to not act in terribly disruptive ways. At their worst, tourists "ruin" places and exploit native habitats. There's an element of the sinister, and a decidedly negative connotation, attached to being a tourist.

Which is not to say, of course, that tourists debase or that they strictly consume; as with any theoretical metaphor, the "identity tourist" is a reduction, based on the stereotypical experience. And I, like nearly all Americans, have been a tourist. I know well the feeling of spending a week in a strange city, taking photographs and buying knickknacks that no local would be caught dead purchasing.

My time with Hemlock was not a vacation. I was an active participant in a discursive network, in a sort of ad hoc tribe. And while it's not entirely clear whether I was Sasha or if I stared so long into Sasha that Sasha stared back into me, a girl existed. She "lived." She created. She was.

Epilogue: Girl, You'll Be a (Whoa?) Man Soon

Soren has now "lived" for nearly a year since his "gender reassignment." I recently moved him to yet another new server at the behest of my new guild master, who relocated our entire membership to what is considered by the *WoW* community to be "the" elite RP server at this current time. When my new guild master, Karissa, asked me to move with the guild, I told her about my previous move—the entire story I've shared here. Her response surprised me: "Damn. That means you're good. REALLY good. They actually thought you were a woman? Wow. That's impressive." I explained my discomfort to her, and she agreed that the weird "bleeding" of RP and "real" was problematic, but she insisted that what I'd actually found out was that I am a talented RPer. She urged me to consider rolling a new female toon, but also asked me not to tell her it was me at first, so she could see herself if I was *really* that convincing. For the record, I haven't. Yet.

Reflecting on the entirety of my experiences with Sasha/Soren across three servers and having interacted with hundreds of players, I'm comfortable offering the following five bits of advice about adopting a virtual identity:

1. It's okay to be a gender/race/class tourist, but think about the cost before you start. Don't make the mistake of thinking there won't be consequences of some sort. There are no free rides.

2. Know the lay of the land. When joining a server, know the designation. If it's RP, know when people are in character and out of character. Don't assume.

3. Similarly, know what you're getting into when you join a guild. It's not the same as joining an instance group or a one-time raid. Guilds in *WoW* do seem to have less permanence than some other games in the past, but even if you become a guild hopper (something I have been known to do with Soren, looking for a home), make sure to get to know the guild you're joining and not

to act too quickly before coming to understand the expectations and standards of your new friends.

4. *WoW* is a richer experience when you do put in the time and effort to find a guild that is a good fit for your style of play and your personality. In spite of the twisted road that Soren/Sasha walked, I still enjoyed it.

5. Have fun! It's easy to over-think gaming situations. If for you that means reading deeply, like I have here, then live and interpret and enjoy. In the end, though, *WoW* is a game. Never lose sight of the fun factor.

Sometimes when I login, and I see Soren, I remember when he wore a pink tabard and had fantastic bangs. Other times, I wonder how many more Naxx runs it will be before I finally get the pants that match the rest of his current armor. You can take the toon out of being a girl, but . . .[5]

[5] All toon and guild names herein have been changed to protect the anonymity of other players.

15
In-Game Identities and Meatspace Mistakes

TIM CHRISTOPHER

I still remember the first time I killed another player.

I was in the Outlands, doing quests. I had to kill Blood Elf Non-Player Characters (NPCs) to get some number of items off them. Since I'm a Hunter, and somewhat reckless, I sent my trusted wolf into a group of about three Blood Elves. I was confident I could take all three. Once they were busy fighting my wolf off, I hit volley, to help my wolf out and to make sure I had all the targets tagged. Shortly after the first Elf died, a new Blood Elf rounded the corner into the fray. I quickly ordered my wolf to attack her, not bothering to look at her name plate. I released a second volley, again assuring my credit for the kill. At this point, a friend of mine looked over my shoulder and asked, "Why are you PvP?"

Two realisms then hit me. The first was that somewhere in that mess of screaming Blood Elves and a gnashing wolf was a player, and not in fact a single Blood Elf on patrol. The second was that said player would likely finish this fight if I didn't. I quickly found the player, ordered my wolf to focus on her, and began to do the same. A short time later I was credited with my first "honorable kill." It was an accident.

The phrase "it's only a game" has less meaning for those involved in online gaming. People play games like *World of Warcraft (WoW)* for a living now. Websites post hourly updates on the value of virtual money to real world dollars. At the time that this is being written, 1,000 gold sells for about $14 on my server.[1]

---

[1] <www.belrion.com/en/wowsvr.php?aid=14&cid=1&gid=4&sid=185>.

Players marry people they meet online. In China, a couple's relationship started with a man saving a woman's in-game character from certain death. The relationship later ended in a divorce complicated by issues of shared in-game resources.[2] The Internet brings us news of real world lawsuits, murders, and illnesses that are reactions to online world events. Academic conferences are held in online games. The real world shrinks, the virtual world grows, and the line between the two continues to fade. As a result, online gamers of all kinds, casual to hardcore, are discovering that more of their online decisions can have offline consequences.

What Is Pseudonymity?

The issue is further complicated by the ability of the *WoW* player to create several characters. This grants the players something new, pseudonymity: the ability to have a number of separate but persistent in-game identities, each with their own reputations, social circles, and personalities. Is it possible to hold a player responsible for the actions of all their characters, and still respect the player's desire to maintain their pseudonymity? It has become increasingly necessary for players to understand just how different their in-game motivations can be—not just for each player, but for each character played—and to further understand the type of real world fallout their virtual world mistakes can spawn.

Let's understand just what constitutes related events within the context of this chapter: real-word events that are a result of actions taken by players in-game. Recently there was a story in the news about one roommate stabbing another because the victim was playing *World of Warcraft* too loudly.[3] In this case the game being played was irrelevant; the victim could have just as easily been watching TV or listening to music. What the victim was actually doing in *WoW* in no way relates to the stabbing. Conversely we have heard a great deal about gold farming. This is the act of gathering, in large amounts, in-game gold with the specific intent of selling it for real world money. Players often complain that this causes the in-game economy to be drastically, and negatively, affected by the real-world economy. Simply put, real-world rich

[2] <http://kotaku.com/112601/couple-go-to-court-over-virtual-goods>.

[3] <http://news.mmosite.com/content/2008-10-30/20081030015238316.shtml>.

people become *World of Warcraft* rich people, without actually earning it in *WoW*. This is a case where in-game and out-of-game very directly affect one another. This is not confined to economic concerns. Personal issues have been the result of conflicts lapsing between the digital and the physical. To date, one of the worst examples was in a different Massively Multiplayer Online Role Playing Game (MMORPG). In this case, the victim had borrowed an in-game sword from the killer. The victim then sold the sword, without the killer's consent. When the killer found out, he stabbed the victim to death.[4] This is an extreme and alarming example of a person's online indiscretions having unimaginable real-world consequences.

The idea of the pseudonym, a very old practice in writing, can shed more light on the discussion. Authors such as Thomas Jefferson used pseudonyms to publish political writings with less fear of persecution. For several decades in the early twentieth century women and minorities used pseudonyms to become published writers. In games like *WoW* players are able to create numerous persistent in-game identities. Each of these identities is akin to a different pseudonym. This ability to create the separate persistent and private identities is what I have come to call "psuedonymity." Weighing the players' perceived right to their psuedonymity against their responsibility for their in-game actions has become a source of much thought for myself, both as a player of *WoW* and as someone who teaches game design courses that often focus on multiplayer games.

It's All Fun and Games, until Someone Loses an Eye (Roman Saying)

The concept of the sacred gamespace has been around far longer than digital games. This term refers to the specific setting of a given game, ranging from the board that chess is played on to the arena a football game is set in. This is synonymous with the term "Magic Circle" used to refer to digital worlds.[5] Good sportsmanship and "friendly rivalry" is built on this concept. But this concept is put to a new test when the people who play these games can so thor-

---

[4] <www.danwei.org/breaking_news/gamer_who_murdered_for_virtual.php>.

[5] See Chapter 4 in this volume for an account of the Magic Circle.

oughly hide their real-world identities. As *WoW* becomes increasingly popular, this becomes more evident. People do things in *WoW* that they would never do in real life. Blizzard has even set up a situation which specifically encourages conflict. They've created a world with two factions that cannot communicate. The narrative of the world often stresses the hostility between the Horde and the Alliance. As a result, this in-world hostility is used as an excuse for in-game hostility. But what about when a Horde character harms a Horde character? Players fall back on oft used excuses like "my character is evil" or "it's part of the game." Both of these may be true, but to what end?

Let me add something from the real world to the discussion. I've been a student and teacher of Tae Kwon Do for over ten years now. When one enters the school, one goes into a lobby. This is where students, family, and instructors mingle and socialize. This floor space is separated by an open doorway from the training room floor. In the training room, no shoes are worn, and little socializing is done. This training room is covered by a thin blue mat, designed to soften the inevitable fall. When on the mat, you are there for a single purpose, to train. On this mat the rules are greatly different from the rest of the world. On this mat one gets hit often and sometimes quite hard. No one should ever complain about being hit while on this mat, due to the fact that the gamespace is inherently distinct from the real world.

When in *WoW*, cities such as Stormwind can be seen as a form of lobby. People go there to socialize, do business, or just gear up. When players leave the city and journey to places like Dragonblight or Grizzly Hills they do so knowing the territory is hostile. The NPCs there will try to kill them, and if the player is PvP, so will the opposing Horde players. Players also know that they are often competing with other Alliance characters for resources. But there are occasions when the ability to accept these conflicts is put to a strenuous test. Players will experience what they call "ganking." This is when they are attacked by a substantially overpowering opposing group of players. Players may also find themselves dealing with other particularly greedy players, who will try to kill or harvest as much as possible, leaving little for anyone else.

When one misbehaves in a gamespace—whether it's the Tae Kwon Do training mat or Azeroth—the consequences can be swift and substantial. If one student at a Do Jang is unacceptably hostile towards another, it may result in suspension or expulsion. In a space such as this there are no uncertainties about who is who. Often *WoW* players hear stories of the use of high level main characters to avenge the defeat of a lower level toon. This form of revenge is only available to those players fortunate enough to have high level characters.

You Can Discover More about a Person in an Hour of Play than in a Year of Conversation (Plato)

The practice of using a play space as a means to learn about people has been used by ancient philosophers and modern psychiatrists alike. Child psychologists will often use play to better understand their patients. The idea that you can learn a great deal about a person from sitting across them in a game of chess has in modern times evolved into the ability to create self-enclosed artificial worlds within a digital game to see how people handle new rules and new roles. In these situations, the purpose is to help learn about the other player, or players.

In a number of projects that I have been involved in, we have explored the idea of gamespace as learning place. The hope was to take the idea of learning by doing into a digital realm. By doing this we believed that players, or students, would feel more encouraged to learn through trial and error.

We often discussed the idea that, since the game could be reset, or end, players would not have to worry about long term consequences. It is this lack of consequences that we hoped would encourage exploration on the part of the student. It is further possible, that when combined with the above mentioned idea of using play to evaluate the student, digital gamespaces have potential to function as particularly potent learning environments.

The very nature of *WoW*, however, has two distinct points of difference with these ideas. The first pertains to understanding the student, or players. Since each player is granted pseudonymity, it is hard to really learn about any specific people. The second issue lies in the *persistence of world*, a defining aspect of online games such as *Warcraft*. This phrase refers to the fact that Azeroth, the setting of *World of Warcraft*, is a constantly running digital environment. When working with games as learning places, the ability to restart if the student fails—a standard feature almost all other types of games—is thought to be very valuable. The persistence of world that *WoW* is built upon means that the player may have to deal with the long term effects of his mistakes.

Once when I was demonstrating *WoW* to a group of new students, the issue of persistence of world came up. I was showing the students the size of the world, and walked my character, a female Gnome, into a city to point out the sheer number of other players. One of the students asked if my character could flirt with someone to see what would happen. I had to explain that my character was the leader of a guild, and as such I was unwilling to risk the potential damage to her social reputation.

Whenever you deal with a character in *WoW*, there is little or no way to tell if they are your neighbor or someone from the other side of the country. While this means that you can't learn about a specific person, it does allow you to learn about people in general. As more people join the game, you get a larger and more varied pool.

Not all players are bad characters. We often lose sight of this because people like to complain. "I divorced my husband because he cheated on me in *WoW*" is a more common headline than "My kids learned the value of kindness from a Gnome." If someone does something that really angers a player in *WoW*, a typical reaction is to sign off and go somewhere to complain. If someone does something kind for a player in *WoW*, then that player just keeps playing. Angry players complain, happy players play. But this does not change the fact that some of what players do to each other online is heinous.

In *WoW* players will repeatedly and brutally kill other low level players. In a setting such as a Do Jang, a high ranking student would never consider attacking a lower ranking student. Whether this is through fear of expulsion, or the restraint of the superior student, is a point of great interest. If fear of punishment is needed to keep people in line, then there is little positive outlook for psuedonymity, or humanity. If a player is kind in *WoW*, there's little chance that they do so for fear of punishment. It is this that may very well indicate that any act of kindness in *WoW* is truly for kindness's sake. An honest character may be a better person than an honest player.

The Do Jang that I attend is populated by varied people from varied walks of life. Many of us never see one another outside of the school. I have at one time been trained in martial arts by a local criminal prosecutor, and with a local FBI agent. We never saw one another outside of class. Despite this distance between many students, when we are in the Do Jang we treat each other with respect. This is not because we may have to deal with one another outside of class, or because we do have to deal with one another in class, but because we are taught by our masters that we should respect others simply for the sake of respect.

While I do not doubt the value of the discipline inherent in a Do Jang, I think there is a second reason for *WoW* players to treat each other with disregard. In *WoW*, players rarely, if ever, have a real-world face to put to the in-game characters they interact with. Perhaps this dehumanizing of each other that is inherent in the use of digital characters is a strong source of careless behavior.

The most effective means of understanding the behavior of *WoW* players is through the ancient philosopher Plato's Allegory of the Cave.[6] Plato tells of a group of people chained in a cave. The entrance to the cave is behind them and all they can see are the shadows on the cave wall in front of them. To these people, all that exists are the shadows. Plato then proceeds to discuss what it would be like for one of these people to be freed, and roam outside of the cave. At seeing the sources of the shadows, the newly freed person would gain an entirely new level of understanding of the world. In many ways, *WoW* players are like the people chained in the cave. It is easy for these players to forget that the simple flat world projected onto their monitors is composed of digital shadows cast by real people. These players must make a point to be aware of the world outside of the cave.

In light of this discussion, another thing to keep in mind about the use of online games like *WoW* is this: don't underestimate what you can learn about yourself. You are among those people playing with, lying to, killing, and protecting these shadows of strangers. After I killed the Blood Elf girl, I did feel sorry. To help ease my guilt, I waited for her to come back to her corpse. I was glad when she risked resurrecting with me standing so near. I then emoted an apology, hoping she would understand it was a mistake, and saluted her, trying to communicate some form of respect. She promptly returned my salute and we went our separate ways.[7]

---

[6] Plato, *Republic*, Book VII.

[7] First of all I should thank my girlfriend, for her patience, counsel, and support as I worked on getting this chapter done and taking my PhD Comps this past semester. Second of all I must thank the shadowy editors. Though we've never met, you offered much sound advice.

Master Philosopher

Battle, Leadership, Power. Familiarize yourself with these topics by reading . . .

The Machiavellian Guild Leader (WOLFENSTEIN): 0/1
There is No War in *Warcraft* (MEDLER): 0/1
Game Developers, Gods, and Surveillance (HOFFSTADT and NAGENBORG): 0/1

Description

A book on *World of Warcraft* could never be complete without a discussion of War! Come on admit it, you turned straight to this section when you saw it in the table of contents. You might have wondered over the years what war has to do with *WoW* anyway, besides its presence in the title. Is war really happening in Azeroth? What role does Blizzard play? The answers the authors in this section provide to such questions aren't always easy to swallow, Reader!

What makes a good guild leader? Can the leadership techniques of famous thinkers like Laozi and Machiavelli help us answer this question? What is "war" anyway? How can it be defined and does the fighting that takes place in Azeroth qualify? What is the concept of "Infowar"? In what way is your privacy infringed as you play *WoW*? Do Blizzard execs act as gods watching over your game?

Rewards

You will receive: **+3 Intellect!**

16
The Machiavellian Guild Leader

MOSES WOLFENSTEIN

"Phase two in thirty seconds, get ready to move!" says the voice over the headphones. The raid leader's tone is brusque and all twenty-four raid members know that if they don't get it this time there are going to be consequences of the 50 DKP (Dragon Kill Points) minus sort. Perhaps this is the third or fourth attempt at taking down Sapphiron that night. The repair bill for the plate wearers is already over 100 gold apiece from numerous wipes, and since the leader is playing as main tank, that means he's taking that cost very personally this evening. The giant ice drake is preparing to lift off of the ground and cast Ice Bolt on three of the party members and during the previous attempt on this boss, everything crumbled shortly after this as the drake pummeled the party with his Frost Breath, killing almost half of the group including most of the healers.

"Alright, move people! Get to the edges and stay out of his damn line of sight!" barks the raid leader. This raid has all the makings of being as emotionally punishing an experience for the players as it has been "physically" devastating for their characters. Yet for some reason all of these players are still playing with this guild, still running the risk of being put through the emotional ringer on any given raid night. At the end of the day there are clearly benefits to the personal cost of living under the iron thumb of a strict raid leader like this, and while there are certainly softer leadership styles that are successful, some players just seem to favor the brutal discipline of a guild run with militaristic fervor.

While the mythos of the *Warcraft* franchise is littered with tales of leaders both inspiring and formidable, for the average player they pale in significance when compared with the guild masters and raid leaders who orchestrate and guide their guilds through some of the most vile and puissant foes that Azeroth has to offer. The leadership demands of *WoW* (and Massively Multiplayer Online Role Playing Games, MMORPGs, more generally) are so intense that corporations like IBM have turned to these virtual worlds to see if these emergent leaders can help shed some light on how businesses of the future might be run.[1] Guild leaders can certainly offer us some novel perspectives on leadership, but they also allow us to look at conundrums of power and promise that have vexed leaders time out of mind.

Leadership is a perennial topic among philosophers, but none have spoken of the demands of leadership with the same level of honesty and brutality as Niccolò Machiavelli. Machiavelli has been reviled as one of the most ruthless and uncompromising thinkers ever to broach the topics of leadership and power, but a more measured consideration of his work in *The Prince* reveals a complicated figure whose advice is often echoed by the practices of successful guild and raid leaders, and whose warnings foreshadow the sort of guild drama that can occur on the fourth wipe on Sapphiron or when that one Shaman your guild was PUGing with (playing in a "pick up group" with at least some strangers) ninjas a purple.

Means and Ends: On Being 1337

Machiavelli is probably best known for a phrase that he never actually wrote; that the ends justify the means. What he actually said needs to be taken in context in terms of both the text surrounding it, and the era in which it was written. Consider the following excerpt where the famous mistranslation occurs (emphasized in italics).

> Everyone sees what you seem to be, few touch upon what you are, and those few do not dare to contradict the many who have the majesty of the state to defend them; and in the actions of all men, and especially of princes, where there is no impartial arbiter, *one must consider the final result.* (p. 60)[2]

---

[1] Byron Reeves and Thomas Malone, *Leadership in Games and at Work: Implications for the Enterprise of Massively Multiplayer Online Role Playing Games* (Report Prepared for IBM, 2007).

[2] All quotes by Niccolò Machiavelli are taken from *The Prince* (Oxford University Press, 1979).

As we look at the translation, we see that Machiavelli was talking about a more nuanced approach to morality than we usually associate with him. Throughout *The Prince* we consistently see the thoughts of a man who recognizes goodness in moral behavior but offers council in accordance with the complex politics and intrigue of his day.

This is evident when Machiavelli references the "majesty of the state" as a way to silence opposition. As a sixteenth-century diplomat, he lived in a time without universal human rights, let alone protection of free speech. Even though a lot of things have changed since Machiavelli's time, his approach to matters of integrity is sometimes evident in *WoW* (not to mention among some of our more unsavory politicians). Most guilds are not democracies, and even if membership is voluntary and the guild master seldom has complete autocratic control, leaders of raiding guilds in *WoW* are not usually transparent regarding decision-making processes with their whole guild. After all, a good record in raiding can definitely buy a certain amount of unquestioning support from guild members and back channel guild politics can get ugly at times.

Machiavelli is not saying that anything goes so long as you come out on top, nor am I suggesting this with regard to guild leadership. Rather Machiavelli is following up on one of the core themes of *The Prince* that he introduces in Chapter 15. People want to see the best features of humanity in their leaders, but because people are not all sunshine and sweetness, successful leaders need to know how and when to play dirty. Machiavelli wouldn't necessarily agree with something the English political philosopher, Thomas Hobbes, claims. In *Leviathan* Hobbes states that, left to their own devices, people would be in a perpetual state of conflict, with "the life of man, solitary, poor, nasty, brutish, and short." However, he was certainly willing to characterize the politics of his day in similar terms even if he held to a Platonic ideal of humans as naturally virtuous before insidious circumstances corrupt this tendency. Modern neuroscience seems to indicate that people are by no means inherently violent or evil, nor necessarily inherently good.[3] However in understanding *The Prince*, it isn't the inherent or natural state of humanity that we need to be concerned with.

---

[3] Stephen Quartz and Terrence J. Sejnowski, *Liars, Lovers, and Heroes: What the New Brain Science Reveals about How We Become Who We Are* (HarperCollins, 2002).

Sixteenth-century Italy was strikingly unstable compared to the conditions most of us live in. This context made it natural to assume the worst about your political allies and opponents. When we sit down to play *WoW* we usually start with a certain background expectation for more civil behavior to carry over from our day-to-day lives, but if you've ever had to listen to Barrens chat for any length of time (or Trade chat on many servers these days), you probably know first hand that you can expect a whole lot less civil behavior on-line than you might expect to find face to face.

Bearing in mind the assumption that many people will be operating on less than noble impulses, we can now see that Machiavelli's basic guideline for truth in leadership is fairly subtle. Rather than promoting the indiscriminate use of deceit or other unsavory methods, Machiavelli is saying that when you have to lie or break a promise in order to maintain your principality (or guild as the case may be), your followers are unlikely to question the legitimacy of your call so long as you meet success. It isn't a question of being justified in your actions, but rather of what you can get away with and why you would choose to. If we step back a pace and consider the core assumption on which Machiavelli builds his stance on honesty alongside a well known instance of raid leadership, we can start to see how many guild and raid leaders might do well to take the sort of pragmatic (and at times unpleasant) approach Machiavelli advocates if their guild mates include some of the less mature or pleasant players in *WoW*.

Loved, Feared, or Hated: Dives and the Onyxia Raid Wipe

At the heart of *The Prince* Machiavelli works around three different feelings that followers can have for their leaders. While it's certainly beneficial for leaders to be loved by their followers, Machiavelli considers it far more beneficial for leaders to be feared. However, he also establishes a natural limit for the behavior of a leader. While being feared can buy leaders a great deal of compliance from their followers, being hated will result in the followers rising up to depose their leader (p. 56). This entire line of thinking is an extension of the basic claims that Machiavelli establishes regarding morality and the conduct of leaders in the eyes of their followers that we've already begun to tease apart in relation to transparency and honesty (or lack thereof).

To bring Machiavelli's idea regarding the benefit of being feared as a leader into the context of *WoW*, we can consider the case of the guild leader Dives of <Wipe Club>. If you don't know Dives by name, you almost certainly recognize his voice if you've been around *WoW* for any stretch of time. He's the seemingly crazy, definitely foul-mouthed, raid leader from the infamous Onyxia wipe who gifted us with the phrases "50 DKP minus!" and "Throw more DoTs" (among others). Many of us had a good laugh over the Onyxia wipe video on YouTube with the goofy Flash animations, but what fewer people know is that after that wipe became a subject of public attention, guild applications to <Wipe Club> exploded. In fact, as Dives mentioned in an interview with the game blog Kotaku, he had to appoint a guild officer for publicity due to the massive influx of guild applications (kotaku.com, 5/19/2006).

While we could take this incident as an indicator that people simply wanted to be part of one of the most notorious guilds in *WoW*, Dives mentioned in the same interview that he also received numerous requests from players in other guilds to come on their Teamspeak and Ventrilo servers and serve up some of his abusive directives. According to a colleague of mine who played on the same server as Dives, these weren't merely requests to be talked down to satisfy some vague sadomasochistic impulses. These were earnest requests from other guilds that wanted no-nonsense raid direction of the sort that Dives provides before the point where his strategy fails and he loses it in the Onyxia incident.

Dives stated in the interview with Kotaku that he had founded <Wipe Club> as a guild for fun. If we take him at his word it raises the interesting question of why his guild mates stick around such an intimidating guild leader, and why players flocked to his guild after the Onyxia wipe became YouTube fodder. Machiavelli would probably see in Dives's abusive behavior justification for his own basic stance on the value of being feared as a leader. When introducing the topic, Machiavelli wrote the following:

> Therefore a prince must not worry about the reproach of cruelty when it is a matter of keeping his subjects united and loyal; for with very few examples of cruelty he will be more compassionate than those who, out of excessive mercy, permit disorders to continue . . . for these usually harm the community at large, while the executions that come from the prince harm particular individuals. (p. 55)

Machiavelli was talking about executing dissenters and other troublemakers here, but we can see the relevance of the same basic principle in the more moderate context of guild and raid leadership. When Dives opens up on his guild mates and starts docking them Dragon Kill Points, he's sending a very clear message that when he's running the raid people better be where they're supposed to be and doing what they're supposed to be doing. First and foremost, Dives wants the guild to be successful here, just as any raid leader would. He also knows for a fact that the more wipes they have on Onyxia, the further morale will drop. Not only can this diminish the raid's chances of taking down the dragon, but it can actually feed back negatively into guild cohesion more generally harming community relations within the guild.

The underlying culture of almost all raiding guilds in *WoW* puts a natural limit on the degree to which Machiavellian principles of leadership cross over into guild politics. Even Dives states that most <Wipe Club> raids are much duller than the Onyxia wipe audio would lead us to believe. In addition, a significant number of raiding players clearly aren't interested in a guild leader that they have to "fear," and many are probably more willing to risk numerous wipes in order to play in a more laid back context. For those players who consider success in the game as the primary objective of playing, having a guild master or raid leader who can hold out and enforce tangible threats is clearly less of a problem. Given the relatively short life span of many guilds in *WoW* it's equally clear that there can be a limit to the level of abuse players are interested in taking either from their leaders or due to a lack of leadership. We probably all know someone who got so fed up with an abusive guild leader that they decided to settle for a less goal-oriented guild. Once "fear" turns to "hatred," the room for fun in your raiding experience evaporates pretty quickly, and at some point the promise of the purples just doesn't seem worth it.

Mercenaries and Auxiliaries: The Perils of PUGing and Battlegrounds

If most guilds in *WoW* are composed of people who share close enough bonds that the sort of extreme political maneuvering Machiavelli calls for would seem out of place, PUGs and battle grounds offer us instances in which we have likely all wished for some more expedient or even retaliatory measures. Consider the following situation. You're in Arathi Basin (AB) and the score is really close, perhaps 800:900. Your side has Blacksmith and the other resources are split down the middle. Suddenly the other side captures your home resource (Farm or Stables, depending on who you play as). You rush back to figure out what the heck is going on only to discover that two of your teammates who were supposed to be guarding the flag are fighting with the other side . . . in the road.

You could all benefit from the win, but these guys are hanging out farming kills instead, and they refuse to stop despite repeated directions from virtually everyone else in the battleground. Now you have to muster some folks from Blacksmith and Lumber Mill to come help recapture your home turf, and while you're out the other side ninjas one resource and moves forces in on the other one. Ironically enough, you queued for an AB precisely because you wanted to avoid the sort of farming behavior that is so endemic in Warsong Gulch. At least there's a time limit in the Basin though, and maybe that Strand of the Ancients will pop in the next few minutes.

Machiavelli had some choice words that offer us some insight into why those two players keep fighting in the road instead of tightening things up for the good of the team. In discussing the different kinds of troops, he distinguished between citizen soldiers, auxiliary troops (troops that are borrowed from someone else), and mercenaries. Battlegrounds and pick-up groups give us a perfect example of the issue Machiavelli raises regarding mercenary troops. In introducing the topic he wrote, "And if a prince holds on to his state by means of mercenary armies, he will never be stable or secure; for they are disunited, ambitious, without discipline, disloyal." He goes on to appraise the captains of these troops saying, "Mercenary captains are either excellent soldiers or they are not; if they are, you cannot trust them, since they will always aspire to their own greatness . . . but if the captain is without skill, he usually ruins you" (p. 42).

Because Blizzard doesn't provide any significant game mechanic for leadership in the battlegrounds, each player basically has the choice to run as their own "captain" when they step in. The result is all too often complete disarray where technically skilled players with good gear (or a class based advantage) but no real devotion to the team run amok farming honor kills, while less skilled/geared players run off solo and invariably get farmed by the other side. Of course, there's variation between different battle groups, and even more variation from instance to instance, but when you face a pre-made team with a "mercenary" or mixed group, it's hard to discount the role of disunity and trust in determining the outcome of the fight, even if the other side is talking on Ventrilo or Team Speak.

We see the same basic issues play out in PUGs all the time. In some instances you might be lucky enough to be the fifth (or tenth or twenty-somethingth) addition to a run composed primarily of one guild. Unfortunately though, in the average PUG, everyone is pretty much out for their own gain which means that unless you happen to have a form of common contract for handling loot (or even for how to pull mobs or run a boss fight) because you've run together before, there's an unfortunately high potential for everything to come apart at the slightest fracture. Sometimes this can mean insanely high repair bills with nothing to show for it. Other times it can mean hours wasted waiting for a group to come together, only for the main tank to suddenly decide that he has better things to do after you've finally managed to fill that last DPS slot.

Machiavelli himself had a particular problem with the use of mercenary and auxiliary troops because he regarded the fact that Italy was a disunited and conquered land during his time as being a result of the use of mercenary or mixed forces in defending it from outside invasion. If you think you've been frustrated when some outsider walked off with that pair of boots that only has a .05% drop rate, imagine what it must feel like for your whole country to get ganked because the leadership decided to PUG the extra defense.

The Bronze Dragonflight: Invisible Leadership

There are good reasons why Machiavelli has fallen out of vogue when people discuss leadership these days. Foremost among them is the fact that we live in a democratic society rather than a monarchy. More importantly though, even if we have evidence to the contrary, we often don't like to assume the worst about people and there can be no doubt that virtually all of Machiavelli's advice is based around the idea that people generally don't act on their better nature. There are still situations in *WoW* (and in life) in which a Machiavellian approach will get you a lot more mileage than a gentler style will, but players in *World of Warcraft* are often not manipulative, scheming, and self interested, and the social structure of guilds often ameliorates some of people's more selfish qualities. Consequently I can't leave the topic of leadership without offering some counterpoint to the admittedly dispassionate and sometimes cruel methods advocated by Machiavelli.

The bronze dragonflight is a prime example from the lore of *Warcraft* of an entirely different approach to the task of leadership. Rather than engaging in high profile positions and directing the affairs of mortals visibly and politically, the bronzes are consistently hidden in odd corners of Azeroth like the Caverns of Time or disguised as unassuming figures like the Gnome Chromie (with the exception of their role in the opening of the gates to Ahn'Qiraj). Your guild may well have a leader who is similar to the bronzes, and this person might not even technically be your guild leader but simply the person who your guild leader talks to in a back channel during turbulent times. To describe the power of such leaders, it's worth turning towards Eastern philosophy, to an author whose true identity is debated and who predated Machiavelli by over a thousand years.

Like Shakespeare, the actual identity or identities of the figure known as Laozi (or Lao-Tzu as the name used to be transliterated) is contested. However the text attributed to this elusive figure is the *Daodejing* (formerly *Tao Te Ching*) and it contains some of the most puzzling and insightful words on human affairs. Many verses of the *Daodejing* speak directly to challenges of leadership, and it provides us with a nice counterpoint to Machiavelli on the fundamental issue of how a leader should be. Verse 17 from the text offers what is in some ways a similar assessment of leadership styles to that offered by Machiavelli. One major difference is that Laozi praises leaders who are loved more than those who are feared. Above all however, verse 17 states that the best leaders "are scarcely known by their subjects," and it ends with the words:

> When the best rulers achieve their purpose
> Their subjects claim the achievement as their own.[4]

Personally, this is the feeling that I've had when my own guild has had its most successful runs. We all feel like we're the ones who

[4] This translation of the *Daodejing* is taken from <taoteching.org>.

did the work and made it happen, and to some degree this is true. At the same time though, I know that we ultimately owe our success to the tireless planning, gear checking, consultation with raid strats, and the dozen other things that our guild and raid leaders have done, invisibly paving our road to victory . . . and purples.

Machiavelli and Laozi represent two of the more divergent perspectives on leadership, and yet when we look to guilds in *WoW* we see manifestations of both perspectives, not to mention a whole range of styles that fall somewhere in between the two. Is one of these leadership styles more likely to bring success than another? Undoubtedly the answer to this question depends greatly on how you define success in your gaming experience. If you consider guild progression to be a sort of empirical gold standard of success, my own casual observations of the top ranked guilds on servers I've played on seem to indicate that successful raid leadership styles vary as wildly as those of the more fail prone. If your standard of success is more geared around a fun social experience, then your personal definitions of fun and social are essential for answering that question.

Regardless, one thing about playing *WoW* is that it provides us with an opportunity to see how different people wear the mantle of leadership and to figure out what type of leadership style works for us. If you already are or aspire to be a guild leader, you may take the path of a Machiavellian autocrat or an elusive Daoist orchestrator. Either way *WoW* can give us the opportunity to try our hands at leadership, and learn something about ourselves in the process.

17
There Is No War in Warcraft

BEN MEDLER

It's in the title. Players kill each other in the thousand every day. Forums are plastered with the hate-filled cries for blood from both the Horde and Alliance factions. War is around each player in *World of Warcraft (WoW)* or at least that is what they're supposed to think. Every race has their nice little fortresses and their guards patrolling the streets. Territory is sectioned into "us" verses "them," where going to the "them" areas is not recommended. There are even huge areas where opposing factions line up and charge at each other, battling until one side is victorious. Yes that's how it looks, but that's not how it's played.

Truth be told, war is not actually going on in *WoW*. This isn't to say that there's no violence—my honor can attest to that—but violence does not mean war. Thrall does not leave Orgimmar to lead players in mighty battles, where many of them perish under the Horde's banner. Some players just sit at the auction house all day, waiting for their auctions to perish.

The philosophy of war has very little to say about situations where soldiers spend most of their time killing each other and jumping back into battle after a short stint as a ghost. What then is *WoW*'s relationship with war and where do the players, or the "soldiers," fit into this relationship? If violence is so prevalent in *WoW*, seeing as one must kill something to level up, how does that factor into the player's experience? We must explore what war actually means and how players act in *WoW* in order to answer these questions. Especially since some players don't always rely on violence to get their enjoyment from the game, making neutrality in this "war" not such a stretch.

The Conflicts of War

A conflict is not a war. Conflict can be defined as individuals or groups taking actions "against each other to attain incompatible goals and/or to express their hostility."[1] *WoW* players have a number of in-game behaviors they perform to achieve their goals (Frostbolt anyone?) or express their hostilities towards other players. They get honor for it too. Thinking of conflict in the typical way—that conflict means war—does the process of defining conflict and war little justice. *World of Warcraft* obviously has plenty of stereotypical conflict situations but, like most Massively Multiplayer Online Role Playing Games (MMORPGs) and Multi-User Dungeons (MUDs), *WoW* also includes a number of economic and social conflicts too. Price gouging at the auction house, dealing with city spammers, and disagreements about guild management are all conflicts present in *WoW*.

Separating war from conflict first involves focusing on violence. Swords slashing, Mages blasting and totems . . . well, totems just sit there, but they still contribute to the overall concept of violence in Azeroth. Conflicts involving violence are different from, say, an economic conflict over prices at the auction house. Carl von Clausewitz, who was a Prussian soldier during Napoleon's reign in France and is a popular author on the subject of war, wrote that war "is an act of violence to compel our opponent to fulfill our will."[2] While a devious Elf at the auction house may undercut her competition in an attempt to compel other players to fulfill her will, this is not a violent act and can be separated from war. However a duel in *WoW*, where members of the same faction battle one another, would be considered war since the players must violently attack one another. War may need violence but it cannot be war's sole defining attribute.

Other definitions of war focus on the role of politics or communities. Keith Otterbein describes war as "armed combat between political communities,"[3] where a political community represents a group within a territory that has an authoritative figure that makes group decisions. Clausewitz also says war is "not merely a political act, but also a real political instrument, a continuation of political

---

[1] Otomar Bartos and Paul Wehr, *Using Conflict Theory* (Cambridge University Press, 2002).

[2] Carl von Clausewitz, *On War* (Plain Label, 1968).

[3] Keith Otterbein, *How War Began* (Texas A&M University Press, 2004).

commerce" (Clausewitz). War is therefore a tool to be used by political communities. Jean-Jacques Rousseau, an Enlightenment philosopher, even goes so far as to say "war then is a relation, not between man and man, but between State and State."[4] This would dismiss any conflict between private citizens as being war, focusing instead on the conflicts between political organizations that govern those citizens.

The morality of war is often linked both to the political definition of war and to the violence attribute of war. For instance, Cicero, a famous Roman philosopher and statesmen, said "no war can be undertaken by a just and wise state unless for faith or self-defense."[5] He also said that war must be announced before it can be considered just. Players on *WoW*'s PvP servers are specifically told that they will be the target of the opposing faction while outside of their own faction's safe areas. However, players are encouraged to attack other players for Honor Points, which may be considered going to war over faith—for instance saying the Horde has a right to occupy their lands, but certainly not self-defense (except for the player being attacked). Hugo Grotius, who is said to be the father of international law, specifically makes that point when he says: "nor can the advantage to be gained by a war be ever pleaded as a motive of equal weight and justice with necessity,"[6] where an example of necessity is self-defense. Does offering Honor Points for killing other players imply justification for the violence that takes place in *WoW*? While this chapter will not discuss the ethics or morality of war it is important to reflect on how *WoW* entices players into accepting its state of constant violence and how the political groups in Azeroth are portrayed as promoting conflicts.

Finally, the definition of war I often use is "a group activity, carried on by members of one community against members of another community, in which it is the primary purpose (or is highly likely) to inflict serious injury or death on multiple non-specified members of that other community."[7] This definition seems to fit closer to the MMORPG style of gameplay which incorporates communities of

---

[4] Jean-Jacques Rousseau, *The Social Contract or Principles of Political Right* (Public Domain, 1762).

[5] Marcus Tullius Cicero, *Cicero's Tusculan Disputations* (Harper and Brothers, 1877).

[6] Hugo Grotius, *On the Law of War and Peace* (Dunne, 1901).

[7] Roy Prosterman, *Surviving to 3000* (Wadsworth, 1972), p. 140.

players. Violence in combination with political organization and anonymity ("nonspecified members") paints a clearer picture of how to describe war. This definition, along with some of the other definitions mentioned, does well to exclude acts such as homicide in the real world or duels in *WoW* from being defined as war.

Violence—*WoW* has that, check. Political communities—that one is debatable. Anonymity—the names over every player's head shout a clear "no" to that attribute of war. Players often talk about spawn camping or revenge killing specific players in *WoW*.[8] Anonymity is definitely not part of the experience of *WoW*. But wait, let's place that to the side for a moment; actual players in *WoW* are anonymous even if their avatars are not. The debatable aspect of how *WoW* compares to war is the political communities. If territory and group decision making define political communities then we can also make other assumptions. These communities must have common goals, a strong group identity, some form of hierarchal leadership to make group decisions, and have the means to deal with the logistics of war (feeding soldiers, building weapons and organizing a campaign). Most present-day states or countries have these properties and thus have the ability to go to war, by definition.

Where does the *WoW* player fit into this definition of war? I don't spend my day making decisions for a large group, deciding how to supply other players with the epic weapons they need or setting up blockades across the borders of The Barrens. Most of the time I am alone, grinding Mobile Objects (mobs), chatting with friends or crafting items. For this very reason we can classify the way players live in *WoW* as similar to the way humans have lived for ninety-nine percent of our species' existence—in small band societies of hunter gathers.

Band of Players

Band societies, unlike more complex forms of human political communities (such as states), are small, nomadic, egalitarian groups of hunter gatherers. Members of a band are treated fairly equally, do not follow a clear leader, and may work as a group

[8] Lisbeth Klastrup, "What Makes World of Warcraft a World? A Note on Death and Dying," in *Digital Culture, Play, and Identity: A World of Warcraft Reader* (MIT Press, 2008).

roaming the land foraging for food. Band societies lack most of the general properties that are needed for war (leadership, territory, group identity, logistical planning). *WoW* players are the same way, no one can tell them what to do, they roam freely and forage resources from the land. They contribute mainly to themselves and little to their host factions.

WoW treats players in a fairly egalitarian way. Every player is a hero in the making. No player has any less chance of defeating a mob or achieving a higher level so long as they work at accomplishing the task. There are no class hierarchies such as nobles, commoners, and slaves (although player guilds sometimes form hierarchies as I discuss below). Non-Player Characters (NPCs) are perhaps on a higher level compared to players—acting as gatekeepers to resources or services—but they have no major power over players. Thrall can't send down orders to his Orc kin to raid the town of Theramore. Players do not have to take orders from anyone and can earn the privileges of any other player if they are willing to invest the time. Even a player's race, which should be considered a player's kin, has little bearing on a player's actions. Nothing in the game forces a player to choose to favor their race over another and faction races intermix.

Players exhibit the practices of nomadic beings and function as single-person band societies. They are self-sufficient, roam where they please, and need not group with others while leveling. It's even hard to stop players from roaming into places where they shouldn't go. One can't threaten them with violence when they step out of line, given that players can't die permanently. What is called "death" in *WoW* is closer to the act of being stunned, requiring the player to perform some action to un-stun themselves. Players can willingly enter into a battle they know they can't win and walk away the moment the battle is over.

Just like nomadic societies, players must follow their food source. Each territory in *WoW* contains mobs within a certain range of levels. Players jump from encampment to encampment as they adventure from one territory to the next, foraging their level's mobs. Even if players wanted to settle down there are no cities or territories that allow player dwellings. The closest thing a player has to external storage is the bank, which functions more like a large backpack being carried between cities. Once a player achieves a high enough level they leave their current encampment and territory behind for greener (and usually more dangerous) pastures. This behavior is equivalent to a nomadic band moving based on animal migration or seasonal changes.

Players hunt and gather resources, the mobs and resources like herbs, in each territory as they scour the land beyond their current temporary encampments. Mobs act like crops or animals because they have such tedious existences that players can clearly see. The killing of mobs is not always framed in the best context[9] but players usually see them as resources to gather. Why wouldn't they? Mobs fade into existence from the ether, have no intelligent rationality (they never remember the past and have no plans for the future), normally are hostile and have no means of conversing with the player. It would be one thing if a player could be invited in for a cup of tea by one of the Scarlet Crusaders but this can't occur; players see mobs as resources that provide sustenance and profit.

Players live most of their leveling experience as a band-like society; they follow their mob resources, lack permanent dwellings and have no meaningful structured hierarchies of authority. Still, players do not always act alone or in small groups which are common to band societies. Player versus Player (PvP) and guilds are other forms of society affiliations where players can participate. Perhaps these affiliations will provide the needed communities and experiences that will define how war is used in *WoW*.

LF(Complex)G

PvP in *WoW* comes in many flavors: duels, the arena, battlegrounds, and world. Dueling and arena PvP are structured like trials of combat, gladiatorial combat for the arena, and definitely do not represent war. Battlegrounds place two teams of opposite faction players against each other in a battle scenario. However, player statistics are tracked in the battlegrounds, where a player can always see who's in the fight and who's winning. This lack of anonymity should not be ignored in this case, especially since players that are killed know the name of their killer and are given the chance to take revenge once that player respawns. Players also do not need to follow a leader in a battleground; everyone can fight how they please. Besides, even if a team loses they still receive

[9] Raph Koster, "The Evil We Pretend to Do," *RaphKoster.com*, <http://www.raphkoster.com/2005/12/30/the-evil-we-pretend-to-do/>.

some sort of compensation. With no clear leaders, no threat of violence and no anonymity, battlegrounds (as well as dueling and arena combat) are not battles in a war.

World PvP generally means battles fought out in the open territories of Azeroth. Spawn camping and revenge killings (and the first act of killing that leads to revenge killings) have already been mentioned, and they define open world PvP (not war). Structured world PvP, where players have to capture static structures like towers or other buildings, can also be found throughout Azeroth. These areas are the closest that *WoW* comes to offering an actual war experience. Faction players that can capture certain structures are given rewards for accomplishing the task. The structures never stay captured, though, and flip back to being contested, or open to attack, after a certain time period. There's a little more anonymity in world PvP because players can enter the fight whenever they are in the area (no scoreboard keeps track of the players). Also, while no true leader is assigned in any structured world PvP, Wintergrasp, a world PvP territory added as part of the *Wrath of the Lich King* expansion, does give military ranks to players as they attack the Keep (similar to the old Honor ranks). However, these only function as driving licenses for the shiny siege weapons.

World PvP falls prey to the same problems that battlegrounds have when defining war. There's no political bureaucracy or logistical planning behind places such as Wintergrasp. Players still know the names of their enemies, they have no clear leadership, and the territories will automatically become available to be recaptured no matter what the players do. This leaves guilds as the last player community that can allow players to participate in war.

Guilds are organizations that allow players to have a sub-affiliation within their host faction. These organizations promote socializing and collaborative play by bringing together groups of players under one banner. These organizations display some properties of a political group: clear leadership, group identity, and at least some logistical means (or group management capabilities). For instance, every guild has a guild leader who may promote other members of the guild into positions of power, creating a hierarchical ranking system of leadership. Guild members also promote their guild's identity by displaying their guild's name under their avatar name and guilds design the color and logo of their own tabard, a piece of clothing specific to guilds that a player's avatar can ware. Finally, guilds can choose to tax their members for guild expenses and guild bank accounts may be purchased to store items used for guild purposes, allowing the guild leadership to handle the logistics of managing the organization.

Guilds are close to being capable of waging war, but they just miss it. They have no territory to defend, acting solely as dependents of their host faction. They also can't declare war on other guilds in their faction, or any similar faction member period. With players having no anonymity and no risk of violence, guild members learn who their rival guild members are. Thus they are no longer "non-specified members of that other community," making their fights more personal than political. Even when a guild declares "war" on a rival faction's guild these fights can be considered personal vendettas or feuds, which are caused by personal conflicts and should not be defined as war. In the end guilds are just sub-groups in their faction, following the same global game rules as everyone else. They're following the rules of factions that are lead by empty NPC figure heads placed there by the rulers of Blizzard.

The State of Blizzard

If players that live in band societies and guilds represent something like a chiefdom, then Blizzard is the state that they live in. The Horde and Alliance are puppet organizations—incapable of taking even the simplest of political action—controlled by the great state of Blizzard. As *WoW*'s developer they are a centralized political organization that lays claim to a territory—all of *WoW*. They have hierarchical command structures, from the main designers to the forum moderators. Blizzard controls the way *WoW*'s cities are protected, the mail system, the way the auction house taxes players, and how the public transportation functions. They control all of the land, can create natural resources on a whim, and allow no permanent dwellings.

Controlling all of the wealth in *WoW* makes Blizzard a Plutocracy, a government ruled by the wealthy. Players can never attain the wealth or power that Blizzard holds, nor gain social status within the system (a player's level has no basis for controlling the functions of the world). The symbolic wealth that the players create in the game is continually taken away from them through the services that Blizzard provides: mail delivery, transportation, auctions, armor repair, and so on.

Blizzard has all the attributes of a political society and can go to war. With whom, you ask? Well I guess with other MMORPGs; wouldn't that make for a fun game? No, if Blizzard is the only community capable of going to war then there is a problem with respect to *WoW*; it can't go to war with itself. Keith Otterbein in *How War Began* specifically points out that political groups can't go to war with themselves. Those conflicts are considered feuds. Unlike in a civil war, which is between two political groups that broke off from one another, Blizzard has complete control over the Horde and the Alliance. Communication between factions is cut off by Blizzard, killing (stunning) players is rewarded by Blizzard, and every player follows the rules as laid out by Blizzard. What really is happening is that Blizzard is promoting the acts of feuding, revenge killings, gladiatorial combat, and homicides for the sheer fact of providing players with an engaging game experience.

What Is It Good For?

We are left then with Blizzard being the only political community in *WoW* capable of engaging in war but, in another sense, incapable. War is not being fought in *WoW*, leaving only personal feuds and glorified duels. Blizzard pokes and prods us players into gutting each other for their, and our, enjoyment. Most players go along with these persuasive ideals, others don't. Other players give up the hack and slash now and again, making use of the parts of *WoW* that I have not discussed yet: when players step back from all the violence and decide to act neutral.

Even though *WoW* is composed mainly of violent conflicts, players find a way to be neutral. The economy in *WoW* is always booming with new crafting recipes and professions added with each expansion. Players do not need to chop another player's head off to find surfing the auction house enjoyable or provide crafting services in the main cities. With the addition of combined auction houses in the neutral goblin cities of Azeroth, separate faction players can even trade with each other (don't they hate each other?). Besides making use of *WoW*'s economy, other players will login to *WoW* just to hang out and talk with their fellow players. Others like to test the game's limits, see how far they can fall or fly around looking for scenic locations. These are all acts that take a neutral stance in *WoW*'s figment war and portray the game as a common social space.

If players can live in *WoW* without needing to resort to violence it makes me wonder why *WoW* and similar MMORPGs rely on the framings of war and do not provide more neutral gameplay. Why not have a tradesmen profession with a stock market and stores, or an ambassador profession that can help mend the broken alliance between the Horde and Alliance factions? These are virtual worlds and yet they are often very constrained. *WoW* could have a simulated United Nations of Azeroth or allow players to have richer interactions with mobs, instead of focusing on hack and slash. Other MMORPGs, MUDs, and virtual worlds have dealt with these issues and some allow more neutral gameplay than others. It would be interesting to see how these issues can be combined into one game experience. I realize a game developer can't put everything into their game and must make sacrifices. However, neutral gameplay is something to think about; players don't always need violence to stay engaged.

In the end, it really depends on whether neutral gameplay in a game can be made fun or not. I can live in a world without war but the crafting system better be fantastic.

18
Game Developers, Gods, and Surveillance

CHRISTIAN HOFFSTADT and
MICHAEL NAGENBORG

Virtual worlds are potential spaces of total surveillance. In theory, every single move or action of the player can be stored, monitored and analyzed by the publisher. The beautiful *World of Warcraft* is no exception. While the interest of players for this aspect of the virtual world is only raised when encountering problems with other players or being sanctioned by one of the Gamemasters, surveillance and privacy in virtual worlds like *WoW* are fields of growing interest for specific scientific disciplines.

From War Games to Information Warfare

The game is called *World of Warcraft*, not *World of Picking Flowers*, for a reason (of course some players gather herbals all the time, but the game wouldn't quite be the same with the latter title). Although *WoW* can be played as a pure Role-Playing Game with focus on social networking, in the background and at the heart of the game there is *war*. This might not be too much of a surprise, since the roots of Massively Multiplayer Role Playing Games (MMORPGs) like *WoW* lay in classic war gaming, the military predecessor of today's entertaining strategy games. In the 1960s and 1970s players became bored with anonymous units on the battlefield and more interested in playing characters they could identity with. This is where role playing took off. The developers of *Dungeons and Dragons*, often referred to as the first Role-Playing Game, were involved in developing war games before creating the pen and paper classic.[1]

---

[1] Patrick Williams et al, "Introduction: Fantasy Games, Gaming Culture, and

If you think about it, the *Warcraft* series evolved from strategic war games to a strategy based Role-Playing Game. In *Warcraft: Orcs and Humans* and *Warcraft II: Tides of Darkness* the player led a group of anonymous characters. With *Warcraft III: Reign of Chaos*, individual heroes were introduced to the series and, finally, in *World of Warcraft* one is playing one elaborated character. Hence, the series nicely followed the steps of the development from abstract war game to character-centered role playing.

Why do we stress this point of war? Because beneath the surface of *WoW*, behind the filigreed facade of a romantic, competitive, and honor-based concept of war, there lies a very modern concept of tactical Information Warfare ("Infowar"). Information warfare can be understood as the use and management of information in pursuit of a competitive advantage over an opponent and is a main topic in today's military research, which brings together war, virtual simulation and information processing.[2]

Although information and communication technology have always played an important role in warfare—think about telegraphy or radios in battle—the Western military now aims for automatization, digitalization and acceleration of modern warfare. While in the first Gulf War the timeframe between the detection of a target and the following bombardment was three days, with today's information technologies the bombardment can take place within ten minutes of preparation.[3] Though *Blizzard* forbids players to use automated auxiliaries like bots, raiding with several add-ons is comparable with keeping track of the battlegrounds on modern jet fighter displays. What makes *World of Warcraft* comparable with Information Warfare is the astonishing quantity and complexity of information provided by Blizzard as well as generated by players, guilds, forums and fan sites and Wikis, the visible in-game information additionally complemented with chat and voice communication.

Social Life," in *Gaming as Culture: Essays on Reality, Identity, and Experience in Fantasy Games* (McFarland, 2006), pp. 1–18.

[2] Friedrich Kittler, "Infowar: Notes on the Theory and History," in Gerfried Stocker and Christine Schöpf, eds., *Ars Eletronica 98. Infowar Information Macht Krieg* (Springer, 1998), pp. 24–29. James Der Derian, *Virtuous War: Mapping the Militay-Industrial Media-Entertainment Network*, second edition (Routledge, 2009). Stephen Graham, "Surveillance, Urbanization and the US 'Revolution in Military Affairs'," in David Lyon, ed., *Theorizing Surveillance: The Panopticon and Beyond* (Willian, 2006), pp. 247–269.

[3] See <www.wired.com/politics/security/magazine/15-12/ff_futurewar>.

The Outer Line of Defense

One should think that *Blizzard's* "Infowar" is fought against attackers from the outside, like hackers committed to identity theft[4] or thieves of either virtual goods or credit card information from players.

Though some hackers may understand it as innovative practice which can lead to improvement of the game, hacking is normally condemned by the general public, at least if it has negative economic consequences for users. Publishers of online games try to get rid of cheating and hacking by including (in their terms of use or other legal documents covering the service provided to the players) permission to monitor the players' computers in order to track third-party cheating programs. In effect the player is only allowed to enter the virtual world if he allows his computer to be searched—like a wayfarer bidding for admission in a medieval town. Blizzard fights a "war on cheating" to ensure that all players have the same gaming experience and they therefore only allow specific, non-automatic auxiliary programs and add-ons. Automatic programs ("bots"), which take control of player's characters, are strictly forbidden.

Although other publishers prohibit this, too, Blizzard was under-fire in public in 2005, when Greg Hoglund reported on his blog that he had discovered spyware functions in the *World of Warcraft* software. He reported that the *WoW* Client was observing all running system processes on his computer, including personal data from mail programs:

> I watched the warden sniff down the email addresses of people I was communicating with on MSN, the URL of several websites that I had open at the time, and the names of all my running programs, including those that were minimized or in the toolbar. These strings can easily contain social security numbers or credit card numbers, for example, if I have Microsoft Excel or Quickbooks open w/ my personal finances at the time.[5]

---

[4] Humphrey Cheung, *Trojan Horse Steals Passwords from World of Warcraft players*, <www.tomshardware.co.uk/trojan-steals-wow-passwords,news-20060.html>. Jeffrey Bardzell et al., *Virtual Worlds and Fraud: Approaching Cybersecurity in Massively Multiplayer Online Games*, <www.digra.org/dl/ db/07311.42219.pdf>.

[5] <www.rootkit.com/blog.php?newsid=358>.

Even if the information was not sent to Blizzard, and was analyzed only on the player's computer, many players regarded this as an illegitimate intrusion. Apparently, most of the players had not read the EULA (end-user license agreement) or Terms of Service, in which the players had accepted this monitoring.

> When running, the *World of Warcraft* client may monitor your computer's random access memory (RAM) and/or CPU processes for unauthorized third-party programs running concurrently with *World of Warcraft*.[6]

In the meantime this passage has been changed. Now players accept that the "free access" to the game is only possible under the conditions set by Blizzard (who are allowed to change the conditions at any time!). And Blizzard is free to change the software on the player's computer by remote access:

> Patches and Updates. Blizzard Entertainment shall have the right to deploy or provide patches, updates and modifications to the Game, as needed or as useful to:
>
> (i) enhance the gaming experience by adding new content to the Game, (ii) incorporating new features to the Game, (iii) enhancing content or features already in the Game; (iv) fixing 'bugs' that may be altering the Game; and (v) determining how you and other players utilize the Game so that the Game can be enhanced for the enjoyment of the Game's users; and (vi) protect you and other players against cheating; and (iii) make the gaming environment safer for you. These patches, updates, and modifications to the Game must be installed for the user to continue to play the Game. For these purposes, Licensor may update the Game remotely, including, without limitation, the Game Client residing on the user's machine, without knowledge or consent of the user, and you hereby grant to Licensor your consent to deploy and apply such patches, updates and modifications to the Game.[7]

Some cases of false violation alarms have appeared, for example, in the case of users of Cedega Linux, which was mistakenly identified as malicious cheat software.

---

[6] Old version of EULA, which can be found at <www.heise.de/newsticker/World-of-Warcraft-Spyware-oder-nicht—/meldung/64962>.

[7] <www.wow-europe.com/en/legal/eula.html>.

The Enemies Within

Besides hindering hackers and cheaters to intrude on the game, it is astonishing that the focus of Blizzard's defense is aligned to control and surveillance of the players *in* the game for purposes of upkeep of fair gameplay and monetary profit. The most important interface between publisher and players are the Gamemasters, who try to control the players' compliance with the EULA and are also addressable for player questions concerning player quarrels and support. Gamemasters normally are invisible—although they can appear visibly as players—and are contacted via an anonymous support channel.

Since Game Masters frequently deal with EULA violations like Gold Farming or Botting, one is reminded of Jeremy Bentham's Panopticon, which has become a favourite subject to study and discuss among philosophers since Michel Foucault's analysis in "Surveillance and Punishment."[8] The Panopticon was conceived by Jeremy Bentham as a utopian prison, where the prisoners were under surveillance by guards stationed in a watch tower. The prisoners could not see the guards, while one guard would be able to see all the prisoners. The prisoners would never know if they were under surveillance or not. And because they wouldn't know, they would always behave as if they were being watched. One can see panoptical structures in the online surveillance techniques of publishers, providers and developers in general, all of which use Spyware to monitor their users.[9]

A great challenge for Blizzard is the containment of commercial trading with the virtual in-game currency gold and with virtual items. Blizzard strictly forbids trading virtual items and money "outside" the game in the real market in order to make real money. But as one can see on platforms like eBay, people nonetheless do. There is a big black market[10] which Blizzard tries to eliminate because they want to be the only ones making money with their

---

[8] Michel Foucault, *Discipline and Punish: The Birth of the Prison* (1995).

[9] Tom Brignall III, "The New Panopticon: The Internet Viewed as a Structure of Social Control," in *Theory and Science* 3:1 (2002). <http://theoryandscience.icaap.org/content/vol003.001/brignall.html>.

[10] IGE, one of the leading professional "MMORPG Services" companies, which sells virtual gold, items and chars worldwide, estimates more than seven billion dollars volume of sales in the next years, making the "secondary market" more profitable than the "first market". See <www.ige.com/about.html>.

game. Compared to other publishers, Blizzard runs a very strict trading and monetary model here.

Elune Be With You!

Now, what role does Blizzard actually play regarding its control functions in the game? Richard Bartle, the co-author of the first Multi-User-Dungeon (MUD), the predecessor of MMORPGs, discusses the role of game designers as gods.

Bartle writes: "Virtual worlds . . . raise awkward questions concerning how they are governed, central to which is the status of the developers of such worlds." Players perceive developers not as a government, but as gods, which Bartle assumes to be the better metaphor, because it would lead to better games. Although Bartle's estimation seems a little arrogant, it emphasizes the necessary independency of the creative developers from the profit-oriented publishers.

Bartle underlines the sovereignty of the developers over the virtual world, which they are able to change any time:

> Virtual world developers routinely use their draconian powers to punish players without trial, exile them, restrict their freedom of speech, destroy their property, infringe their privacy—sometimes for reasons of protecting the virtual world from its players and sometimes for no apparent good reason whatsoever. ("Why Governments Aren't Gods and Gods Aren't Governments," <www.uic.edu/htbin/cgiwrap/bin/ojs/index.php/fm/article/view/1612/1527>, accessed May 2009)

The description of game designers as gods seems to be more of a wish than a realistic estimation, but Bartle tries to defend his thesis—"Virtual world designers need to be considered gods, not governments, because that's what virtual world designers are"—with two arguments.

First of all, he claims, governments can dispense their rights while gods can't. And secondly, governments are elected from ordinary people; gods are not and therefore cannot lose their rights or be disempowered.[11]

---

[11] Bartle bases this argument on an article by C. Doctorow: "Why Online Games Are Dictatorships." See <www.informationweek.com/news/internet/webdev/showArticle.jhtml?articleID=199100026>.

Of course, the reality of the computer games market looks different now. Nowadays the commercial success of a game decides the fate of developing studios: publishers and players have a lot of power and options to topple the supposed gods. We think that the role of game designers and publishers is well characterized by the figure of the Machiavellian "prince," which Foucault describes in his writings on "Governmentality" as a fragile form of governing.

> For a prince has only two things to fear: one is internal and concerns his subjects; the other is external and concerns foreign powers. From the latter he protects himself with reliable troops and reliable allies—and he will always have reliable allies if he has reliable troops. Moreover, he will always enjoy quiet within his kingdom if there is quiet outside of it, unless it is disturbed by conspiracy.[12]

Blizzard has to make huge efforts to remain the sovereign of Azeroth, the virtual *World of Warcraft*. This becomes apparent when we observe that Blizzard is not interested in hindering virtual fraud between players in the game, but only tries to boost its own objectives and its sovereignty. Therefore Blizzard tries to be quite invisible to the players, too, as there is not much communication with the fans or players in the forums. If it comes to support, Blizzard even censors complaints about technical problems in the forums, blaming everyone else but themselves.

Whoever wants to simulate the role of Blizzard should try the game MMORPG *Tycoon*[13] in which the player is able to use similar surveillance and censorship functions as Blizzard.

Spy versus Spy?

Blizzard is not able to spy all the players' activities on its own. So the Blizzard customer service team encourages players to report on other players. In 2006, the customer service team announced they had already banned more than a hundred thousand accounts.[14] Compared to other MMORPGs, in *World of Warcraft* there is no

---

[12] Niccolò Machiavelli, *The Prince* (Bantam, 2003), Book 19, p. 71.

[13] <www.vectorstorm.org/get-games/full-games/mmorpg-tycoon/>.

[14] Sal Humphreys, "Ruling the Virtual World: Governance in Massively Multiplayer Online Games," in *European Journal of Cultural Studies* 11:2, pp. 149–171.

reward system for player-to-player surveillance, while in Sony's *Everquest* players can become guides who solve minor conflicts between players and hence practice minor observation duties.

But we shouldn't overstretch the picture of Blizzard as a bad guy encouraging players to be insidious traitors.

Blizzard provides the facility for players to build social networks within the game, such as short-term battle groups as well as long-lasting guilds. There are several surveillance techniques integrated and available via add-ons that allow guild leaders to observe the players in the guild and to apply sanctions if needed. Guilds and groups develop social etiquettes and group rules, which differ from each other: while one guild enforces role playing and playful social interaction, another guild may emphasize raiding, which demands high time commitment and a high training and preparation standards for their members. With help from in-game add-ons like "DamageMeter" or "DKP," guild or raid leaders are able to make individual achievements visible and reward them. "It is DKP, I argue, that generates, in large part, the motivation and political cohesion necessary for a guild to be able to successfully engage the end-game content of MMORPGs"[15]

Finally, the visibility of the individual efforts of the players is determining when it comes to loot sharing. This group-based surveillance is supposed to play an important role in the in-game "Information War," highlighting its positive aspects (providing a fair, achievement-oriented reward system) as well as its negative aspects.

Indeed players often report on social pressure and mutual control on playing and interacting regularly, because this is the only path to success in the end game. This mutual social control shouldn't be seen as entirely negative, as it helps co-ordinating groups and social interaction and hence provides a fertile gameplay. This shows that surveillance in games should be portrayed as Janus-faced phenomenon, which can be positive and negative. In this panopticon, not only are the guards invisible, but the players—the inmates—can be guards, too.

---

15 <http://joystick101.org/blog/wp-content/uploads/2007/10/dkp1.html>. Also see Krista-Lee Meghan Malone, *Governance and Economy in a Virtual World: Guild Organization in World of Warcraft*, Thesis (MS in Anthropology), University of Wisconsin, Milwaukee, 2007.

Grand Master Philosopher

Physics, Reality, and Technology in and out of Azeroth.
Familiarize yourself with this topic by reading . . .

Bits of Ogres, Bytes of Orcs (PRYMUS): 0/1
Future Pasts of Magic and Deceit (SPENCER and JANSSEN): 0/1
Can I Have Unlimited Power in *WoW*? (MICHAUD): 0/1

Description

Some of the more abstract, and difficult, inquiries into the nature of reality are reserved for the branch of philosophy known as "metaphysics." You might remember being introduced to some metaphysical topics as an apprentice. In this section, Reader, the metaphysical speculation is taken a bit further.

WoW players are often accused of being disconnected from reality. But what is "real" anyway? Does *WoW* present evidence of a society that has reached the technological singularity envisioned by science fiction writers? Are there rules of the universe that cannot be broken, even in *WoW*? What rules *can* be broken in the gameworld? Is Azeroth even different from the real world? Or does the real world influence Azeroth and vice versa?

Rewards

You will receive: **+3 Intellect!**

19
Bits of Ogres, Bytes of Orcs

KYLIE PRYMUS

Philosophers have some strange conversations. I mean really strange. Strange enough that our sanity is frequently called into question. Get a couple of philosophers playing *World of Warcraft* and you can rest assured that both the intelligibility and practicality of their discussion will taper off dramatically. But since you're reading this book you've probably done your share of face melting and gold farming, so I'm going to assume you're okay with the strange and unusual.

I got involved in just such an abstruse conversation once after killing an Orc in the Barrens. "I've slain an Orc!" I proudly proclaimed to a colleague.

"No," he replied, "you initiated a computer program that displayed an animation of an 'Orc' 'dying'."

Yes, he actually gestured those scare quotes.

"Orcs aren't real," he declared. In true philosophical form I responded with a question: "What does 'real' mean?" That question is at the heart of a philosophical field known as metaphysics.

What in the world is metaphysics? Metaphysics is, simply, what's in the world.

Specifically, what are the key components of the universe? The ancients came up with the idea of dividing the world into four categories: earth, air, fire, and water. Modern scientists will say the universe is composed of atoms and not-quite-understood subatomic particles. But the term "atom," in fact, was coined 2,500 years ago by a Greek philosopher named Democritus (460 B.C.E.–370 B.C.E.) to describe the smallest building block of the universe. Can the entire universe be described as complex interactions between basic physical particles?

Perhaps, but chances are if someone tells you that *WoW* is just a complicated computer program, you'll disagree. There's more to the world than what our five senses tell us, just as there's more to *WoW* than pressing keys to produce elaborate animations. What about consciousness? What about emotion? Are they real? Few would deny that they *seem* to exist, but if you ask whether they are completely separate from the other building blocks of the universe, well, then you're thinking like a metaphysician.

Back to that, ahem, "dead" "Orc." Is it real? In purely physical terms I can describe what I did as pressing a few buttons that executed a series of computer commands. These commands were sent to a program stored on a centralized server and made changes to that program, changes which were then broadcast to any computer in the world that happened to be paying attention. Or I can say that a pre-defined pattern of electrical currents racing through a circuit board was recognized and replicated on other circuit boards throughout the world. But that seems to miss the point.

What about my colleague, the Azerothian non-realist (a fancy philosophical phrase I just invented—one of the perks of being a philosopher!—that simply means he doesn't believe Azeroth is real)? How would he describe an Orc? He would say an Orc is an identifiable pattern of atoms—patterns that we recognize as biological and would include, among other things[1], green skin and large teeth. However there have never been examples of such patterns of atoms existing so Orcs aren't real. And they most certainly can't be slain!

Now we're arguing over semantics. To put things a bit more simply he might say the Orc doesn't really exist because it's *just* a computer crunching numbers. But that leads us to the granddaddy of metaphysical questions: are *numbers* real? Fortunately for you I wouldn't touch that one with at ten-foot Hellreaver.

By now this may all sound like I'm beating a dead Orc. Philosophers have been arguing over this stuff for millennia and now we've got Azeroth to add more nuances to the debate. Actually, we've got 400+ Azeroths to add to it because each realm hosts a dif-

---

[1] Determining these "other things," the specific characteristics that define a unique species, is the province of a biological field known as taxonomy. Taxonomy has its roots in—you guessed it— metaphysics!

ferent Azeroth, a different possible world. What happens on Uther stays on Uther—unless you transfer your main to Kalecgos.

So then even if Azeroth is real, which is the real Azeroth? Well, now you're beginning to see how much fun metaphysics can be. . .

Going *Meta*—What Happens in Outland, Doesn't Stay in Outland

It's Tuesday morning and the halls of Ironforge are empty. Not a soul is hanging out at the normally frame-rate punishing auction house; an eerie silence envelops the Great Forge. Where are all the Player Characters (PCs)? Perhaps there was a great raid. Some Horde über-guild could have organized a massive siege of the city and wiped out all of its inhabitants. If that were the case we'd be seeing Tauren and Trolls dancing around the city. There are none. Maybe there's been a repeat of the infamous Corrupted Blood Plague and players throughout the city have fallen victim to a high level raid-dungeon disease. A nice theory, but there are no corpses littering the streets.

Actually it's quite obvious to most any *WoW* player why Ironforge is abandoned on this—and every—Tuesday morning: server maintenance. Azeroth and all of its inhabitants are taken offline for a few hours so that technicians in the "real world" can perform diagnostics to ensure everything continues to run smoothly. To explain a certain phenomenon within the game world we had to appeal to forces outside of the game world. Philosophers call this process of looking outside of one's intended area of interest for answers "going meta."

"Meta" is a Greek word meaning *after* or *beyond*. The term metaphysics was first coined to describe a section of writings by the ancient Greek philosopher Aristotle (384 B.C.E.–322 B.C.E.), a section that was untitled but came *after* his writings on physics. The *Physics* deals with precisely that. For example, in Book VII Aristotle talks about motion in very Newtonian ways: objects must get their motion from somewhere so he analyzes the various sources of motion possible in objects and animals. Contrast this with the sort of questions he delves into in Book II of the *Metaphysics*, foremost of which is whether there is a so-called first cause. If all objects have to trace the origins of their movement to something prior to them, can this go back infinitely, or is there a first cause, an unmoved mover?

Modern science is not immune to these questions either, despite the fact that our knowledge of physics has expanded by leaps and bounds. We have instruments that can register such subtle weight changes that the small fluctuations of gravity in different parts of the planet must be taken into account, and time can be measured down to the attosecond—that's 0.0000000000000000001 seconds (eighteen zeros between the "." and the "1")!

However, while our physics might be pushing level 80 (with the perpetual promise of more expansions and higher level caps to come), our metaphysics is still firmly in the newbie zone. Metaphysicians are surely impressed by all this scientific accuracy, but they still want to ask questions *about* that accuracy. You can measure attoseconds, but is there a smallest unit of time? You can tell the difference between a helium and hydrogen atom by weight alone, but was Democritus right—is there a smallest, indivisible building block of the universe?

At first glance you might think these metaphysical questions are superfluous, just for fun, and not at all relevant to the "real" work of physics. This would be a grave mistake, and *WoW* can help us see why. The term "meta" doesn't just apply itself as a prefix to physics. You can go meta-*anything*. In philosophy we talk about metaphysics, metaethics, metalogic and yes, even metaphilosophy. Whether we realize it or not, when we play *WoW* we very frequently have conversations about, and are affected by, things that are meta*game*.

Weekly server maintenance is but one example of metagame information—it's not something in the game world but something about (beyond, after) the game world. When I have to back out of a raid because my son or daughter got sick, or I get booted because of a power failure and the entire raid wipes, those are metagame explanations. I can't explain my failure solely in terms of the game; it wasn't that I didn't have good enough gear or lacked experience with this particular mob pull. The reason I failed can only be explained by talking above the level of the game. By the same token, sometimes our failings in science cannot be explained in the language of science but have to go beyond that language. That's when we bring in metaphysics.

A last but very practical example. We often hear people complaining about *WoW* and other Massively Multiplayer Online Role Playing Games (MMORPGs) that they're too addicting and that they never end. Many players set goals for themselves, (physical) goals which are impeded by (metaphysical) metagame information. How many of us have been or known people who wanted to have a max level character of every class? It seems an impossible goal for all but the most dedicated—by the time you get close, Blizzard raises the level cap! Similarly, as soon as the scientist cuts the attosecond in half the metaphysician steps in and raises the bar yet again.

It's important to know our metagame limits before setting goals for ourselves within the game. Similarly it's important to get our metaphysical theories straight if we hope to accomplish our scientific goals.

The Problem of Other Minds—When Is an NPC Really a PC?

Metaphysics isn't limited to abstract world-behind-the-world questions. In metaphysics we find some of the coolest topics in all of philosophy, questions that make your brain tingle and twist, conundrums that change the way you look at the world. They may be some of the hardest to answer, but they are an important part of understanding how we participate in the world.

It's one thing to question the limits of space and time—how relevant are attoseconds to your daily life anyhow?—but quite another to question the nature of conscious thought. I'm specifically referring to questions about whether we can ever be sure that others have conscious thoughts on a par with our own. This is a very old topic known as the problem of other minds and it arises because of an obvious truth. We can *see* other bodies. We can touch them and smell them, hear them and taste them. But we have no direct sensory experience of other minds. How do we know other people have thoughts and feelings the way we do?

Living in an age in which we spend hours interacting with others in a virtual world for fun is likely to make us forget that there was a time when all of this was very new and very spooky. The first time I made plans with a friend over e-mail, back before the "Internet" was so much as a buzzword, I half-way didn't expect him to show up at the appointed time because I wasn't entirely convinced that I'd been communicating with him. All I'd been doing was typing words on a computer screen!

Now, interacting with others virtually is commonplace and in *WoW* we have very explicit signs to let us know which characters are Non-Player Characters (NPCs) and which are PCs—who's "real" and who isn't. Yet I'll bet that 99.9 percent of regular *WoW* players could identify a PC from an NPC on sight with no name tags displayed. PCs, generally, move differently than NPCs. They run everywhere. They jump. A lot. Their behavior doesn't follow the rather simple scripting of NPCs.

Do you think Blizzard could program an NPC to behave so much like a PC that it would fool most players? Disregarding chat and whispers (they would give it away too easily), could we find ourselves interacting with a bot we thought was a person? Probably not. Maybe if they snuck one or two in there without telling anyone we'd be fooled for a while, but if we knew they were out there (just as we know NPCs exist—and they outnumber PCs!) we would very quickly learn to distinguish them. As human beings with minds we are very good at spotting physical things that suggest to us that something else has a mind. How do we do that?

You might think this is a psychology question and, on a certain level, it is. But this is metaphysics so we're going beyond. Metapsychology. Sure we know how to spot behaviors that indicate a mind, but how did we decide in the first place that those behaviors indicate minds?

The most commonly accepted explanation is known as the *argument from analogy*. I stub my toe—a physical action that anyone can observe. I feel pain, something only I can observe. I grimace and cry out, again observable by everyone. Every time I stub my toe and grimace and cry out I also experience pain. Those are three distinct events yet are almost always connected—the order is somewhat irrelevant. Thus if I observe another person stubbing their toe and grimacing I assume, by analogy, that where the two observable actions are the third (pain) probably is as well.

My Jewelcrafter doesn't stand still behind a counter in Orgrimmar waiting for other PCs to come by and open a trade window. Doing so is not only boring, it's an incredibly ineffective way of hawking my wares. I hawk my goods in the trade channel or deposit them at the auction house. Because I, an actual thinking person, have certain goals and an aversion to boredom and inefficiency I assume that other characters I see who stand around behind counters waiting for others to trade with them are NPCs, not PCs. I don't need the green name above their head to indicate that they're not conscious. I can use the argument from analogy—other PCs wouldn't do that because *I* wouldn't do that.

We have an advantage in *WoW* that we lack in the offline world. We could, in theory, check and see if any particular character is being controlled by a human or not, most likely by digging into the code, and therefore be certain who has a consciousness and who doesn't. Offline all we have is the argument from analogy. Psychologists and neuroscientists do the best they can to try and identify minute similarities and differences between individual humans and between humans and animals, but there are still metaphysical questions that need to be answered. How close does the analogy have to be? Does a person who doesn't grimace or cry out when they stub their toe not feel pain? If an MRI shows that certain neurons in my brain fire when I feel pain, then should I assume when similar neurons fire in other people they also feel pain? What counts as similar enough? Are the brains of fish similar enough? What about a person in a coma, or someone who is "brain dead?"

Ask yourself the following question: in the absence of visible, color-coded nametags and chat windows, how would you determine who was a PC and who an NPC? Perhaps most importantly, what would you do in cases where you weren't sure?

This is where the problem of other minds is most difficult, on the practical level when determining how to treat cases that are ambiguous. It affects serious moral questions such as euthanasia, abortion, and animal rights and will continue to do so regardless of how much purely scientific knowledge we accumulate.

If you wouldn't fathom attacking a low-level, flagged PC in a PvP zone, what would you do if you weren't sure whether the mobs you were farming were PCs or not? What criteria would you use to distinguish between them?

In the offline world all we have is the argument from analogy. There are no shortcuts, neither t-shirt nor model number to indicate whether a particular person or animal has or lacks consciousness. Nor is it possible to look behind the scenes, to examine the code and tell who does and does not think. Therefore if we want to address ambiguous cases we need to be more clear on exactly what behaviors or systems—what actions or gear—is "good enough" for us to believe that an object is conscious.

Counter-factuals and Possible Worlds—Why My Realm Is the Place to Be

If you think the problem of other minds indicates that philosophers have a tendency to focus on strange conundrums then this next issue is going to take the Gnomish Engineering award for quirkiness in the face of adversity. No contemporary philosopher had a stronger reputation for making outlandish (or should I say Outlandish) claims than David Lewis (1941–2001). Lewis, a metaphysician, concluded in his seminal work *On the Plurality of Worlds* that the only way out of a long-standing logical and linguistic problem was to make a pretty far out metaphysical claim: that there are innumerable parallel universes almost identical to ours except for minute differences representing every possible choice we could make.

Honestly. A well-respected Princeton professor asserting the existence of parallel universes. It seems ludicrous, but somehow *WoW* makes it all sound plausible. Follow me on a little thought experiment.

I'm standing at the gates of Ahn'Qiraj. It's January 22nd, 2006 and the gates are firmly closed. Patch 1.9, which added the gates and the raid dungeon they protect, was released three weeks prior, but opening them requires a very long, very high raid-level quest chain. Watching the gates open was kind of a big deal, but as of January 22nd it was impossible to do. What do I mean by impossible to do? I mean it hadn't been done. Not on my realm, not on anyone's.

There are several ways that one could define what I mean by "impossible" in this case. One might think to look at the requirements and determine the absolute minimum time it would take if all high end guilds on the realm knew precisely what to do and speed ran it. That would be a scientific way of answering the question. A Blizzard employee might, for example, make the claim that it would take a minimum of twenty days to meet the requirements given perfect adherence to the rules, therefore it's impossible for the gates to be open on January 22nd, nineteen days after the patch went live. But that assumes a lot of knowledge that, in the real world of metaphysics, we just don't have.

Here's another way. I stand at the gates on the Uther realm on January 22nd and I observe that the gates are not open. I make the further claim that the gates could *not* be open. It's impossible for them to be open at this point in time. On January 23rd I observe, again on Uther, that the gates are still not open but my further conjecture has changed: the gates are not open, but they *could* be.

We make statements beginning with "could have" or "could not have" all the time. Philosophers call these statements *counter-factuals*. "I got out of bed at 8:00 this morning but I could have slept in until 9:00." What does that mean? You didn't do it, so how can there be any truth to the statement "I could have?" It's counter-factual because it's contrary to the actual fact of what happened. How can something contrary to fact be true? Lewis wrestled with this problem because since Aristotle's day we've devised a fairly rigid notion of truth. To say that something could be true or false there needs to be some way, even hypothetical, that one could check and verify it. How do you verify the truth of a possible past event that didn't happen?

On January 23rd the gates of Ahn'Qiraj opened—on the Medivh realm. I had no characters on the Medivh realm and even if I made one it would be practically impossible for me to survive the journey to Silithus, much less participate in the massive battle that was happening. Yet when my Uther-locked toon stood on the barren fields before the gates that day and said "the gates are closed but they *could* be opened" what made that statement true was that there was a possible world—a parallel universe, an alternate server—in which the gates were, in fact, opened. I could determine, in theory, whether the statement was true—I could look at that other realm and see. On January 22nd no realm had opened the gates. On January 23rd one realm had.

Lewis believed in possible worlds because it was the only way he could find that, theoretically, our counter-factual statements could be true or false. Even if it were impossible for me to log into other servers or hear about what was going on in them, it was still either true or false that the gates opened on Medivh on January 23rd. I could even take a step back. On January 23rd I as a player had not witnessed the opening of the gates, but I could have. In another possible world I rolled my toon on Medivh instead of Uther and therefore would be enjoying the battle.

In real life we don't have the ability to see other possible worlds. But for Lewis if the statement "I woke up at 8:00 but could have slept until 9:00" were true then that meant there is another possible world in which you did, in fact, sleep in until 9:00.

For this reason, quirky as his views may have been, Lewis probably would have loved *WoW*. And I bet he would have been a voracious realm-hopper.

Too Big a Byte to Chew?

These are just a few of the many issues metaphysics wrestles with, but do they bring us any closer to determining if Azeroth is metaphysically real? It mirrors the real world in many metaphysical ways: there are in game and metagame levels, the potential for confusion over which characters are controlled by a conscious mind, and even the possibility of multiple parallel worlds. Do these imply "realness?"

Perhaps the question "Is Azeroth metaphysically real?" is made in the wrong philosophical spirit. If there are just as many metaphysical problems within Azeroth as there are in the offline world, the more important question becomes whether we have any basis for calling the "real" world real at all! Inasmuch as we are still struggling with metaphysics—with defining the extreme ends of science, our awareness of other minds, what it means for things to be possible or impossible—perhaps we have no basis for claiming the offline world is real, at least no more real than Azeroth is.

As you may have guessed I used the occasion of the dead Orc not as a chance to prove to my colleague that *WoW* and other MMORPGs are just as real as what we call reality, but rather to show that what we call reality is no more well-defined than Azeroth itself. At least within Azeroth we suffer from fewer illusions about where we stand. In fact, that knowledge may make Azeroth even *more* real than the so-called real world.

20
Future Pasts of Magic and Deceit

LEON SPENCER and ANNA JANSSEN

In *World of Warcraft (WoW)*, everyone's fighting each other. It says so right in the name. The Alliance fights the Horde, players fight players, the Scryers fight the Aldor, Booty Bay fights piracy, technology fights nature and ultimately, death fights life. So it's as well-named as it's well-sold; tens of millions of players are fighting for and against dozens of in-world factions, as well as hundreds of thousands of guilds and other player-driven organisations.

At first glance a new member of those tens of millions will likely feel they're observing a world of base, ignoble traits: bloodlust, vengeful hatred, and greed, and thus the pseudo-medieval trappings of the world seem entirely appropriate. But if that player were to look a little closer, if he were to read the quest text before clicking "Accept," if he were to wait to take in his surroundings, it might occur to him that rather than a horizon full of untouched forests and simple villages of stone and wood, the skyline could more aptly feature great shimmering skyscrapers thrusting out of layered grids of gleaming hovering traffic—an Alderaan, not a Middle Earth.

We're going to take a step back and show you how this could be by taking a new journey through the long-forgotten history of Azeroth, one that delves as deep into its past as it does into our future. We're talking about the final entanglement of technology and society, the most exciting and relevant debate going on today in the philosophical school of future studies: the Technological Singularity. We're going take a long look at Azeroth, because while the Singularity itself might be inevitable for us, we would never want it to turn out for us how it has for them, a world that seems to be trapped in time, bound by ties created with the very finest crafts of war.

The Evolution of the Species

Tracing the evolution of a species means finding fossils and footprints of the missing links, finding their ancestors. It involves a lot of very intensive, careful, laborious work for palaeontologists. Fortunately, it's a much easier proposition when you're tracing the evolution of a species's technology. Fossils and footprints are everywhere, apparent in everything. Computers have keyboards with QWERTY layouts because typewriters needed to work without jamming up. You can type 'LOL' with yours and have it mean something to your guild, because the US Army used so many acronyms during World War II that their GIs created thousands in parody and showered them over the airwaves. Footprints everywhere.

The most obvious footprint in the mud for technology, however, is not leaving muddy footprints. The roads of Rome don't merely exist millennia later; they are still in active use. Transportation means goods, services, and culture spread forming the basis of any civilisation and thus the wheel is the most primary invention. How you get around matters, not just for picking up but also for your society as a whole. So the first clue that Azeroth isn't just some medieval world is the fact that they have internal combustion engines.

They also have steam engines, motorbikes, tanks, aeroplanes, bombers, steam boats, airships, trams, helicopters, electric lights, batteries, and robots. These, and many other examples of contemporary technology, are all very much in evidence in Azeroth, most of which are the result of Goblin or Gnomish engineering. From these observations, one must conclude that the technology of Azeroth is at least at the level of our own.

A growing trend in our technological development has been one towards an ideal called "ubiquitous" or "pervasive" computing, whereby people use technological devices without actually being aware that they are using them, let alone the specifics of which device, where it is located, or how it works. Take the evolution of the mobile phone: simpler models require that you interact with the device directly, using buttons and getting constant feedback as you try and place a call. More complex models can perform voice recognition, and work with a wireless headset—all you need to be aware of is the headset itself, which you can activate and tell whom you would like to call. You don't need to know where the phone is, what model it is, what it's doing, if it even exists at all; it's ubiquitous.

It's not so much of a stretch to think of issuing a computer command with verbal and gestural inputs much like "casting a magic spell." What is using a computer if not exercising demiurgic power? The aesthetic that magic conjures is one of control, because users like to feel in control of their otherwise intimidating systems. The more complex and powerful, and expensive, the system, the more they need to feel in control. And considering that programmers are the most likely people to be fans of fantasy books and role-playing games, we're forced to conclude that a magical paradigm for computer interaction isn't just possible; it's inevitable. Terminology from fictitious and historical mythologies litter modern computer systems—terms like "icon," "wizard," "daemon," and "magic number." On reflection, such terms appear more at home in a quest description than a serious business machine.

And magic is everywhere on Azeroth. From the great world tree Teldrassil, a whole island supported on a single, enormous trunk, to the floating city of Dalaran, from a Mage's first *Fireball* to the Dragon Aspect Malygos's *Arcane Breath*, magic is powerful, destructive and potent. The great science fiction author Arthur C. Clarke's third law, as originally published in his essay "Hazards of Prophecy: The Failure of Imagination," in *Profiles of the Future* (1962), states: "Any sufficiently advanced technology is indistinguishable from magic." And on reflection, perhaps it's not simply the gulf of understanding that creates this illusion, but also that the imagination required to advance technology is fuelled with, and thus influenced by, the fantastic.

Now let's talk about mana. In *World of Warcraft*, it's the energy that powers magic users, it slowly replenishes by itself, or it can be replenished simply by drinking water (of some kind). A magic user can only have a maximum amount of mana. The laws of physics state that work done means energy was spent, so energy has to have been generated somewhere in the equation. A hydrogen fuel cell, currently by far the most promising "alternative" energy source, is powered by hydrogen and oxygen. Water is hydrogen and oxygen.

So, the magic user imbibes the water or breathes the air, nanobiotechnological systems in their body convert that hydrogen and oxygen to electricity, which powers a battery, which cannot be filled higher than one hundred percent. When a magic user casts a spell, some form of tiny embedded computer system hears and processes their movements, then uses the stored energy to create the desired effect. Not only is this a possible way of using technology, it's the most desirable. Clean, efficient, self-sufficient, portable, extensible, powerful, and most of all, extremely cool; there is nothing about Azeroth's magic that wouldn't sell. It's exactly the kind of technology you would expect from a post-singular society.

This Is the Singularity

You might be familiar with the idea of a Quantum Singularity, commonly a black hole, from physics. A singularity is a space-time event, after which, it is impossible to predict what will occur because the normal laws break down. For a Quantum Singularity, that means physical laws like gravity and electromagnetism. But what if there was a different type of singularity that could break down, for instance, the laws of economics and sociology, completely changing what people can do forever. This is the Technological Singularity, and much like a black hole, after a world passes through the event horizon, there is no going back and there is no way to look forward.

The shape of the Technological Singularity is simple to describe: it is the point at which artificial intelligence exceeds human intelligence. Today, computers and brains each have certain distinct advantages: computers are very quick and accurate for almost any algorithm, may use fine-grained control over the execution of those algorithms, and may trivially transfer knowledge from one to the other, while our brains are unmatched at pattern recognition, creativity and flexibility. When a being is created that has the best of both worlds—instant, networked, parallel creative problem solving—the world passes through the Singularity.

At this point that artificial intelligence (AI) could build a more advanced AI, which could do the same. Moore's law, which currently governs the technological development of our modern society—computer processor speeds double every eighteen months—would go right out the window. Moreover, a computer program has many advantages a human lacks: it is trivial to transfer knowledge instantly and exactly from one process to another, and those processes may be optimised, shared, networked, and finely controlled. An entity equipped with both these and a human's heretofore unmatched capability for pattern recognition and creative thought could improve itself to the physical limits of the universe, and no problem would be unsolvable.

Such an artificial intelligence, or perhaps a downloaded natural intelligence called an *infomorph*, would be capable of inhabiting any arbitrary number of networked ubiquitous computers, and perhaps even capable of controlling or influencing people, exactly like a god, or a ghost, or a demon in Azeroth. Azeroth's gods are the proof positive of their passing through the singularity. And "Daemons" are, after all, what system administrators call background processes or services on computer systems.

These digital gods on Azeroth ultimately come down to those on the side of creation, embodied by the Titans, and destruction, endorsed and supported by the many demons of the Burning Legion. The Titans were obviously the progenitors of the Technological Singularity, described as the creators of the present world. The Burning Legion, comprised of various artificial intelligences and perhaps corrupted infomorphs may be the ultimate realisation of Mary Shelly's most famous nightmare, or perhaps even features of the Titans' post-singular world.

Three Mysterious Questions

Why Just Azeroth?

It's no secret that the Orcs and Draenei, among other races and individuals, originate from another planet. We have discussed various transportation methods available in the *World of Warcraft*, but we've left the biggest until last: spaceships. One of the most important marks of a post-singular society is space colonisation; it might be the only mark that matters when it comes to measuring how advanced a civilisation is. In 1964 a Soviet Russian astronomer, Nikolai Kardashev, created the ultimate score card for measuring the advancement of a people, elegant in its simplicity, based on the only real limitation the universe has to offer the sufficiently advanced: energy. His measure, the Kardashev Scale, rates how much power a civilisation can harness in a very Russian way.

A civilisation is Type I on his scale when it can harness the entire power capabilities of a whole planet, Type II when it can harness all the power of a star, and Type III when it can harness all the power from a galaxy. This puts us, humanity, at somewhere near 0.7, still a Type 0 civilisation. Which is okay, really, because we are still pre-singular, but the singularity breaks all the curves—including energy demand.

A major part of this break will be the unchaining of space exploration. For the first time in our history, humans will have unlimited resources to explore the frontier just outside our Terran doorstep: the solar system, the galaxy and far, far beyond. This new galactic migration will not just be driven by human curiosity, and the quest for new challenges, but by individuals simply looking for new homes. Individuals, we can predict, will wish to leave earth and seed the galaxy: either with values akin to those of earth, or opposed to.

But the races of Azeroth are hardly space colonists. The Exodar is a beautiful ship, but it crashed. What is the point of warring over territory and resources when space offers infinite territory and resources for anyone with the technology?

Why Are You Fighting?

A post-singularity doctor can cure any disease, including aging and most forms of death, which perfectly explains healing potions, priests, and spells like Cure Disease, which takes an instant to cast and can cure anyone of anything, and Resurrect. So, Azeroth is dead on target when it comes to post-singular medical technology. But any species, when a new level of security is reached, has a tendency to breed like rabbits—for instance, the post-World War II baby boom.

But there are no skyscrapers in Azeroth. The few cities are simple medieval keeps that could support only a scant ten thousand people. There clearly isn't the high population density that would be the result of great medical technology.

Because Azeroth is not safe. The advancement of the species is about the ability to control the environment, to put a halt on natural selection, to make the weakest of your species stronger than the strongest of any lesser species. The victory of tool-users long ago was to subjugate nature; the sharpest claw is not as deadly as a bullet, the hardest natural armour is nothing compared to steel and any swarm can be overcome with tactics.

A bear, no matter how ferocious, cannot pose a threat to a city. It would pose so little threat that more people would want to save that bear from harm than would want to kill it. Nature is now just one of a number of aesthetic preferences rather than a factor of the biosphere of the planet. Natural disasters still happen to remind us that we have not yet succeeded in conquering nature, but each new disaster spurs generations of scientists and engineers to create ways to predict, defend against, and finally, to control weather and tectonic systems.

But in Azeroth, towns are threatened by animals on a day-to-day basis. In the fight of people versus nature, nature more than often wins out. And that is just the struggle of people against natural forces, but Azeroth is a land torn by war. It seems as if Azeroth is continually thrown into one conflict or another, with artificial intelligences, with themselves in the concourse of politics, and with extra-terrestrials. How could this be?

Why Gold?

Money makes the world go 'round. But what about the *World of Warcraft*? In our modern society, regardless of your level of awareness of it, economic change impacts everyone. So it should come as no surprise that economic trends will continue to shape the post-singular world.

One of the most significant impacts of the Technological Singularity, theorized by some philosophers, is the development of a post-scarcity economy. Post-scarcity is a concept that has been around a while. The Federation's economy in Star Trek would be a popular example, and Cory Doctorow's book *Down and Out in the Magic Kingdom* takes a very thorough look at a more contemporary implementation of such a system.

Post-scarcity means a world in which you can have anything you want, because everything is abundantly plentiful. Traditional economies work on the idea of trade: I have something I don't need that you do, and you have something I need that you don't, so we trade. With the creation of sophisticated artificial intelligence, in conjunction with advanced technology, it should be possible to eliminate shortages of vital items such as food, fuel, and water. Much like the replicators on Star Trek, you ask a computer for something, and bwwwwm, it appears. Nanotechnology means having the ability to assemble things from atoms up. In a post-scarcity economy there would never be shortages on the supply end, so the concept of trade would become obsolete.

Every player knows trade is alive and well on Azeroth. The auction houses are continually buzzing with it. Gold buys supplies, training, enchantments, gems, mounts, bags, and any gear you don't feel like questing for. For heroes, gold is very important. But what about for the rest of the citizenry? The inhabitants of Azeroth do not necessarily have any need for gold. After all, they give it away pretty much freely to wayward questers passing through their towns.

In Azeroth it is magic that puts food on the tables of the world's inhabitants, and magic too fuels the engines of any non-biological transportation. Magic burns training into your brain instantly, straight out of *The Matrix*. So why would Azeroth's inhabitants require gold?

The Horrible Answer

In contemporary society most individuals live a fairly structured life; childhood is usually dominated by school, with some recreation. As one matures, work dominates daily life, and recreation becomes secondary. It is not until retirement, after some sixty years, that we are entirely free to choose how we spend our time. Even that freedom is contingent upon having the money to do what we want, so having that freedom is quite uncommon. In the cases where retirees are financially solvent, many people become bored and restless without routine. Researchers have yet to conclude whether being raised from birth with such freedoms would eliminate this restlessness.

Boredom, however, is a concept unfamiliar to Azeroth denizens. Every day is another battle, for the humblest farmer or the mightiest mage. Whether it's simply surviving, or fighting, trading, crafting, politicking, or exploring the fabric of space and time, in Azeroth it's difficult not to stay busy.

Why? Maybe the world's inhabitants long ago exhausted every form of entertainment. Perhaps the Titans, the engineers of Azeroth's Technological Singularity, the ageless immortals who alone comprehend the sophistication of their world, found a new and macabre way of keeping the population entertained. Maybe they didn't stop at engineering the Singularity, but continued to create the perfect distraction: ceaseless, changing, involving, and evolving warfare. George Orwell's seminal work *Nineteen Eighty-Four* describes a similar twisted control. This conflict is also the apparent source of stagnation within Azeroth, that strange and unique paradox.

Counting Down to Forever

Technological singularities sound far out, a fantastic idea as unreal as a videogame, but according to some models, we have already passed the first layer: Information Technology. Networked computers have completely changed just about everything forever. It was impossible to predict how, and now it's impossible to go back. From your personal correspondence to the nature of warfare, the first layer of the singularity tore through the world like a horde of Orcs, and now everything changes so very much faster, snowballing, careening blindly into the heady future. It's a fantastic time to be alive.

And, what some models of the Technological Singularity predict, the final two will come within fifty years of this writing. The second layer will be biotechnological in nature, as wearable, ubiquitous, implantable, and finally, biological computers take information technology to its natural conclusion and we all become Mages. We become the computers. And then in the final layer, through artificial intelligence, the computers will become us. And then nothing will be impossible.

But it's important, while we fall faster and faster into the future, to take stock. To think about how we want to be when the singularity hits us fully, about what kind of society we will become. Will we set out to explore and tame this wild galaxy, to spread art and love and massively multiplayer online role playing games throughout the cosmos, or will we ignore the lessons Azeroth teaches and amuse ourselves in an endless masochistic war? It's philosophy that matters. The nature of time means that even the smallest intention now can mean drastic changes then. We need to be ready to assume our rightful place, to advance the cause of life, to ensure wild freedom and endless possibility for ourselves and our species, from now until the stars die out.

Because by then my Druid will be so freaking badass.

21
Can I Have Unlimited Power in *World of Warcraft*?

NICOLAS MICHAUD

A Mage narrowly escapes death by blinking away from an angry dragon, a Shaman calls down lightning to strike her foe, a Death Knight rides its horse over the water while its pursuers drown . . . within the *World of Warcraft (WoW)* it seems that anything is possible. The basic laws of nature that rule me need not apply when I am out slaying Orcs as a Night Elf Warrior.

It's likely that part of the reason I play the game is because I don't have to follow the rules that oppress me in my normal life. All the things that I wish I could do are legitimate options when playing *WoW*. I can levitate, walk on water, cast elemental spells, instantly teleport, and control the minds of others, just to name a few things I can't do in the real world. But, how far does this go? Is it true that in-game anything is possible as long as the creators allow it? Which rules can be broken in the game universe, and which rules are so deeply a part of the fabric of the universe that they cannot be broken, even in *WoW*?

It seems that we can break all of the laws of physics in *World of Warcraft*, but can we break all of the rules that govern our universe? Perhaps the laws of physics are optional in-game, but what about rules that some philosophers argue are even more fundamental to the fabric of the universe—math and logic? Is it possible that even those two pillars of the structure of the universe become fluid and flexible for those playing *World of Warcraft*? Keep in mind that we're not trying to answer the question "Can we do these things in the real world?" but instead "How far can the rules that govern us in the real world be bent in the gameworld?"

There's a sense in which the characters of *WoW* exist in a different universe with different rules. The designers of *WoW* and other similar games have created closed systems in which different rules apply. You cannot fully enter those worlds any more than the Lich King can exit the game and grab a latte at the local Starbucks. So although the game is not the "real" world and you only have limited access, the universe in which those characters exist is a kind of closed system in which the entities embedded in it must follow the rules. This is similar to our own universe from which we cannot escape and in which we must follow the laws of physics.

Can Gnomes Break the Laws of Physics?

The first fact to note is that the laws of physics do not work the same way in *WoW* as they do in real life. Players in *WoW* seem to regularly violate laws of physics, perhaps most fundamentally through the use of magic. Spell casters do all sorts of things that seem impossible in the external world. In the real world you cannot levitate any more than you can turn yourself into a bear or create a succubus. So, at first glance you can say that players in *WoW* can violate the laws of physics. It seems that the Law of Gravitation need not apply in the game, for example. One can simply levitate and violate what seems to be one of the most fundamental rules of our universe. One wonders, then, if all of the laws of physics can similarly be dismissed.

A physicist examining this argument might disagree with my original assessment. He or she might point out that, while seeming laws such as gravitation are violated, they are not violated in a way that compromises physics, even in-game. Consider the problem from this angle: although we cannot violate the laws of gravitation in the external world, we can fly. Simply put, we can apply other natural laws in such a way that gives us the ability to violate a law, *seemingly*. So maybe it's similar for characters in the game. Characters do not just levitate in the game with no cost; they must expend mana to do something. The physicist may argue that the most fundamental law in physics is still maintained, at least conceptually—the Law of Conservation of Energy and Matter. Although we may not understand the means of exchange between mana and levitation, there is an exchange, a kind of energy is applied to "violate" the law. But, it may be that this violation is, in-game, more akin to building an airplane and flying than simply making something from nothing.

The Law of Conservation of . . . Mana?

Consider this more fundamental law of physics—the Law of Conservation of Energy and Matter. Can characters in-game violate this fundamental rule of our external universe? I believe that they can. The Law of Conservation of Energy and Matter tells us that in a closed system energy cannot be created or destroyed—energy can only be changed from one form to another. In other words, the total amount of energy in the universe cannot change. So, we can use energy and manipulate it, but we cannot destroy it, or create it out of nothing. But in the game world it is also a closed system. Within it different rules can apply, but is the Law of Conservation one which only exists in *WoW* if the creators decide to write it in?

Although it seems at first as if within the game the Law of Conservation must be followed, there are also ways in which it is violated. Consider the creation of mana itself. This mana is used to do things and manipulate the in-game environment. Mana is used as energy and results in work being done. But the mana itself seems to come from nowhere. Sometimes characters can drink something to gain mana, so it can be said there is an energy transfer, but most of the time mana just seems to regenerate itself. We might argue that the characters themselves generate the mana, but from what? They do not have to eat to generate mana or do anything at all to generate mana, so it seems to come from nowhere. The same thing seems to be the case for focus, rage, and rune power. Alright, the laws of physics may be optional in *WoW*, but what about the rules of math?

Do Goblin Engineers Follow the Rules of Mathematics?

First off, one might argue that math is a somewhat contextual notion. Mathematics can be described as a coherent system grounded on a set of rational axioms. In other words, some might argue that you can develop almost any system of math you want. Different systems would be based on different basic rules, or axioms, from which the rest of the system is derived. Different systems, then, could be developed by choosing different axioms as the basis of our mathematical system. Someone may then argue that in *WoW* we can have a completely different kind of math from what we normally use by starting with a different set of axioms than we normally use for our mathematical concepts.

This is a difficult potion to swallow, though. Is it really reasonable to agree that all of our mathematical notions are purely contextual? Do rules of math go out the window once we are playing a game with different rules? It seems that even the most fundamental of mathematical concepts, then, would be purely relative. My intuitions tell me that the rules of math cannot be this relative, but I need more than just my intuitions to prove it.

In defense of my intuition, let's consider one of the most basic functions of math—addition. Is it possible that the basic summation of two quantities can equal more or less than the conjunction of its parts? Imagine that the creators of *WoW* decide that they do want to create their own system of math, in-game. So, they structure the system so that the normal function of addition works in a different way than we normally conceive. Let's imagine that they structure it so that when your Warrior hits she does ten points of damage. Now, normally, in our world, if the Warrior hits twice then 10 + 10 = 20. So we would expect that within the game the total amount of damage done for two hits would be 20 points. But, they have structured it differently. Your Warrior does hit for ten points, but when taken in conjunction with a second hit the two add up to 40 total points of damage. It could be said, then, that within the game 10 + 10 = 40. This certainly seems like something that they could do. There is no rule that could stop them from programming the game so that every time two sets of ten are taken together they equal forty. In the language of the game the rule of addition seems to be one which can be violated.

We can object though. You might argue that, although the game is structured to work that way, the language of math is not actually violated because in reality two sets of "10" are not actually added up. The programmers are just replacing our normal symbolization "20" for "10" to make it seem as if they are changing the rules of math, when in reality they are only just saying "10" when they actually mean "20." More importantly, you might argue that there is no way that they could program the game so that they could violate the basic rules of quantification. You could say that, no matter what number they call it, if 40 points of damage are done, there is no way that 10 + 10 can actually equal 40.

It seems as if these basic quantitative intuitions cannot be violated. No matter what name you call a quantity, you cannot actually change the nature of the quantity. For example, if you place your two hands together, palms touching, you know that you have the same number of fingers on both hands. You can call that number 5 (five fingers on each hand) or you can call it ten, or blue, or fizzcrank, but the word you use to describe the quantity does not change the fact that you have the same number of fingers on each hand. Nevertheless, it does seem as if the programmers of *WoW* could have some fun even with basic arithmetic and perhaps it is just our limited human perspective that prevents us from fully understanding the ways alternative consistent mathematical systems work in the game. Let's give them the benefit of the doubt and say that characters within the game can both live by different rules of physics and math, but what about what some philosophers consider to be the most fundamental rule of the universe… logic.

Try Teaching A Tauren Logic . . . (Where's a Plus Int. Potion When you Need One?)

There are two laws of logic that some consider to be foundational: the Law of Excluded Middle and the Law of Non-Contradiction. The Law of Non-Contradiction is generally considered to be so foundational that we cannot even rationally consider its falsity. Classical logic, the logic that is most commonly used in reasoning and taught in school, relies heavily on these rules and even our every day reasoning often assumes their truth. The Law of Excluded Middle tells us that something is either the case or not the case, there is nothing in-between. For example, you are either playing *WoW* or not playing *WoW*, there is no middle option. The Law of Non-Contradiction tells us that something cannot both be the case and not the case at the same time. So, for example, you cannot be playing *WoW* and not playing *WoW* at the same time. One wonders, though, if these laws actually structure reality or if they are just our way of understanding the world.

Let's start with the Law of Excluded Middle. This law assumes that in our statements things cannot be "kinda" the case. You can't kinda be a Tauren, or kinda be mining, or kinda be flying a gryphon. If you think about this, though, you might reject this idea. You could argue that you *can* kinda be an Elf, a Half-Elf, for instance. You might argue that if a Human and a Blood Elf have a child then the result is a kind of middle ground between the two. A Half-Elf is neither an Elf nor not an Elf; it is in a middle space between the two. A classical logician though, would reject this argument and say that a Half-Elf is not an Elf, it is a Half-Elf. So it falls squarely into the camp of "not an Elf" and not in some non-existent middle ground. But, the problem might be a bit deeper.

Consider the fact that you can play a Human character who is balding. At what point is he bald? Clearly, if your Human character has no hair he is bald, but what if he has some hair? Normally, we start calling people bald when they still have hair, they just don't have as much, especially on the tops of their heads. So we say they are "bald." But how many hairs do you have to lose to be called "bald?" The answer isn't "all of them." The answer is somewhere between not-bald and totally bald. Some philosophers would argue that this middle space between not-bald and totally bald proves that the Law of Excluded Middle must be wrong—there is a space between bald and not bald, the state of "balding."[1] There are numerous cases like this in which you are in a middle state—for example, when you walk into an inn there is a point in the doorway in which you are not inside the inn and, at the same time, you are not outside the inn. Or if you sit in a chair there is a point when you are not quite sitting all the way down but you are not standing either. So you are neither inside the inn nor not inside the inn and you are neither sitting nor not sitting.

Critics argue that these are just problems with the way we use words. They argue that if we were to really take a look at problems like "balding" we would realize that if by "bald" we mean "the state of having no hair" then there is no middle ground; either you "have no hair" or you "have hair." So they claim we are just playing games with words that have vague meanings. But, non-classical logicians have some very good reasons for wanting to reject the Law of Excluded Middle so let's consider an even more fundamental law of logic—the Law of Non-Contradiction.

What's in the Empty Box . . . Nothing or an Epic Item?

It seems impossible for us to violate the Law of Non-Contradiction. The law is simple: something cannot be the case and not the case

[1] This problem is generally known in philosophy as the "sorites paradox." It

at the same time. Even in-game, how is it possible to violate this law? What possible programming can be done to make it so that I am a Tauren and not a Tauren *at the same time?* You might argue, in a way similar to the Half-Elf example that a Half-Tauren is both Tauren and not Tauren at the same time, but this seems to just be playing games with language, again. Could programmers actually program it so that something in-game is both true and not true at the same time? Could they program it, for example, so that you can both be casting a spell and not casting a spell at the same time, or flying and not flying at the same time?

One of the strongest reasons for us to argue that, in our world, the Law of Non-Contradiction must be true is because of all of the problems that result if it isn't true. Imagine that you reject the Law of Non-Contradiction. Well that means that when you say something is true it can also not be true. This doesn't mean that you may be wrong; this means that what you are claiming is true is both true and false. So if you say to someone "I like *WoW*" you could also mean at the same time "I don't like *WoW*." How can we even begin to think of this? Here's a further complication: how does the Dialethist (one who believes the Law of Non-Contradiction is false) make statements like "Dialethism is true" without it also being possible that he means "Dialethism is false" at the same time?[2]

Contradictions seem to result in some serious problems. For classical logicians the problem is pretty severe. For certain formal reasons, a contradiction results in what is called "explosion."[3] Basically, if we introduce a true contradiction into our belief set, we can postulate anything as being true. You might think of this problem in a non-formal way: if I allow for the possibility that one thing I believe is both true and false at the same time, I can allow for *anything* to be true, regardless of how silly it is. This is due to the fact that for anything I believe, it seems that the opposite can be true also. The rule which prevents me from believing that the truth of something prevents its falsity is no longer strong enough to hold in any case. If, for example, your Dwarvish friend believes in true

---

was posed by Eubulides of Miletus, who asked, "When does a collection of grains of sand become a heap—the first grain, or second, or third . . . ?"

[2] Dialethism has been defended and popularized by Graham Priest. See his article, "What Is So Bad About Contradictions?" *Journal of Philosophy* (1998).

[3] Graham Priest, J.C. Bell and Bradley Armour-Garb, eds., *The Law of Non-Contradiction* (Oxford University Press, 2007).

contradictions and says to you "I wish that I was taller" you could reply "yes, but you believe that something can be true and false at the same time so do you also mean that you wish that you were *not* taller? If you believe in one true contradiction, what's to prevent all true statements from also being false at the same time?"

Can there be an exception made, though, for violating the Law of Non-Contradiction in-game in *WoW*? Could the programmers make something true and not true at the same time? I think it is important to assert that "yes" they probably could play with language and program the game to tell you things like "you are not flying" when you are flying or as you cast a spell have your combat screen state "you are not casting a spell." But, this does not change the fact that, even within the game, you are actually flying or actually casting a spell. Like the case with math, this just changes what we are calling something. We could say we are "not flying" when we are flying, but this does not create a true contradiction.

The real problem is that it may be impossible for us to even begin talking about how a true contradiction can be made. It seems *so* impossible that even when we imagine that it could be done in the world of the game, we don't know what it actually means. Graham Priest presents us with a story that might help decide if true contradictions are possible in the world of the game. In his story, "Sylvan's Box" he presents a fictional tale in which a man finds a box which contains something and nothing at the same time.[4] The man shows the box to his friend and they discuss what they should do with it. After the story, Priest asks the reader a couple of questions. He asks us how many people are in the story and what they are talking about and he points out that we can answer all of these questions without the result of explosion. He argues that even if his characters were to find this box, they don't have to say stuff in the story like "I have found a box which has something and nothing in it; therefore, I can conclude anything else I'd like to be true such as 'there are talking lollipops inhabiting Pluto'." More importantly, he argues that we can talk about this imaginary box without coming to crazy conclusions about talking lollipops on Pluto. Perhaps there can be boxes in *WoW* which contain something and nothing at the same time. They obviously would be BoP Epic items.

---

[4] Graham Priest, "Sylvan's Box," *Notre Dame Journal of Formal Logic* 38 (1997), pp. 573–582.

I Can't Understand True Contradictions. Try it Again . . . In Orcish

The final problem is, then, a simple one. Perhaps characters in *WoW* can violate all laws of physics, mathematics and logic, even the Law of Non-Contradiction as long as the creators of the universe make it possible. But, one wonders if we are just saying they can without giving any real meaning to our statements. Sure, the creators of *WoW* can *say* that you can loot a box that contains both something and nothing, but what does this actually mean? Think about it for a moment: if you open the box in *WoW* the text may say "this box contains nothing" but if you take something out of it, no matter what the text *says* the box actually did contain something. It seems like the creators would just be lying to us about what the box contains. Perhaps games like *World of Warcraft* are separate universes in their own right and it is possible for them to violate these foundational rules, but how could we even understand what this means? I am sure the Gnomes can find a way, but Humans may lack sufficient creativity.

The problem above is the fundamental problem of contradictions. It does seem that we can say all kinds of things about contradictions. But, does this mean that contradictions can be understood? Even if, within the game, violations of the Law of Non-Contradiction are possible, we would not be able to make sense of them.

Some philosophers think this is good reason to believe that contradictions cannot be true. Other philosophers argue that just because we cannot understand true contradictions doesn't mean that they cannot exist. I can say the following, though, with relative confidence: understanding true contradictions would take more than just more knowledge or understanding, it would require a whole different way of thinking that is probably impossible for us. So, even if they are possible, we will never know or understand. Our reality, and, therefore, our understanding of the world within *WoW* are restricted by our own limited perspective.

Denizens of Azeroth

Phill Alexander is a level 80 Blood Elf Hunter and PhD candidate in the Rhetoric and Writing program at Michigan State University. He researches online discourse communities and gender, race, and class in video games, which is indeed just a clever way of claiming that playing *WoW* for hours on end is "research." He's totally rolling need, because that—whatever dropped—*is* a hunter weapon.

Allan Baumer is a guy going to Georgia Tech. He is a graduate student obtaining a masters in Human-Computer Interaction with a focus on digital media. His strongest interest is narrative and how it develops in digital spaces. Allan was trained in analyzing film at the University of Central Florida (a BA!) and worked on various projects involving interactive entertainment. He digs writing things, cursing, mix CDs, webcomics, rolling dice, laughing with friends, and good times. He aspires to learn how to not explode things when cooking and being a more awesome person.

Paul Brown teaches English and Media at a high school in Northeast England. He has an MA in Computer Game Studies and is continuing his work on player motivation through a PhD at the University of Manchester. He has also written for *The Legend of Zelda and Philosophy*. Paul recently smuggled an Orc out of Azeroth with the intention of showing him a better, more peaceful way of life and teaching him the art of butling. He is pleased to announce that Grunt is much happier and makes a surprisingly good butler.

Pauline Chan is a Master's candidate in the Digital Media Studies program at Georgia Institute of Technology, where she has chosen to couple a lifelong interest in narrative (for which she received a B.A. in English Literature from the University of California, Irvine) with an equally persistent love for digital representations and virtual communities. She also moonlights as two separate level 80 resto druids in *World of Warcraft*, and role-plays on a number of alts when not raiding or taking up another ridiculous reputation grind. As a result, she has adopted a rather fierce attachment to coffee (though can be persuaded by tea as well).

TIM CHRISTOPHER is completing quests to earn the title of "Doctor" in the area of game studies in the Arts and Technology program at the University of Texas at Dallas. He teaches classes in game design mechanics and serious gaming at UT Dallas. Tim's alter ego Linc has earned the title "explorer" and is now working on the title "chef." He's always seen in the company of either his trusted wolf Xelda, or his two headed dog Kirkandspock. Linc's areas of interests include skinning, leather working, and cooking. Linc enjoys raiding with friends as well as hunting in Northrend.

When AFK, **JON COGBURN** teaches Philosophy at Lousiana State University. He WTS copies of *Philosophy Through Video Games* (Routledge, 2008), which co-writing with trusty NPC (or is it the other way around?) Mark Silcox left him both OOM and in an extended state of Global Cooldown. Luckily, playing and writing about WOW MP5NC and HP5. Now he is GTG. Even though the RW is a PvP realm, let it never be said that Jon Cogburn is a PKer. QFT.

DARIO COMPAGNO is hopefully soon finishing a vain PhD in discredited Semiotics at the University of Siena, searching for the elusive concept of the author in twentieth-century structural and analytical theories and in computer game worlds such as Azeroth and Hyrule. Both in *WoW* and real life, Dario loves to play the Druid: changing his aspect like a chameleon, he's always sneaking through angry professors who unsuccessfully try to prevent him from reaching his PC or a console. Dario imagined the guiltless Schopenhauer playing Zelda in *The Legend of Zelda and Philosophy*, and he has wonderfully edited together with Patrick Coppock *Computer games, between Text and Practice*, an amazing special issue of the prestigious e-journal *EC*.

PATRICK J. COPPOCK is an eternal collector of avatars and game credits whose ludic career started with Hangman and OXO at grammar school in Belfast, Northern Ireland, where he also hammered out an honours degree in psychology at QUB. Then, for twenty-six years he roamed deep valleys and high mountains in Norway in search of trolls, oil, and new adventures. While there, he gold-farmed a MA and PhD program in applied lingustics at NTNU, Trondheim, researching sign language videophones, MOO's and MUD's as process-oriented writing, before moving on to Bologna, Italy, as visiting scholar of semiotics at the department of communication disciplines at UNIBO, where his wife Patrizia works. He is at present tenured researcher in theory and philosophy of languages at the University of Modena and Reggio Emilia, fifteen leagues to the north, working with colleagues in the north, south, west and east to build a game philosophy research network: <http://gamephilosophy.org>.

Luke Cuddy teaches philosophy in Southern California. He has contributed to several other books of the Popular Culture and Philosophy series and he edited *The Legend of Zelda and Philosophy*. If he has to search for the missing chapters of *Green Hills of Stranglethorn* again he's just going to off his toon.

Sean C. Duncan is a doctoral candidate in the Department of Curriculum and Instruction and a member of the Games+Learning+Society Initiative at the University of Wisconsin,-Madison. He researches design thinking in online gaming communities, learning with games, and digital media literacy. Unfortunately, he still can't find Mankrik's wife.

Monica Evans is an Assistant Professor of computer game design at the University of Texas at Dallas. Her research interests include critical game studies, serious and educational games, and narrative structures for interactive systems. She would love to teach a course in the proper way to raid Naxxramas, but keeps getting distracted by complex philosophical issues. You can reach her by email only if you're exalted with Texas.

Juan Ferret is an Assistant Professor at the University of Texas at El Paso. Besides doing research on philosophy of physics (the problem of time and motion, particularly) and Latin American philosophy (classic Maya and Nahua), he enjoys being chased by the Horde all over Feathermoon.

Kevin N. Haw splits his time between writing computer code and speculative fiction and once turned down a job offer from the company that eventually became Blizzard Entertainment. Which is all well and good, as he avoided the tax implications of such a decision. He invites you to visit his website at <http://www.KevinHaw.com> to view his ongoing projects.

Christian Hoffstadt has just finished his PhD at the Institute of Philosophy at the University of Karlsruhe, Germany. His key research areas include epistemology, meta-theory, media philosophy (film, game studies), philosophy and contemporary culture, and philosophy of medicine. While rumors say that he was completely lost in Azeroth for about two years, in actual fact he ground the intellectual widths of Azeroth to improve his scientific skills for the ultimate quest—to figure out the philosophical difference between strong game commitment and addiction.

Debra Jackson received her PhD in Philosophy from Purdue University but feels more loyalty to her Common Blood guildies than to the Boilermakers. She is an assistant professor of philosophy at California State University, Bakersfield, and is currently grinding rep toward tenure when not raiding, farming, or completing dailies. Her research interests include feminist philosophy, critical theory, philosophy of law, and how to maximize her dps.

Anna Janssen, a work-for-hire sniper who for tax purposes is a post-graduate co-ordinator for the University of Sydney's world-famous Faculty of Medicine. Endlessly fascinated by the simplest things, her browser's history lists websites on cryptozoology, basic chemistry, conspiracy, band biographies, psychology, bad fantasy novels, *Star Trek: Voyager*, the stock market, and astronomy. When she isn't writing or researching, she's designing clothes and jewellery, playing bass, admiring the attention span of kittens, editing her single-page 'zine, *Colophon*, or drawing her award-winning *Popecomic*, or updating her videogame blog Naked Gamer, <http://nakedgamer.net>.

Eli Kosminsky first picked up *World of Warcraft* as a Gnome-sized high school freshman, never expecting to find anything but a distraction from the mundane real world. Although he's a well-trained Undead Warlock in Azeroth, his main identity has much to learn, and is currently a student at MIT. While attending classes, Eli is repeatedly disappointed to find that his backpack contains neither a PvP trinket to dispel his nasty sleep debuffs, nor the crystallized souls of his fallen adversaries.

Ben Medler has been known to try and school Murlocs on the finer points of socio-politics. These talks never go well. While a Digital Media PhD student at the Georgia Institute of Technology Ben has studied a number of areas in relation to games including: conflict, decision making, player identity, and analytics. While he promotes the ability to be neutral in games he has been known to shout "For the Horde!" a little louder.

Nick Michaud is told by other philosophers that he should actually go to work on occasion. Instead, he is usually playing *WoW*. Given this fact, if you want to say "Hi," you have a far better chance of doing so by logging on than calling his office. You can find him on Medivh playing his Night Elf Warrior "Elegy" in his Guild the Pez Dispensers of Justice with Chris "I Play *WoW* Because a Hot Chick Asked Me To . . . What's Your Excuse?" Balestra; Nick "AFK" Grover; Josh "I Don't Need Your Help" Smith; Nick "Your Mom!" Rosaci; Lara "I'm in a Guild?" Stalvey, Michael "What the *$&# is Josh Doing!?" Salvato, and Jessica "Wait, I want to Hug it!" Watkins. He couldn't get killed by, I mean killed with, people he loves more.

Michael Nagenburg's first computer was a Commodore 64 and he has not stopped playing video games since the mid-1980s. Still, he somehow managed to study philosophy at the University of Karlsruhe. Although he started Pen and Paper role playing in the mid-1990s, he did his doctoral thesis on privacy and ICT technology in 2004. Currently, he is working at the Interdepartemental Center for Ethics in the Sciences and Humanties at the University of Tübingen, Germany. His research topics include privacy, surveillance, and video games. Being an ethicist he chose the side of the underprivileged and demonized people of Azeroth, the Horde. However, he never really found the time to play *WoW* for a very long time. Nevertheless he published a couple of papers on *WoW* with Christian Hoffstadt, who provides him with a lot of insight into the world of Azeroth.

John Nordlinger is a member of the Horde and head of gaming research at Microsoft. He often writes and lectures about ethical and educational issues arising from videogames.

Kylie Prymus has managed to put over 400 points into his dissertation writing trade skill, specializing in the relationship between ancient virtue theories and modern Internet communication. When not hawking his wares in auction houses up and down the East Coast he resides in Pittsburgh and maintains a critical gaming blog.

Phil Serchuk is a level 80 Blood Elf Warlock on Hakkar. When not melting faces or battling the Scourge, Phil spends his free time roleplaying as a PhD candidate in philosophy at the University of Toronto. Although his main spec is logic and philosophy of language, Phil sometimes experiments with off-specs in philosophy and computer science. He is not now nor has he ever been a ninja.

Miguel Sicart is a level 60 Assistant Professor at the Center for Computer Games Research, IT University of Copenhagen. His research and hunting areas include ethics, game design, and political games. He has founded a non-violent cult in Argent Dawn, now extinct due to internal clashes, and has published *The Ethics of Computer Games*.

Mark Silcox is an assistant professor of philosophy at the University of Central Oklahoma. He is the co-author (with Jon Cogburn) of *Philosophy through Video Games* (2008). He belonged to the design teams for the video games *Aidyn Chronicles: The First Mage* and *Earth and Beyond*. He wishes to state for the record that he is in no way prejudiced against the Orcish race—in fact, many of his oldest friends are Orcs. But marriage is between an elf and a woman-elf.

Leon Spencer is an independent videogame designer, an industry-shattering subversive rock star who spreads controversy with one hand and gathers the love of grateful millions with the other. For the honors degree he holds in design computing, he devised an engine to breathe life and story into lifeless background characters in videogames—specifically video-games like *World of Warcraft*. When he isn't freeing mankind from the tyranny of religion, he's artfully harming people he dislikes. Visit <http://chaoseffect.com> if you want more, and if you work for a studio, offer him a job.

Audrey Whitman is a graduate student in the Digital Media Masters Program at Georgia Institute of Technology, where she manages a project studio developing games on immigration. Her background is in Technical Writing and Media Studies (from Carnegie Mellon University); but her interests currently lie in the design and development of massively multi-player online games, the communities that emerge around them, and the pedagogic role of play. She enjoys industrial music, math jokes, swearing, and giant boots. Chances are, she has more tattoos than you do.

Moses Wolfenstein is a doctoral student at the University of Wisconsin, Madison, in the department of Educational Leadership and Policy Analysis, as well as a member of the Games+Learning+Society research group there. His dissertation work revolves around the question of how guild leadership in *World of Warcraft* can inform the study of school leadership. When he's not trying to grind academic rep with the faculty at UW, he's probably trying to grind rep with the Sons of Hodir in Northrend. Can't those guys just get a tabard?

Index